Computer Simulation of Compression-Ignition Engine Processes

Computer Simulation of Compression-Ignition Engine Processes

V Ganesan

Universities Press

Universities Press (India) Private Limited

Registered Office
3-6-747/1/A & 3-6-754/1, Himayatnagar,Hyderabad 500 029 (A.P.), India
Email: info@universitiespress.com

Distributed by
Orient Blackswan Private Limited

Registered Office
3-6-752, Himayatnagar,Hyderabad 500 029 (A.P.), India

Other Offices
Bangalore / Bhopal / Bhubaneshwar / Chennai
Ernakulam / Guwahati / Hyderabad / Jaipur / Kolkata
Lucknow / Mumbai / New Delhi / Patna

First published 2000
Reprinted 2013

ISBN 978 81 7371 283 8

Set in Times New Roman 10/12 by
OSDATA, Hyderabad 500 029

Printed at
Graphica Printers, Hyderabad 500 013

Published by
Universities Press (India) Private Limited
3-6-747/1/A & 3-6-754/1, Himayatnagar,
Hyderabad 500 029 (A.P.), India

I dedicate this book to my revered gurus,

Professor B S Murthy and Professor T R Jagadeesan

CONTENTS

PREFACE

Internal Combustion Engines can be broadly classified into spark-ignition (SI) and compression-ignition (CI) engines. The spark-ignition engine dates back to 1876 when August Otto first developed the SI engine and compression-ignition engine to 1892 when Rudolf Diesel invented the CI engine. Over the last one century, engines continued to develop, as our knowledge of engine processes has increased. New technologies became available and demand for new types of engines arose. Further, environmental constraints on engines changed. The last twenty five years or so have seen an explosive growth in engine research and development as the issues of air pollution, fuel cost, and market competitiveness have become increasingly important. A very large amount of literature on engines is available which is yet to be adequately organized and summarized.

It is well known that over the last one decade, computers were extensively used for simulation data and modelling purposes and for building powerful, integrated database systems. Computer simulation procedures have been built by theoretical foundations and used in a large number of applications. In recent years the availability of fast digital personal computers have revolutionised the world. Hence, the systems which were hitherto not amenable for simulation techniques have come under the purview of simulation studies. One such area is the computer simulation of compression-ignition engines.

In engineering, simulation process has come to mean developing and using the appropriate combination of assumptions and equations that permit critical features of the process to be analysed. The modelling of engine processes continues to develop as our basic understanding of the Physics and Chemistry of the phenomena of interest steadily expands, and as the capability of computers to solve complex equations continues to increase. Computer simulation activities can make major contributions to engine design at different levels of generality or detail, corresponding to a different stages of model development.

As of now two basic types of models have been developed. They can be categorized as thermodynamic or fluid dynamic in nature depending on whether the equations which give the model its predominant structure are based on energy conservation or on a full analysis of the fluid motion. Other labels given to thermodynamic energy-conservation-based models are: zero-dimensional, phenomenological and quasi-dimensional. Fluid dynamic based models are often called multi-dimensional models due to their inherent ability to provide detailed geometric information on the flow field, based on the solution of the governing flow equations.

This book has been written as a text and a professional reference. Further, to the best of the author's knowledge no such textbook along with the software is available for teaching under-graduate and post-graduate students. This book attempts to provide a simplified framework for the vast and complex map of technical material that exists on compression-ignition engines, and at the same time include sufficient details to convey the complexity of the engine simulation. Of course, no one text can include everything about engine simulation. The emphasis here is on the thermodynamics, combustion physics and chemistry, heat transfer and friction processes relevant to compression-ignition engines with simplifying assumptions. Since, details are covered from the fundamentals, it is hoped that it will be a valuable tool for both under-graduate and post-graduate students as well as practising engineers.

This book is arranged in the following sequence. The first four chapters deal with the fundamentals and basics on adiabatic combustion and isentropic process. The fifth chapter is meant for the review of fundamentals and basic nomenclatures associated with the CI engine. Chapters 6 to 9 deal with the CI engine simulation in a step-by-step approach.

In Chapter 6, the details of ideal cycle simulation (ICS) has been dealt with employing thermodynamic relations and using air as a working medium. This is to make the reader familiarize himself with thermodynamic analysis of the Diesel cycle and to get him into the groove of engine simulation.

In Chapter 7, fuel-air cycle simulation (FCS) has been carried out using appropriate equations. This will make the reader understand the effect of adding fuel in the analysis, and help him to appreciate the influence of various operating parameters on engine performance. Some parametric studies have been made, and are given in the form of tables.

In Chapter 8, progressive combustion simulation (PCS) using rate equations and a zero-dimensional model, have been incorporated. Heat transfer has been taken into account by means of, again, empirical relations. This will take the reader a little closer to the actual engine.

In Chapter 9, the actual cycle simulation (ACS) has been attempted, taking into account the gas exchange process and friction. A number of parametric studies have been carried out and the results are provided in various tables.

It is hoped that this step-by-step approach will make the reader understand and appreciate the complexities involved in the computer simulation of compression-ignition engines.

Appendices include relevant equations and data. Tables are also provided with required data wherever necessary. Further, a hard copy of the computer program is also given so that the students and the teachers may take advantage of the same. If anyone requires a floppy this can be supplied at a nominal cost. It is the desire of the author that the reader should develop his own code. Those who understand the theory provided in various chapters can very easily write the various sub-routines giving the necessary input data and make his program work and compare the results given in various tables. Hence, it is strongly advised that the reader should make attempts in this direction.

Many individuals have assisted me in various ways as I have worked on this book over the past three years. I am grateful to my colleagues in the I.C. Engines Laboratory at Indian Institute of Technology, Madras, for their encouragement and support. Many of my **P**unctilious and **h**ighly **D**evoted scholars, have helped me in the preparation of text materials and I am very grateful to them for the same. I am particularly thankful to my QIP scholar, Mr. J. M. Mallikarjuna for his support in running the program and making various tables and graphs in the book. The interest he took in this regard is very much appreciated. I wish to thank the Centre for Continuing Education of the Indian Institute of Technology, Madras for the help rendered in the preparation of this book.

I am especially indebted to my secretary, Ms. Vijayashree and son G. Venkatasubramanian who have put their heart and soul to bring out this book by helping me in DTP and other computer operations. Without their unstinting help it would not have been possible to bring out this book in this fashion.

My wife Rajalakshmi, son Venkatasubramanian and daughter Aparna have encouraged me throughout this long and time-consuming work which took many hours away from them. Without their continuing support it would never have been finished; for their patience and faith that it would ultimately come to fruition, I will always be grateful.

V. GANESAN

LIST OF SYMBOLS

Symbol	Description
A, A_p	area of the piston
A_{ex}	wide open exhaust valve area
A_{in}	wide open inlet valve area
ACS	actual cycle simulation
A/F	air-fuel ratio
AL	coefficient for the calculation of C_p
bp	brake power
B	bore
BDC	bottom dead centre
BL	coefficient for the calculation of C_p
$C_{\rm m}$	mean piston speed
C_p	specific heat at constant pressure
$C_{\rm pa}$	specific heats of air
$C_{\rm pf}$	specific heats of fuel
$C_{\rm vr}$	constant volume specific heats of the reactant mixture
$\overline{C_v}(T)$	mean value of specific heat constant volume
$C_{\rm w}$	specific heat of water
CL	coefficient for the calculation of C_p
DL	coefficient for the calculation of C_p
f	amount of bypass exhaust gas in exhaust driven supercharger
$F_{\rm mep}$	friction mean effective pressure
fp	friction power
F	force
FCS	fuel-air cycle simulation
G	number of intake valves per cylinder
$\overline{h}$	specific enthalpy
$h_{\rm c}$	heat transfer coefficient
$h_{\rm fg}$	heat of vapourization

H	intake valve diameter
H_{add}	heat added
H_p	enthalpy of product
H_{rp}	heat of reaction at constant pressure
H_r	enthalpy of reactant
H_w	enthalpy of water
ibc	start of injection
ip	indicated power
IC	internal combustion
ICS	ideal cycle simulation
k	specific heat ratio
k_p	specific heat ratio of the products
k_r	specific heat ratio of the reactants
K	number of cylinders
L	connecting rod length
M	mass
M	piston skirt length
m_p	mass of products
m_r	mass of reactant
n	mass fraction
n	number of working stroke per minute (rpm/2) per cylinder
N	number of moles of various species
N	speed in rpm
N_a	moles of air entering the carburetor
N_m	moles of fuel vapour and air in engine during compression stroke
N_{mo}	kilomoles of air-fuel vapour in a mixture containing 1 kmol of fuel
N_p	kilomoles of products formed from the combustion of $N_m + N_x$
N_p	moles of gaseous products
N_p	moles of products after combustion
N_{po}	kilomoles of products formed from the combustion of N_{mo}
N_r	moles of gaseous reactants
N_r	moles of reactant before combustion
N_w	number of moles of water
N_x	kilomoles of residual exhaust from previous cycle
p	pressure
p_a	atmospheric pressure
p_e	pressure at the instant combustion ends
p_i	pressure before the spark passes
p_{imf}	inlet manifold pressure
p_m	manifold pressure
p_{mef}	mean effective pressure
P_{im}	indicated mean effective pressure
P_p	final pressure of the products
PCS	progressive combustion simulation
PR_{crit}	critical pressure ratio
q_a	Heat added

q_r	Heat rejected
Q_p	energy release at constant pressure
Q_v	energy release at constant volume
r	compression ratio
R	gas constant
RAF	relative air-fuel ratio
Re	Reynold's number
S	stroke
S	total entropy
S_r	scavenging ratio
SI	spark-ignition
t_{in}	inlet water temperature
t_{out}	outlet water temperature
T	temperature
T'	equilibrium temperature
T_a	ambient temperature
T_e	temperature at the instant combustion ends
T_i	initial temperature before the spark passes
T_m	manifold temperature
T_m	temperature of the fresh fuel-air mixture in the intake pipe
T_p	temperature of products
T_r	temperature of reactants
TDC	top dead centre
$\overline{u}$	average specific internal energy
U_{rp}	heat of reaction at constant volume
V	volume
V_{bdc}	total cylinder volume
V_{disp}	displacement volume
V_r	cut-off ratio
V_{tdc}	clearance volume
W_{comp}	work done during compression stroke
W_{exp}	work done during expansion stroke
W_{loop}	intake-exhaust loop work
w_{net}	net work output per unit quantity of air
W_{net}	work input to the gear driven supercharger
W_{spch}	net work output of the cycle
W_{turb}	work input to the exhaust driven supercharger
Y_{cc}	chemically correct amount of oxygen per mole of fuel
Y_{min}	minimum oxygen required for combustion per mole of fuel
Z	working fluid velocity
$\Delta\theta_c$	combustion duration in terms of crank angles
Δp	pressure change during a small interval of time
Δp_c	pressure change as a result of combustion
Δp_p	pressure change as a result of piston movement
ΔS	change in enthalpy
ΔU	change in internal energy

η_c	isentropic efficiency of the compressor
η_t	turbine efficiency
η_{th}	thermal efficiency
γ	specific heat ratio
λ	thermal conductivity of gas
ϕ_i	function to calculate entropy
θ	crank angle
θ_c	crank angle when combustion ends
θ_i	crank angle at the start of ignition

1 INTRODUCTION

1.1 Simulation

Simulation is a broadly used and somewhat ill-defined term from the engineering point of view. According to Webster's international dictionary "*to simulate*" means "*to feign, to attain the essence without the reality*". However, the simplest meaning of simulation is "*imitation*". These dictionary meanings do not bring out a clear picture of the word "simulation" for engineering applications. Therefore, a definition of the word is desired in this context. With some trepidation, the author defines simulation as follows:

Simulation is the process of designing a model of a real system and conducting experiments with it, for the purpose of understanding the behaviour of the system.

Computer simulation has gained a greater importance these days because of the availability of fast digital computers. It can be defined as follows:

Computer simulation is the process of formulating a model of a physical system representing actual processes and analyzing the same. Usually, the model is a mathematical one representing the actual processes through a set of algebraic, differential or integral equations and the analysis is made using a computer.

In modern research, computer simulation has become a powerful tool in that it saves time and is also economical compared to experimental study. A proposed theory can be analyzed quickly using a computer and the cost of setting up an experimental apparatus can be postponed until optimization is achieved. However, it may be noted that simulation is only a step prior to experimentation and the results obtained from simulation studies must be validated with experimental results to establish the reliability. Once validated, computer simulation can provide a deep insight into the performance characteristics of the system. This statement is particularly true in the case of internal combustion engine studies.

1.2 Advantages of computer simulation

In an internal combustion (IC) engine, the processes involved are extremely complex. Until the last decade, the design of an engine relied heavily on previous experience and know-how. As a result of this, in engine design, extensive testing of the prototype is considered necessary. Selecting the best design from such testing is a task of considerable magnitude. Because of these difficulties, analysis by means of computer simulation has become quite popular in recent years. Further, computer simulation offers the following advantages:

(i) It serves as a tool for a better understanding of the variables involved and their effect on engine performance.

(ii) It systematizes knowledge obtained through expensive engine testing.

(iii) It considerably reduces the time-consuming tests by narrowing down the variables that must be studied.

(iv) It helps in optimizing the engine design for a particular application, thereby reducing cost and time.

1.3 Objective of this book

The main objective of this book is to present the theory and computer programs necessary for simulating the performance of a conventional hydrocarbon-fuelled compression ignition (CI) engine, for any fuel of the form $C_xH_yO_z$.

The model describes the processes occurring within the working fluid of a compression ignition engine and provides an indication of the limits and trends of the performance, as a function of some system variables. This will enable one to see what one could expect from an engine working within such system variables.

1.4 Step-by-step approach

A four-stroke compression ignition engine works on the four-stroke, five-event principle. The five events are given below.

(i) Suction
(ii) Compression
(iii) Combustion
(iv) Expansion
(v) Exhaust

These five events are completed in two revolutions of the crank shaft of the engine. Simulation in this book is attempted in a step-by-step approach.

Step I: As a first step, the engine is assumed to work with air as the working medium in an ideal air-standard diesel cycle. We will call this analysis an ideal cycle simulation (ICS). Here, heat addition and heat rejection are supposed to take place by means of a heat transfer process at constant pressure and constant volume, respectively.

Step II: As the second step, ideal cycle simulation is modified by taking fuel into account, incorporating adiabatic flame temperature calculations for heat addition/combustion analysis. In this analysis, instead of air, the working medium is assumed to be a mixture of fuel and air. We will call this analysis as fuel–air cycle simulation (FCS). Here, combustion is assumed to take place at constant pressure and under adiabatic condition.

Step III: In this step, the adiabatic flame temperature calculations are modified by assuming combustion to be progressive, i.e., heat release is not instantaneous but spreads over a period of time. In other words, the duration of combustion is taken into account. In CI engines, the heat release analysis can be done either by means of progressive combustion at constant pressure, or as means of zero-, one- or two-dimensional heat release models. In this book, two types of analysis have been explained. The first one is the progressive combustion at constant pressure. The second one is the progressive combustion using a zero-dimensional single-zone model. Further, extension to one- or two-dimensional models using two- or multi-zone approach is also possible. We will call this analysis progressive combustion simulation (PCS). However, in recent years, attempts have been made to use multi-dimensional models. This requires high speed, high memory computers.

Step IV: In this final step, using simplified assumptions, the engine heat transfer can be taken into account by means of empirical equations. Gas exchange processes are introduced in order to analyze the engine intake and exhaust. We will call this analysis actual cycle simulation (ACS). In this step, intake and exhaust processes using fluid dynamic equations, heat transfer and friction are included by means of empirical equations.

By means of this step-by-step simulation, the values of pressure, volume and temperature at salient points in the cycle are calculated. Work output as well as thermal efficiency is evaluated. Provisions have been made in the computer program for making parametric studies. This step-by-step approach, it is hoped, will make the reader appreciate the complexities involved in actual engine simulation.

Compared to other processes, the combustion process is not amenable to thermodynamic analysis. However, an attempt has been made to bring combustion analysis within the purview of thermodynamics.

In order to get a basic understanding of the combustion process pertaining to engines, the next two chapters are devoted to providing a background for analyzing the combustion phenomena using thermodynamics. These chapters deal with reactive processes and adiabatic flame temperature calculations, respectively.

2

REACTIVE PROCESSES

2.1 Introduction

When a fuel comes into contact with oxygen or air under the proper environment, a chemical reaction takes place. The reaction can be *exothermic*, where heat energy is released; or sometimes *endothermic*, where heat energy is absorbed. The heat energy released in an exothermic reaction can be used, for example, to run an internal combustion engine. In the analysis of internal combustion engine processes, we are interested in the study of exothermic reactions involving those substances that can be used as fuels. In other words, we would like to inquire into chemical reactions upto the extent that these reactions are a source of heat energy for heat engines, especially the internal combustion engines.

Many books talk about *reactive processes.* Let us see what is meant by a *reactive process.* A process involving *chemical reaction* can be considered as reactive process. Then, what is a chemical reaction?

A *chemical reaction* may be defined as a rearrangement of the atoms of the reactants due to the redistribution of electrons to form products that are different from reactants. The implication of this definition is that the number of atoms of each element participating in a reaction remains unchanged, i.e., the conservation of matter. This principle will be used in writing the equations for chemical reactions.

It is known that a chemically correct or stoichiometric mixture of hydrocarbon fuel and air reacts to produce only H_2O or CO_2 or both.

For example:

$$H_2 + 0.5\,O_2 \rightarrow H_2O,$$
$$CO + 0.5\,O_2 \rightarrow CO_2,$$
$$CH_4 + 2.0\,O_2 \rightarrow CO_2 + 2\,H_2O,$$
$$C_8H_{18} + 12.5\,O_2 \rightarrow 8\,CO_2 + 9\,H_2O,$$

$$C_{10}H_{22} + 15.5\,O_2 \rightarrow 10\,CO_2 + 11\,H_2O,$$
$$CH_3OH + 1.5\,O_2 \rightarrow CO_2 + 2\,H_2O,$$
$$C_2H_5OH + 3.0\,O_2 \rightarrow 2\,CO_2 + 3\,H_2O.$$

Note: All the above fuels can be used in IC engines.

2.2 Heat of reaction

Under conditions that promote combustion, the active constituents of a fuel react with oxygen. This combustion process involves the oxidation of the carbon and hydrogen present in the fuel. The combustion process is a complex reaction or, more exactly, a rapidly occurring series of reactions.

Whenever combustion occurs, the energy associated with the chemical bonds in the fuel and oxygen molecules is released. The chemical energy is converted into heat energy and appears first as a heating effect in the product gases. The final temperature of the products of combustion depends on a number of factors. The important ones are as follows.

(i) the fuel and its composition,
(ii) the pressure and temperature of the reactant mixture,
(iii) the state of the fuel, whether liquid or gaseous, and
(iv) the external constraints imposed on the reacting system, i.e. whether the combustion takes place at constant volume or at constant pressure.

In order to calculate the final temperature of the products of combustion, the energy characteristics of the fuel should be known. The energy characteristics of fuels are variously known as *enthalpies of combustion, heating values, heat of combustion* and *heat of reaction*. In this book, the term *heat of reaction* will be used.

2.2.1 Definition of heat of reaction

The heat of reaction at constant volume, U_{rp}, and at constant pressure, H_{rp}, is defined as the energy added to bring the products of combustion to the initial temperature, viz. 298 K, when a unit quantity of fuel and chemically correct oxygen burn at constant volume or at constant pressure, respectively.

The implications of the above definition are as follows.

(i) U_{rp} and H_{rp} are both negative.
(ii) U_{rp} and H_{rp} are properties of the fuel.
(iii) U_{rp} and H_{rp} refer specifically to chemically correct fuel-oxygen mixtures reacting at 298 K.

It may be noted that both U_{rp} and H_{rp} are measurable quantities.

For the analysis of engine combustion, we will define two related energy terms, Q_v and Q_p; where the term Q_v stands for energy release at constant volume and Q_p, the energy release at constant pressure.

2.2.2 Definition of Q_v and Q_p

The energy released at constant volume, Q_v, and that released at constant pressure, Q_p, are defined as the heat energies released, when the products are cooled to the temperature, T, of the reactants when a unit quantity of fuel burns at constant volume or at constant pressure, respectively.

Note: Q_v and Q_p are both positive. They are properties of the reactant mixture, referred to any temperature. They are calculated from the heat of reaction.

2.3 Measurement of U_{rp}

Let us assume that a chemical reaction takes place in a closed rigid container of fixed volume. Let the subscripts r, p and v denote the reactants, the products and the volume, respectively. The first law for a closed system can be written as

$$Q_v - W = \Delta U. \tag{2.1}$$

Since there is no change in the volume of the system, i.e. $W = 0$, eq.(2.1) becomes

$$Q_v = \Delta U. \tag{2.2}$$

The change in internal energy due to the chemical reaction is given by

$$\Delta U = \sum \left[(N_i \bar{u}_i)_p - (N_j \bar{u}_j)_r \right] \tag{2.3}$$

$$= U_p - U_r.$$

The subscripts i and j stand for the various species in the products and reactants, respectively, and N represents the number of moles of these species (fuel, oxygen, carbondioxide, etc.), and $\bar{u}$ is the specific internal energy in kJ/kmol.

Since there are at least two reactants and often there is more than one product of reaction, the summation sign is used in eq.(2.3).

The quantity U_{rp} is measured using a constant-volume bomb calorimeter. A schematic diagram of the bomb calorimeter is shown in Fig.2.1.

A measured quantity of the fuel along with excess air is introduced into a rigid vessel, which is designed to withstand the high pressure of combustion

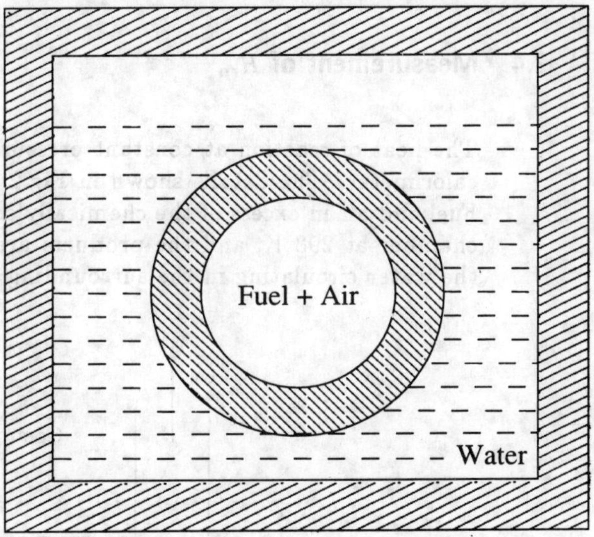

Fig.2.1 *Bomb calorimeter*

without deformation. If there is a deformation, work will be done on the vessel by the product gases and the results reported will become spurious. The vessel is placed in a large tub containing water at room temperature and is left for a period so that temperature equilibrium as well as thorough mixing of fuel and oxygen is achieved. The fuel is ignited by a spark plug. Heat is transferred to the water through the walls of the vessel. The entire system, which is insulated against heat transfer to the surroundings, comes to temperature equilibrium at some temperature T'. A correction is applied to reduce the temperature, again, to the initial temperature, viz. 298 K.

If we designate the change in internal energy ΔU as U_{rp}, then from eq.(2.3)

$$U_{rp}(298) \quad = \quad U_p(298) - U_r(298). \tag{2.4}$$

For octane (C_8H_{18}), the value of U_{rp} can be calculated as

$$U_r(298) = [\overline{u}_{C_8H_{18}} + (12.5 + x)\overline{u}_{O_2} + 3.76(12.5 + x)\overline{u}_{N_2}]_{298}, \tag{2.5}$$

$$U_p(298) = [8\overline{u}_{CO_2} + 9\overline{u}_{H_2O} + x\overline{u}_{O_2} + 3.76(12.5 + x)\overline{u}_{N_2}]_{298}, \tag{2.6}$$

where x denotes the number of moles of excess oxygen and 3.76 is the ratio of N_2 to O_2 in air, calculated on molal basis. Substituting eqs.(2.5) and (2.6) in eq.(2.4), we have

$$U_{rp} = [8\overline{u}_{CO_2} + 9\overline{u}_{H_2O} - \overline{u}_{C_8H_{18}} - 12.5\overline{u}_{O_2}]_{298}. \tag{2.7}$$

If the specific enthalpies of the various constituents are known, U_{rp} can be estimated from eq.(2.7).

2.4 Measurement of H_{rp}

The heat of reaction at constant pressure, H_{rp}, is measured in a steady-flow calorimeter. The details shown in Fig.2.2 are reduced to the bare essentials. Fuel and air in excess of the chemically correct requirement enter the reaction chamber at 298 K, and the products are cooled to the inlet temperature by the water circulating in the surrounding jacket.

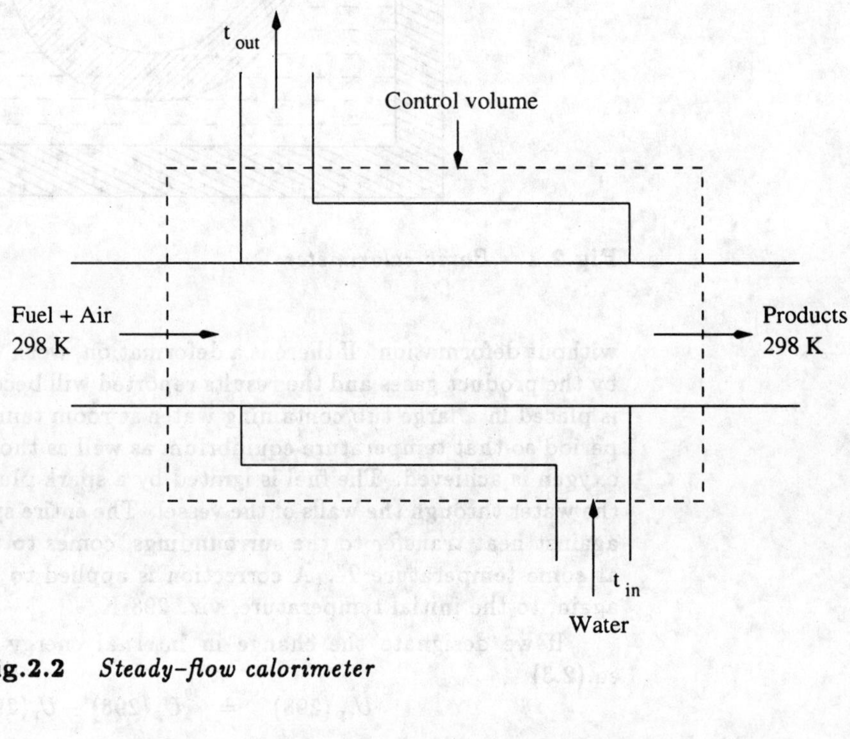

Fig.2.2 *Steady–flow calorimeter*

If the changes in the kinetic and potential energies are negligible, as is usually the case, for a steady-flow conservation of energy

$$H_r(298) + H_w(t_{in}) = H_p(298) + H_w(t_{out}), \tag{2.8}$$

$$H_w(t_{in}) - H_w(t_{out}) = H_p(298) - H_r(298). \tag{2.9}$$

The left-hand side of eq.(2.9) can be written as

$$N_w C_w(t_{in} - t_{out}). \tag{2.10}$$

The subscripts r, p and w refer to the reactants, products and cooling water, respectively. The terms t_{in} and t_{out} refer to the inlet and outlet water temperatures, respectively. The left-hand side of eq.(2.9) represents the energy added to bring down the temperature of the product to 298 K, which according to the definition is H_{rp}. Therefore,

$$H_{rp} \quad = \quad N_w C_w (t_{in} - t_{out}), \tag{2.11}$$

where N_w is the number of moles of water passing through the jacket per unit mole of the fuel burnt. Clearly, H_{rp} is negative because t_{in} will be less than t_{out}. Now, H_{rp} can be written as

$$H_{rp} \quad = \quad H_p(298) - H_r(298). \tag{2.12}$$

For example, when decane (diesel); $C_{10}H_{22}$, is burnt, the two terms on the right-hand side of eq.(2.12), with x denoting the moles of excess oxygen, can be written as

$$H_r(298) = \left[\bar{h}_{C_{10}H_{22}} + (15.5 + x)\bar{h}_{O_2} + 3.76(15.5 + x)\bar{h}_{N_2}\right]_{298}, \tag{2.13}$$

$$H_p(298) = \left[10\bar{h}_{CO_2} + 11\bar{h}_{H_2O} + x\bar{h}_{O_2} + 3.76(15.5 + x)\bar{h}_{N_2}\right]_{298}, \tag{2.14}$$

and hence H_{rp} for decane is given by

$$H_{rp} = \left[10\bar{h}_{CO_2} + 11\bar{h}_{H_2O} - \bar{h}_{C_{10}H_{22}} - 15.5\bar{h}_{O_2}\right]_{298}. \tag{2.15}$$

The point to be noted in the measurement of U_{rp} and H_{rp} is that the reactant mixture contains excess air, and not chemically correct oxygen. There are three reasons for making measurements using excess air:

(i) Air is readily available while oxygen is not.

(ii) A chemically correct fuel-oxygen mixture would heat the equipment excessively.

(iii) Excess air is used to ensure complete combustion.

Since the reactant and product gas mixtures enter and leave the device at the same temperature, the excess oxygen and nitrogen terms on the right-hand side of eqs.(2.5) and (2.13) will cancel out [see eqs.(2.7) and (2.15)], and it will appear as though the heat of reaction was measured for a chemically correct fuel-oxygen mixture.

If we know H_{rp}, we can calculate U_{rp} and vice versa. Subtracting eq.(2.4) from eq.(2.12), we have

$$H_{rp} - U_{rp} \quad = \quad (H_p - U_p) - (H_r - U_r). \tag{2.16}$$

The temperature subscript has been dropped since it is understood always to be 298 K. For gases, we can write

$$\bar{h} - \bar{u} \quad = \quad RT \tag{2.17}$$

where R is the universal gas constant, since the enthalpy $\bar{h}$ and internal energy $\bar{u}$ are in units per mole. For liquids and solids

$$\bar{h} - \bar{u} \approx 0.$$

The difference between the constant-pressure and constant-volume heat of reaction may then be written as

$$H_{rp} - U_{rp} = (N_p - N_r)RT. \tag{2.18}$$

With $R = 8.314$ kJ/kmol-K and $T = 298$ K, the value of the product RT will be 2477.57, which can be approximated to 2480. Thus,

$$H_{rp} - U_{rp} = 2480(N_p - N_r), \tag{2.19}$$

where N_p and N_r denote, respectively, the mole number in the product and in the reactant mixture of the gaseous species for a chemically correct fuel-oxygen mixture.

Let us now work out an example to calculate the H_{rp} and U_{rp} values. These calculations will reveal the effect of H_2O on the products in the liquid or gaseous form. If H_2O is in the liquid form, the values are higher and thereby are termed as higher calorific value of fuel. If H_2O in the product is in the gaseous form, they are called the lower calorific value of the fuel.

2.5 Calculation of higher and lower heat value of fuels

- Consider the fuel C_8H_{18}. We can write the reaction equation as

$$C_8H_{18} + 12.5O_2 \rightarrow 8CO_2 + 9H_2O,$$

$$N_r = 1 + 12.5 = 13.5,$$

$$N_p = 8 + 9 = 17.$$

From Table 2.4, for gaseous C_8H_{18} and gaseous H_2O in the product

$$H_{rp} = -5089100 \text{ kJ/kmol}.$$

We can now calculate U_{rp} using eq.(2.19):

$$\begin{aligned} U_{rp} &= -5089100 - 2480 \times (17 - 13.5) \\ &= -5097780 \text{ kJ/kmol (see Table 2.2)}, \end{aligned}$$

a change of less than 0.2%.

It can easily be shown that the effect of condensing the water vapour in the product on H_{rp} and U_{rp} values is quite substantial. Let

H_{rp} = the constant-pressure heat of reaction with gaseous H_2O,

H'_{rp} = the constant-pressure heat of reaction with liquid H_2O.

Then

$$H_{rp} - H'_{rp} = N_{H_2O} \times \overline{h}_{fg}(H_2O).$$

With

$$\overline{h}_{fg}(H_2O) = 43956 \text{ kJ/kmol},$$

$$H_{rp} - H'_{rp} = 9 \times 43956$$

$$= 395604 \text{ kJ/kmol},$$

therefore

$$H'_{rp} = -5089100 - 395604$$

$$= -5484704 \text{ kJ/kmol}.$$

Similarly, U'_{rp} is given by

$$U'_{rp} = H'_{rp} - 2480 \times (N_p - N_r)$$

$$= -5484704 - 2480 \times (17 - 13.5)$$

$$= -5493384 \text{ kJ/kmol},$$

a change of more than 7.0% (compared to U_{rp}).

- Consider the fuel, $C_{10}H_{22}$. We can write the reaction equation as

$$C_{10}H_{22} + 15.5O_2 \quad \rightarrow \quad 10CO_2 + 11H_2O$$

From Table 2.4, for gaseous $C_{10}H_{22}$ and gaseous H_2O, we have

$$H_{rp} = -6312300 \text{ kJ/kmol},$$

$$U_{rp} = -6312300 - (21 - 16.5) \times 2480$$

$$= -6323460 \text{ kJ/kmol (see Table 2.2)}.$$

a change of less than 0.2%.

Let H_{rp} denote the constant-pressure heat of reaction with gaseous H_2O in the product, and let H'_{rp} denote the constant-pressure heat of reaction with liquid H_2O in the product. Now

$$H_{rp} - H'_{rp} = N_{H_2O} \times h_{fg}(H_2O).$$

With $h_{fg}(H_2O) = 43956$ kJ/kmol, we have

$$H_{rp} - H'_{rp} = 11 \times 43956 = 483516 \text{ kJ/kmol}.$$

Then,

$$H'_{rp} = -6312300 - 483516$$

$$= -6795816 \text{ kJ/kmol},$$

a change of more than 7.0%.

Similarly, it can be shown that the change in the U_{rp} value will also be of the same order.

The above calculations show that while securing heat of reaction values from published tables, greatest care must be exercised to note the condition of H_2O in the product. As mentioned earlier, normally, the term *lower* calorific value refers to H_{rp} or U_{rp} for the case of *gaseous* H_2O in the product and the term *higher* calorific value to those for the case of *liquid* H_2O in the product.

Tables 2.1 and 2.2 list the U_{rp} values for various fuels that can be used in the calculation of temperature rise due to heat of reaction in internal combustion engines. Similarly, Tables 2.3 and 2.4 list the H_{rp} values for various fuels. When the U_{rp} and H_{rp} values listed in the table are divided by the molecular weight, the units are converted to kJ/kg with numerical results that differ only slightly. It may be noted that the constant heat of reaction per unit mass is a characteristic of the hydrocarbon series.

Table 2.1 U_{rp} constant-volume heat of reaction values for the case of liquid H_2O in the product

Fuel	Formula	Mol. wt.	Liquid fuel		Gaseous fuel	
			kJ/kmol	kJ/kg	kJ/kmol	kJ/kg
Methane	CH_4	16	—	—	−880522	−55033
Ethane	C_2H_6	30	—	—	−1545568	−51519
Propane	C_3H_8	44	−2187764	−49722	−2201184	−50027
n-Butane	C_4H_{10}	58	−2936380	−50627	−2855300	−49229
n-Pentane	C_5H_{12}	72	−3484496	−48396	−3508516	−48729
n-Hexane	C_6H_{14}	86	−4133612	−48065	−4162532	−48402
n-Heptane	C_7H_{16}	100	−4782828	−47828	−4816748	−48167
n-Octane	C_8H_{18}	114	−5432244	−47651	−5471064	−47992
n-Nonane	C_9H_{20}	128	−6688460	−52253	−6125380	−47855
n-Decane	$C_{10}H_{22}$	142	−6731176	−47403	−6779696	−47744
Methanol	CH_3OH	32	−901132	−28160	−936032	−29251
Ethanol	C_2H_5OH	46	−1540276	−33484	−1667908	−36259
Benzene	C_6H_6	78	−3439736	−44099	−3559068	−45629

Table 2.2 U_{rp} constant-volume heat of reaction for the case of gaseous H_2O in the product

Fuel	Formula	Mol. wt.	Liquid fuel		Gaseous fuel	
			kJ/kmol	kJ/kg	kJ/kmol	kJ/kg
Methane	CH_4	16	—	—	− 797570	−49848
Ethane	C_2H_6	30	—	—	−1421140	−47371
Propane	C_3H_8	44	−2021860	−45951	−2035280	−46256
n-Butane	C_4H_{10}	58	−2629000	−45327	−2647920	−45654
n-Pentane	C_5H_{12}	72	−3235640	−44939	−3259660	−45273
n-Hexane	C_6H_{14}	86	−3843280	−44689	−3872200	−45026
n-Heptane	C_7H_{16}	100	−4451020	−44510	−4484940	−44849
n-Octane	C_8H_{18}	114	−5058960	−44377	−5097780	−44717
n-Nonane	C_9H_{20}	128	−5667100	−44274	−5710620	−44614
n-Decane	$C_{10}H_{22}$	142	−6274940	−44189	−6323460	−44531
Methanol	CH_3OH	32	− 818180	−25568	− 853080	−26659
Ethanol	C_2H_5OH	46	−1503760	−32690	−1543480	−33554
Benzene	C_6H_6	78	−3403220	−43631	−3434640	−44034

Table 2.3 H_{rp} constant-pressure heat of reaction for the case of liquid H_2O in the product

Fuel	Formula	Mol. wt.	Liquid fuel		Gaseous fuel	
			kJ/kmol	kJ/kg	kJ/kmol	kJ/kg
Methane	CH_4	16	—	—	− 885482	−55343
Ethane	C_2H_6	30	—	—	−1551768	−51726
Propane	C_3H_8	44	−2192724	−49835	−2208624	−50196
n-Butane	C_4H_{10}	58	−2842580	−49010	−2863980	−49379
n-Pentane	C_5H_{12}	72	−3491936	−48499	−3518436	−48869
n-Hexane	C_6H_{14}	86	−4142292	−48166	−4173692	−48531
n-Heptane	C_7H_{16}	100	−4792748	−47927	−4829148	−48291
n-Octane	C_8H_{18}	114	−5443404	−47749	−5484704	−48111
n-Nonane	C_9H_{20}	128	−6700860	−52350	−6140260	−47971
n-Decane	$C_{10}H_{22}$	142	−6744816	−47499	−6795816	−47858
Methanol	CH_3OH	32	− 902372	−28199	− 939752	−29367
Ethanol	C_2H_5OH	46	−1542756	−33538	−1672868	−36367
Benzene	C_6H_6	78	−3443456	−44147	−3565268	−45709

Table 2.4 H_{rp} constant-pressure heat of reaction for the case of gaseous H_2O in the product

Fuel	Formula	Mol. wt.	Liquid fuel		Gaseous fuel	
			kJ/kmol	kJ/kg	kJ/kmol	kJ/kg
Methane	CH_4	16	—	—	− 797570	−49848
Ethane	C_2H_6	30	—	—	−1419900	−47330
Propane	C_3H_8	44	−2016900	−45839	−2032800	−46200
n-Butane	C_4H_{10}	58	−2622800	−45221	−2644200	−45590
n-Pentane	C_5H_{12}	72	−3228200	−44836	−3254700	−45204
n-Hexane	C_6H_{14}	86	−3834600	−44588	−3866000	−44954
n-Heptane	C_7H_{16}	100	−4441100	−44411	−4477500	−44775
n-Octane	C_8H_{18}	114	−5047800	−44279	−5089100	−44641
n-Nonane	C_9H_{20}	128	−5654700	−44177	−5700700	−44537
n-Decane	$C_{10}H_{22}$	142	−6261300	−44094	−6312300	−44453
Methanol	CH_3OH	32	− 814460	−25452	− 851840	−26620
Ethanol	C_2H_5OH	46	−1498800	−32583	−1541000	−33500
Benzene	C_6H_6	78	−3399500	−43583	−3433400	−44018

Note: For H_2O $\overline{h}_{fg}$ (25°C, 298.16 K) = 43956 kJ/kmol.

Exercise

Write a computer program to calculate the heat of reaction in kJ/kmol and in kcal/kg for the following fuels, for the eight conditions given in the table:

$$C_8H_{18},\ C_{10}H_{22},\ CH_3OH,\ C_2H_5OH,\ CH_4,\ CO,\ H_2.$$

Constraint	Fuel	H_2O in the product
Constant volume	Liquid	Liquid
Constant volume	Liquid	Gaseous
Constant volume	Gaseous	Gaseous
Constant volume	Gaseous	Liquid
Constant pressure	Liquid	Liquid
Constant pressure	Liquid	Gaseous
Constant pressure	Gaseous	Gaseous
Constant pressure	Gaseous	Liquid

3

ADIABATIC FLAME TEMPERATURE

3.1 Introduction

Virtually every problem involving combustion will involve the calculation of adiabatic flame temperature. The final temperature that can be achieved is maximum for those systems where the combustion is complete and the system is adiabatic. In this chapter, we discuss the technique for the calculation of the adiabatic flame temperature.

The adiabatic flame temperature of a combustion system depends on many factors. The major ones are:

(i) the fuel(s),
(ii) the chemical composition of the reactant mixture,
(iii) the pressure of the reactant mixture,
(iv) the temperature of the reactant mixture,
(v) the constraints on the system, viz. whether the combustion takes place at constant-volume or at constant-pressure.

Fuels with different hydrogen-to-carbon ratios produce different flame temperatures. Likewise, as the composition of the reactant mixture varies (lean, chemically correct or rich), the flame temperature also varies.

Fuel–oxygen mixtures produce higher temperatures than fuel–air mixtures with an equivalent oxygen content; the nitrogen present in air is essentially inert and, as such, does not contribute to the combustion reaction but merely absorbs energy.

A higher initial temperature of the reactant mixture before combustion increases the flame temperature. Constant–volume combustion does not transfer work to the surroundings in contrast to constant-pressure combustion; hence, the adiabatic flame temperature at constant-volume is much higher than that at constant-pressure. Further, the reactant pressure can also affect the flame temperature.

Accurate calculation of the flame temperature involves a set of complicated equations. However, for two reasons we will confine our attention only to a simple set of equations:

(i) Accurate calculation tends to obscure the physics of what is taking place.

(ii) Approximate flame temperature computation often produces *good enough* values, although we cannot say how good until approximate and accurate values are compared.

The adiabatic flame temperature calculations, if done manually, are carried out by trial and error. This can be done very easily by a systematic search with a computer. The main emphasis in this chapter will be towards this end.

3.2 Complete combustion in C–H–O–N systems

Assuming complete combustion, we can decide the composition of the combustion products merely by inspecting the reactant mixture. For a reactant mixture that contains C, H, O, N atoms, we will formulate the rules as follows:

(i) All hydrogen is first oxidised to H_2O.

(ii) All carbon is initially oxidised to CO.

(iii) If any oxygen remains, part of the CO is oxidised to CO_2.

(iv) If there is sufficient oxygen to oxidise all the carbon to CO_2, the excess appears as O_2.

(v) All nitrogen appears as N_2, i.e. nitrogen is assumed to be inert.

Keeping in mind the above rules, let us consider the general case of any fuel represented by the formula $C_xH_yO_z$.

Let us denote C_x as N_{mC}, H_y as N_{mH_2} and O_z as N_{mO_2}. Here N_{mC}, N_{mH_2} and N_{mO_2} denote, respectively, the number of moles of carbon, hydrogen and oxygen atoms in a mole of fuel.

Let Y_{cc} denote the chemically correct amount of oxygen per mole of fuel required for combustion. Then, as per the above rules,

$$Y_{cc} = N_{mC} + 0.25N_{mH_2} - 0.5N_{mO_2} \tag{3.1}$$

Let Y_{min} denote the minimum amount of oxygen required in the reactants per mole of fuel, i.e. the minimum amount of oxygen required to convert H_2 to H_2O and C to CO.

We can express this as

$$\begin{aligned} Y_{min} &= 0.5(N_{mC} - N_{mO_2}) + 0.25(N_{mH_2}) \\ &= Y_{cc} - 0.5N_{mC}. \end{aligned} \tag{3.2}$$

Hence, for a reactant mixture containing

$$1 \text{ mole}^{\dagger} \text{ of fuel } + YO_2 + 3.76YN_2$$

the product mole numbers can be written as

$$\left.\begin{array}{ll} \underline{Y_{\min} \le Y \le Y_{cc},} & \underline{Y \ge Y_{cc},} \\ N_1 = 2(Y_{cc} - Y), & N_1 = 0, \\ N_2 = 2(Y - Y_{\min}), & N_2 = N_{mC}, \\ N_3 = 0.5N_{mH_2}, & N_3 = 0.5N_{mH_2}, \\ N_4 = 3.76Y, & N_4 = 3.76Y, \\ N_5 = 0, & N_5 = Y - Y_{cc}. \end{array}\right\} \quad (3.3)$$

N_1 through N_5 can be used as subscribed variables in the computer program, so that the subscripts 1 to 5 can be made to denote

$$1 = CO, \; 2 = CO_2, \; 3 = H_2O, \; 4 = N_2, \; 5 = O_2. \quad (3.4)$$

With the above background, we will now examine the calculation of adiabatic flame temperature for

(i) constant-volume combustion, and
(ii) constant-pressure combustion.

It is easy to develop the system of equations for a particular fuel and then pass on easily to the general formulation of the solution for any fuel.

Calculations, if done manually, will be quite tedious and time-consuming. Hence, it is always better to write a computer program for the calculations. In the next few sections we will develop the necessary background theory for the same.

3.3 Constant-volume adiabatic combustion

An illustration of the problem is given in Fig.3.1. The reactants at temperature 298 K and pressure P_r are ignited and both the flame temperature T and the final pressure P_p are to be calculated. Since pressure and temperature are intensive quantities, the size of the vessel is of no concern, and they are independent of the system.

† A mole is the amount of substance of a system that contains as many elementary entities as there are carbon atoms in 0.012 kg of carbon. The elementary entities must be specified and they may include atoms, molecules, ions, electrons and other particles or a specified group of such substances.

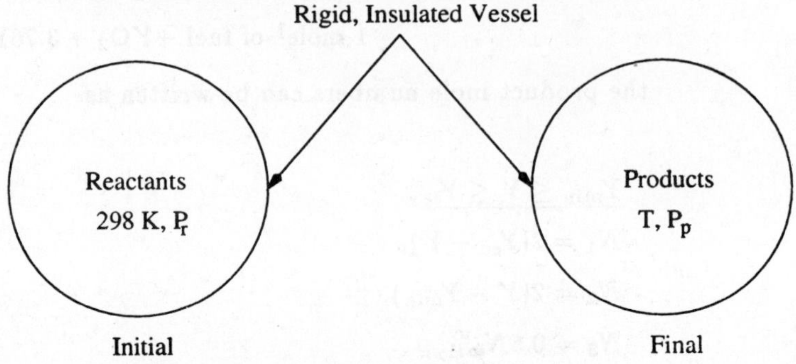

Fig.3.1 ***Constant-volume adiabatic combustion***

Let us choose to work with a reactant mixture containing one mole of fuel. The fuel we select for illustration is C_8H_{18}. The reactants will be

$$C_8H_{18} + YO_2 + 3.76YN_2.$$

Since the combustion takes place in a rigid insulated vessel, there is no work and heat transfer. Hence, the energy equation can be written as

$$U_r(298) \quad = \quad U_p(T) \tag{3.5}$$

For C_8H_{18} the heat of reaction at constant-volume is [refer to eq.(2.7)]

$$U_{rp} = [8\overline{u}_{CO_2} + 9\overline{u}_{H_2O} - \overline{u}_{C_8H_{18}} - 12.5\overline{u}_{O_2}]_{298} \tag{3.6}$$

Case (i) $Y \geq Y_{cc}$

Here,

$$U_r(298) = [\overline{u}_{C_8H_{18}} + Y\overline{u}_{O_2} + 3.76Y\overline{u}_{N_2}]_{298}, \tag{3.7}$$

$$U_p(T) = [8\overline{u}_{CO_2} + 9\overline{u}_{H_2O} + (Y - 12.5)\overline{u}_{O_2} + 3.76Y\overline{u}_{N_2}]_T. \tag{3.8}$$

The above four equations [eqs.(3.5) to (3.8)] are now manipulated as follows. Substituting eqs.(3.7) and (3.8) into eq.(3.5), we get

$$[\overline{u}_{C_8H_{18}} + Y\overline{u}_{O_2} + 3.76\overline{u}_{N_2}]_{298}$$

$$= \quad [8\overline{u}_{CO_2} + 9\overline{u}_{H_2O} + (Y - 12.5)\overline{u}_{O_2} + 3.76Y\overline{u}_{N_2}]_T. \tag{3.9}$$

From eq.(3.6) we can write

$$\overline{u}_{C_8H_{18}} \quad = \quad [8\overline{u}_{CO_2} + 9\overline{u}_{H_2O} - 12.5\overline{u}_{O_2}]_{298} - U_{rp} \tag{3.10}$$

Substituting the value of $\overline{u}_{C_8H_{18}}$ from eq.(3.10) into eq.(3.9) and simplifying, we get

$$-U_{rp} = 8\Delta\overline{u}_{CO_2} + 9\Delta\overline{u}_{H_2O} + 3.76Y\Delta\overline{u}_{N_2} + (Y - 12.5)\Delta\overline{u}_{O_2}, \tag{3.11}$$

where

$$\Delta\overline{u}_i = \overline{u}_i(T) - \overline{u}_i(298). \tag{3.12}$$

It may be noted that the left-hand side of eq.(3.11) is a measurable quantity and the right-hand side contains pairs of internal energy differences.

Case (ii) $Y_{\min} \leq Y \leq Y_{cc}$

Equations (3.5) to (3.7) remain unchanged. In place of eq.(3.8), we can now write

$$U_p(T) = [2(12.5 - Y)\overline{u}_{CO} + 2(Y - 8.5)\overline{u}_{CO_2} + 9\overline{u}_{H_2O} + 3.76Y\overline{u}_{N_2}]_T \tag{3.13}$$

Proceeding as in the previous case, we have

$$\begin{aligned} -U_{rp} = {} & 9\Delta\overline{u}_{H_2O} + 3.76Y\Delta\overline{u}_{N_2} + 2(12.5 - Y)\overline{u}_{CO}(T) \\ & + 2(Y - 8.5)\overline{u}_{CO_2}(T) + (12.5 - Y)\overline{u}_{O_2}(298) \\ & - 8\overline{u}_{CO_2}(298) \end{aligned} \tag{3.14}$$

For generality and in accordance with eq.(3.11), we need to transform the eq.(3.14) into a form that contains only pairs of internal energy differences on the right-hand side. We can do it by adding and subtracting the terms

$$2(12.5 - Y)\overline{u}_{CO}(298) \quad \text{and} \quad 2(Y - 8.5)\overline{u}_{CO_2}(298)$$

on the right-hand side of eq.(3.14). We can group them and obtain

$$\begin{aligned} & -U_{rp} - 2(12.5 - Y)(\overline{u}_{CO} + 1/2\overline{u}_{O_2} - \overline{u}_{CO_2})_{298} \\ & = 2(12.5 - Y)\Delta\overline{u}_{CO} + 2(Y - 8.5)\Delta\overline{u}_{CO_2} + 9\Delta\overline{u}_{H_2O} + 3.76Y\Delta\overline{u}_{N_2}. \end{aligned} \tag{3.15}$$

The important point at this juncture is to recognise the term

$$(\overline{u}_{CO} + 1/2\overline{u}_{O_2} - \overline{u}_{CO_2})_{298}$$

as the heat of reaction U_{rp}, for the dissociation of CO_2.

Now, U_{rp} can be computed using the relation

$$U_{rp} = H_{rp} - 2480(N_p - N_r).$$

The value of H_{rp} which is a positive heat of reaction for CO_2 can be found from standard handbooks to be 282800 kJ/kmol. Therefore,

$$
\begin{aligned}
(U_{rp})_{CO_2} &= 282800 - 2480(1.5 - 1) \\
&= 281560 \text{ kJ/kmol } CO_2 \\
&\approx 281600 \text{ kJ/kmol } CO_2.
\end{aligned}
$$

The results of the two cases of Y, viz. $Y \geq Y_{cc}$ and $Y \leq Y_{cc}$, are given by eqs.(3.11) and (3.15), respectively. Since $N_1 = 0$ for $Y \geq Y_{cc}$, we could add the term $N_1\Delta\bar{u}_{CO}$ on the right-hand side of eq.(3.11) without affecting its validity. Similarly, we can add $N_5\Delta\bar{u}_{O_2}$ on the right-hand side of eq.(3.15). When this is done, eqs.(3.11) and (3.15) take the form

$$Q_v = N_1\Delta\bar{u}_{CO} + N_2\Delta\bar{u}_{CO_2} + N_3\Delta\bar{u}_{H_2O} + N_4\Delta\bar{u}_{N_2} + N_5\Delta\bar{u}_{O_2} \tag{3.16}$$

or, in a simpler notation,

$$
\left.
\begin{aligned}
Q_v &= \sum N_i\Delta\bar{u}_i \quad (i = 1, 2, 3, 4, 5), \\
Q_v &= -U_{rp} - 281600 \times N_1, \\
\Delta\bar{u}_i &= \bar{u}_i(T) - \bar{u}_i(298).
\end{aligned}
\right\} \tag{3.17}
$$

Equation (3.17) represents the general expression for any constant-volume adiabatic combustion problem.

The final pressure P_p is obtained from

$$P_p = P_r \frac{N_p T}{N_r\ 298},$$

where N_p and N_r denotes the number of moles of the gaseous products and reactants, respectively.

3.4 Constant-pressure adiabatic combustion

An illustration of the problem is given in Fig.3.2. Since the constant-pressure combustion is assumed to take place in diesel engines, the fuel selected is $C_{10}H_{22}$ and the reactant in this case is

$$C_{10}H_{22} + YO_2 + 3.76YN_2$$

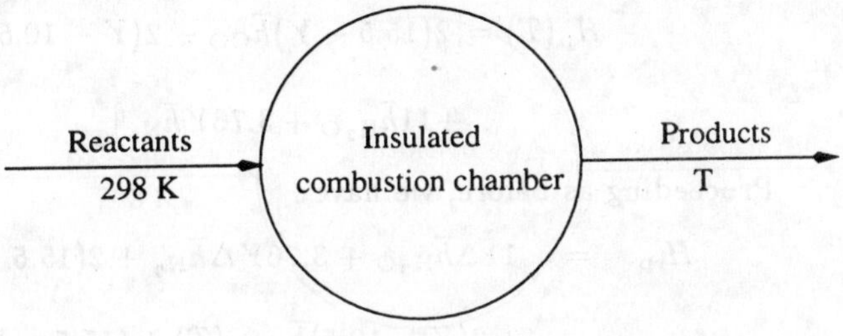

Fig.3.2 *Constant-pressure adiabatic combustion*

The reactants enter an insulated combustion chamber at a temperature of 298 K. The problem is to find the temperature, T, of the products. Since there is no heat transfer, the energy equation can be written as

$$H_r(298) \quad = \quad H_p(T). \tag{3.18}$$

Let us choose to work with a reactant mixture containing one mole of fuel. The fuel we have selected for illustration is $C_{10}H_{22}$.

The heat of reaction for $C_{10}H_{22}$ is [refer to eq.(2.15)]

$$H_{rp} = \left(10\bar{h}_{CO_2} + 11\bar{h}_{H_2O} - \bar{h}_{C_{10}H_{22}} - 15.5\bar{h}_{O_2}\right)_{298}. \tag{3.19}$$

Case (i) $Y \geq Y_{cc}$

We have

$$H_r(298) = \left(\bar{h}_{C_{10}H_{22}} + Y\bar{h}_{O_2} + 3.76Y\bar{h}_{N_2}\right)_{298}, \tag{3.20}$$

$$H_p(T) = \left(10\bar{h}_{CO_2} + 11\bar{h}_{H_2O} + 3.76Y\bar{h}_{N_2} + (Y - 15.5)\bar{h}_{O_2}\right)_T. \tag{3.21}$$

These four equations, eqs.(3.18) to (3.21) are manipulated as follows:

Substituting eqs.(3.20) and (3.21) into eq.(3.18), solving eq.(3.19) for the term $\bar{h}_{C_{10}H_{22}}$ and then eliminating that term from eq.(3.20) results in

$$-H_{rp} = 10\Delta\bar{h}_{CO_2} + 11\Delta\bar{h}_{H_2O} + (Y - 15.5)\Delta\bar{h}_{O_2} + 3.76Y\Delta\bar{h}_{N_2}, \tag{3.22}$$

where

$$\Delta\bar{h}_i \quad = \quad \bar{h}_i(T) - \bar{h}_i(298). \tag{3.23}$$

Note that the left-hand side of eq.(3.22) is a measurable quantity and the right-hand side contains pairs of enthalpy differences.

Case (ii) $Y_{\min} \leq Y \leq Y_{cc}$

Equations (3.18) to (3.20) remain unchanged. In place of eq.(3.21) we now have

$$H_p(T) = \left[2(15.5 - Y)\bar{h}_{CO} + 2(Y - 10.5)\bar{h}_{CO_2} + 11\bar{h}_{H_2O} + 3.76Y\bar{h}_{N_2}\right]_T \tag{3.24}$$

Proceeding as before, we have

$$\begin{aligned} H_{rp} = {} & 11\Delta\bar{h}_{H_2O} + 3.76Y\Delta\bar{h}_{N_2} + 2(15.5 - Y)\bar{h}_{CO}(T) \\ & + 2(Y - 10.5)\bar{h}_{CO_2}(T) + (15.5 - Y)\bar{h}_{O_2}(298) \\ & - 10\bar{h}_{CO_2}(298) \end{aligned} \tag{3.25}$$

We need to bring eq.(3.25) into a form that contains only pairs of enthalpy differences on the right-hand side. This can be done by adding and subtracting the terms

$$2(15.5 - Y)\bar{h}_{CO}(298) \quad \text{and} \quad 2(Y - 10.5)\bar{h}_{CO_2}(298)$$

on the right-hand side of eq.(3.25). On rearranging the terms, we obtain

$$\begin{aligned} & -H_{rp} - 2(15.5 - Y)\left(\bar{h}_{CO} + 1/2\bar{h}_{O_2} - \bar{h}_{CO_2}\right)_{298} \\ & = 2(15.5 - Y)\Delta\bar{h}_{CO} + 2(Y - 10.5)\Delta\bar{h}_{CO_2} + 11\Delta\bar{h}_{H_2O} + 3.76Y\Delta\bar{h}_{N_2} \end{aligned} \tag{3.26}$$

The important point is to recognise the term

$$\left(\bar{h}_{CO} + \frac{1}{2}\bar{h}_{O_2} - \bar{h}_{CO_2}\right)_{298}$$

as the heat of reaction H_{rp} for dissociation of CO_2. This reaction has a positive heat of reaction amounting to 282800 kJ/kmol CO_2, a value that can be found in handbooks.

Now compare eqs.(3.22) and (3.26). As $N_1 = 0$ for $Y \geq Y_{cc}$, we could add the term $N_1\Delta\bar{h}_{CO}$ on the right-hand side of eq.(3.22) without altering its validity. Similarly, when $Y_{\min} \leq Y \leq Y_{cc}$, $N_5 = 0$, so the term $N_5\Delta\bar{h}_{O_2}$ can be added on the right-hand side of eq.(3.26). When this is done, eqs.(3.22) and (3.26) take the form

$$Q_p = N_1\Delta\bar{h}_{CO} + N_2\Delta\bar{h}_{CO_2} + N_3\Delta\bar{h}_{H_2O} + N_4\Delta\bar{h}_{N_2} + N_5\Delta\bar{h}_{O_2} \tag{3.27}$$

or, in a simplified form,

$$\left.\begin{aligned} Q_p &= \sum N_i\Delta\bar{h}_i \qquad (i = 1, 2, 3, 4, 5), \\ Q_p &= -H_{rp} - 282800 \times N_1 \\ \Delta\bar{h}_i &= \bar{h}_i(T) - \bar{h}_i(298) \end{aligned}\right\} \tag{3.28}$$

3.5 Calculation of adiabatic flame temperature

Let us first consider the case of constant-volume combustion. For this process, Q_v is given by eq.(3.17), which is

$$Q_v = \sum N_i \Delta \overline{u}_i \qquad (i = 1, 2, 3, 4, 5).$$

$\overline{u}_i$ can be expressed in terms of $\overline{C_v}$ and T. Since the internal energy increases with temperature, and the slope also increases with temperature, the Newton–Raphson iterative scheme provides a rapidly converging systematic search for the flame temperature.

Rewriting eq.(3.17), we get

$$\sum [N_i \overline{u}_i(T) - N_i \overline{u}_i(298)] - Q_v = 0 \tag{3.29}$$

For the Newton–Raphson iterative scheme, we require the derivative of this function with respect to T, which is nothing but

$$\sum N_i \overline{C_v}(T) \tag{3.30}$$

Appendix B gives a brief discussion of the Newton–Raphson method of solution. Appendix C describes the formulation of algebraic expressions for enthalpy, internal energy and heat capacities of gases. The expression for internal energy, $\overline{u}(T)$, for example, is given as follows:

For $400 \leq T \leq 1600$

$$\overline{u}(T) = AL + (BL - R)T + CL \ln(T). \tag{3.31}$$

For $1600 \leq T \leq 6000$

$$\overline{u}(T) = AH + (BH - R)T + CH \ln(T). \tag{3.32}$$

The heat capacity $\overline{C_v}(T)$ is given as follows

For $400 \leq T \leq 1600$

$$\overline{C_v}(T) = (BL - R) + \frac{CL}{T} \tag{3.33}$$

For $1600 \leq T \leq 6000$

$$\overline{C_v}(T) = (BH - R) + \frac{CH}{T} \tag{3.34}$$

The values of the coefficients $AL, BL, \ldots$ and $AH, BH, \ldots$ for various gases are listed in Tables 3.1 and 3.2, respectively. Since the expression for internal energy [eq.(3.32)] does not extend upto 298 K, H_{rp} and U_{rp} values at 298 K are listed in Table 3.3 for four gases.

In order to calculate the flame temperature, the Newton–Raphson iterative scheme could be conveniently employed. For this, start with a hypothetical value of the flame temperature. Then, the new-flame temperature is obtained from

$$T_{new} = T - \frac{[U_p(T) - U_p(298) - Q_v]}{\overline{C_v}(T)}. \quad (3.35)$$

If the difference between T and T_{new} is within, say, 5 degrees, the iteration can be stopped.

For constant-pressure combustion, instead of $U_p(T)$, the values of $H_p(T)$ are computed using the relation given in Appendix C.

For example:

For $400 \leq T \leq 1600$

$$\overline{h}(T) = AL + BL \times T + CL \ln(T). \quad (3.36)$$

For $1600 \leq T \leq 6000$,

$$\overline{h}(T) = AH + BH \times T + CH \ln(T). \quad (3.37)$$

Similarly, instead of $\overline{C_v}(T)$ the values of $\overline{C_p}(T)$ are computed using the relation

$$\overline{C_p}(T) = BL + CL/T, \quad \text{for } 400 \leq T \leq 1600, \quad (3.38)$$

$$\overline{C_p}(T) = BH + CH/T \quad \text{for } 1600 \leq T \leq 6000. \quad (3.39)$$

T_{new} is calculated using the relation

$$T_{new} = T - \frac{[H_p(T) - H_p(298) - Q_p]}{\overline{C_p}(T)} \quad (3.40)$$

These calculations are illustrated by means of examples in section 3.6.

Let us now consider the general case. Assume that the reactants are at temperature T_r and not at 298 K. Thus, we should calculate Q_p and Q_v at the temperature T_r. Since both Q_p and Q_v involve heats of reaction, we inquire into the variation of H_{rp} and U_{rp} with temperature. The difference can be ignored except for large changes in temperature. For example,

$$H_{rp}(T_r) - H_{rp}(298) \approx (N_pC_p - N_rC_p)_{cc}(T_r - 298) \quad (3.41)$$

where the subscript cc refers to a chemically correct reaction. Usually, T_r differs from 298 by only a few hundred degrees. Furthermore, the difference

Table 3.1 Values of coefficients AL, BL, CL and DL for 400 K$\leq T \leq$ 1600 K used in the calculation of C_p,C_v,u and ϕ

Gas	AL	BL	CL	DL
CO	299180.0	37.85	−4571.9	−31.10
CO_2	56835.0	66.27	−11634.0	−200.00
H	357070.0	20.79	−7.9	−3.90
H_2	326490.0	40.35	−8085.2	−121.00
H_2O	88923.0	49.36	−7940.8	−117.00
N_2	31317.0	37.46	−4559.3	−34.82
O	265120.0	24.60	−2729.2	13.86
O_2	43388.0	42.27	−6635.4	−55.15
OH	217810.0	37.36	−5561.4	−44.06
NO	111050.0	37.81	−2874.8	−15.70
N	326040.0	17.19	5371.4	64.67

Table 3.2 Values of coefficients AH, BH, CH and DH for 1600 K $\leq T \leq$ 6000 K used in the calculation of C_p,C_v,u and ϕ

Gas	AH	BH	CH	DH
CO	309070.0	39.29	−6201.9	−42.77
CO_2	93048.0	68.58	−16979.0	−220.40
H	357010.0	20.79	0.0	−3.82
H_2	461750.0	46.23	−27649.0	−176.60
H_2O	154670.0	60.43	−19212.0	−204.60
N_2	44639.0	39.32	−6753.4	−50.24
O	298360.0	23.17	−6910.3	21.81
O_2	127010.0	46.25	−18798.0	−92.15
OH	298750.0	42.86	−17695.0	−92.24
NO	138670.0	39.92	−7061.8	−33.90
N	486400.0	26.91	−18159.0	−20.31

Table 3.3 H_{rp} and U_{rp} values at 298 K

Heat of reaction	CO_2	H_2O	O_2	N_2
U_{rp} (kJ/kmol)	9364	57316	17200	15780
H_{rp} (kJ/kmol)	6886	54838	14722	13302

between $N_p C_p$ and $N_r C_p$ is seldom large. As a consequence, it is legitimate to ignore the temperature variation in H_{rp} and U_{rp}.

Then, for the general case of constant-volume adiabatic combustion with reactants at T_r, the flame temperature is given by

$$\left.\begin{aligned} Q_v &= \sum N_i[\overline{u}_i(T) - \overline{u}_i(T_r)], \\ Q_v &= -U_{rp} - N_{CO} \times 281600, \end{aligned}\right\} \tag{3.42}$$

and for constant-pressure adiabatic combustion

$$\left.\begin{aligned} Q_p &= \sum N_i[\overline{h}_i(T) - \overline{h}_i(T_r)], \\ Q_p &= -H_{rp} - N_{CO} \times 282800 \end{aligned}\right\} \tag{3.43}$$

For the general case, the necessary expressions for the Newton–Raphson iteration appear now for constant-volume combustion as

$$T_{new} = T - \frac{[U_p(T) - U_p(T_r) - Q_v]}{\overline{C_v}(T)} \tag{3.44}$$

and for constant-pressure combustion as

$$T_{new} = T - \frac{[H_p(T) - H_p(T_r) - Q_p]}{\overline{C_p}(T)} \tag{3.45}$$

While developing a computer program, the calculations for $H_p(T)$, $U_p(T)$, $C_p(T)$ and $C_v(T)$ can be done by means of function subprograms.

3.6 Solved examples

1. Compute the flame temperature when a chemically correct mixture of liquid C_8H_{18} and air initially at 400 K and 1 atm, burns at constant volume.

   The reactant mixture is

$$C_8H_{18} + Y_{cc}O_2 + 3.76Y_{cc}N_2,$$

where Y_{cc} is the chemically correct oxygen to fuel ratio. Here

$$N_{mC} = 8, \quad N_{mH_2} = 18, \quad N_{mO_2} = 0.$$

Therefore,

$$\begin{aligned} Y_{cc} &= N_{mC} + \frac{N_{mH_2}}{4} - \frac{N_{mO_2}}{2} \\ &= 8 + \frac{18}{4} = 12.5. \end{aligned}$$

Thus, the reactant mixture is

$$C_8H_{18} + 12.5\ O_2 + 47\ N_2,$$

and the product mole numbers are

$$\begin{aligned} N_{CO} &= N_1 = 0, \\ N_{CO_2} &= N_2 = 8, \\ N_{H_2O} &= N_3 = 9, \\ N_{N_2} &= N_4 = 47, \\ N_{O_2} &= N_5 = 0. \end{aligned}$$

with $Q_v = -U_{rp} - N_{CO} \times 281400$.

In Table 2.2, U_{rp} for C_8H_{18} is given as -5058960 kJ/kmol. As $N_{CO} = 0$, $Q_v = +5058960$ (liquid fuel and gaseous products). Between 400 and 1600 K, the value of $\overline{u}_p(T)$ is given by

$$\overline{u}_p(T) = AL + (BL - R)T + CL\ \ln(T)$$

The values of AL, BL and CL are taken from Table 3.1. As $N_1 = 0$ and $N_5 = 0$, the summation is done only for three species: N_2, N_3 and N_4. This yields

$$\begin{aligned} U_p(T) &= N_{CO_2}[AL + (BL - R)T + CL\ln(T)]_{CO_2} \\ &\quad + N_{H_2O}[AL + (BL - R)T + CL\ln(T)]_{H_2O} \\ &\quad + N_{N_2}[AL + (BL - R)T + CL\ln(T)]_{N_2} \\ &= 8 \times [56835 + (66.27 - 8.314)400 - 11624\ln(400)] \\ &\quad + 9 \times [88923 + (49.36 - 8.314)400 - 7940.8\ln(400)] \\ &\quad + 47 \times [31317 + (37.46 - 8.314)400 - 4559.3\ln(400)] \\ &= 1338331\ \text{kJ} \end{aligned}$$

Let us assume the flame temperature to be $T = 3000$ K. For temperatures between 1600 and 6000 K

$$\begin{aligned}
U_p(T) &= N_{CO_2}[AH + (BH - R)T + CH\ln(T)]_{CO_2} \\
&\quad + N_{H_2O}[AH + (BH - R)T + CH\ln(T)]_{H_2O} \\
&\quad + N_{N_2}[AH + (BH - R)T + CH\ln(T)]_{N_2} \\
&= 8 \times [93048 + (68.58 - 8.314) \times 3000 - 16979 \times \ln(3000)] \\
&\quad + 9 \times [154670 + (60.43 - 8.314) \times 3000 - 19212 \times \ln(3000)] \\
&\quad + 47 \times [44639 + (39.32 - 8.314) \times 3000 - 6753 \times \ln(3000)] \\
&= 6446774.07 \text{ kJ}
\end{aligned}$$

$\overline{C_v}(T)$ is calculated from

$$(B - 8.314) + C/T \text{ (kJ/kmol K)}$$

where $B = BL$ for $400 \le T \le 1600$ K,
$= BH$ for $1600 \le T \le 6000$ K.

This gives

$$\begin{aligned}
C_v(T) &= N_{CO_2}(BH - 8.314 + CH/T)_{CO_2} \\
&\quad + N_{H_2O}(BH - 8.314 + CH/T)_{H_2O} \\
&\quad + N_{N_2}(BH - 8.314 + CH/T)_{N_2} \\
&= 8(68.58 - 8.314 - 16979/3000) \\
&\quad + 9(60.43 - 8.314 - 19212/3000) \\
&\quad + 47(39.32 - 8.314 - 6753.4/3000) \\
&= 2199.74 \text{ kJ/kmol K}
\end{aligned}$$

The new flame temperature is given by

$$\begin{aligned}
T_{new} &= T - [U_p(T) - U_p(T_r) - Q_v]/\overline{C_v}(T) \\
&= 3000 - \frac{6446774.07 - 1338331.3 - 5058960}{2199.74} \\
&= 2977.5 \text{ K.}
\end{aligned}$$

This T_{new} is compared with the assumed T of 3000 K. If the difference between them is less than say ± 5, then T_{new} is taken as the adiabatic flame temperature. Otherwise, taking T_{new} as T, the process is repeated calculating $U_{\text{p}}(T), C_v(T)$ and T_{new} till convergence is achieved. With

$$\begin{aligned} T = T_{\text{new}} &= 2977.5 \text{ K}, \\ U_{\text{p}}(T) &= 6397297.534 \text{ kJ}, \\ \overline{C_v}(T) &= 2198.16 \text{ kJ/kmol K}, \\ T_{\text{new}} &= 2977.49 \text{ K}. \end{aligned}$$

As the last value of T_{new} is within ± 5 of the previous T_{new}, this last T_{new} is taken as the adiabatic flame temperature of C_8H_{18}. Thus,

$$\textbf{Adiabatic flame temperature} = \textbf{2977.49 K.}$$

2. Compute the flame temperature when a chemically correct mixture of liquid $C_{10}H_{22}$ and air initially at 400 K and 1 atm, burns at constant pressure.

For $C_{10}H_{22}$, the reactant mixture is

$$C_{10}H_{22} + Y_{cc}\ O_2 + 3.76\ Y_{cc}\ N_2$$

$$\begin{aligned} Y_{cc} &= N_{mC} + \frac{N_{mH_2}}{4} - \frac{N_{mO_2}}{2} \\ &= 10 + \frac{22}{4} - \frac{0}{2} = 15.5 \end{aligned}$$

The reactant mixture is

$$C_{10}H_{22} + 15.5O_2 + 58.28N_2$$

and the product mole numbers are

$$\begin{aligned} N_{CO} &= N_1 = 0, \\ N_{CO_2} &= N_2 = 10, \\ N_{H_2O} &= N_3 = 11, \\ N_{N_2} &= N_4 = 58.28, \\ N_{O_2} &= N_5 = 0, \end{aligned}$$

with

$$Q_p = -H_{\text{rp}} - N_{CO} \times 282800.$$

From Table 2.4, the H_{rp} value for $C_{10}H_{22}$ (liquid fuel and gaseous products) is -6261300 kJ/kmol. As $N_{CO} = 0$, $Q_p = 6261300$ kJ/kmol. Between 400 and 1600 K, the value of $H_{\text{p}}(T)$ is given by the relation

$$h_{\text{p}}(T) = AL + BL \times T + CL \ln(T)$$

The values of AL, BL and CL are taken from Table 3.1. Here, for a chemically correct mixture,

$$N_1 = 0 \quad \text{and} \quad N_5 = 0$$

Hence, for summation only three species, i.e. N_2, N_3 and N_4 are considered, with

$$N_2 = 10, \quad N_3 = 11, \quad N_4 = 58.28.$$

This yields

$$\begin{aligned} H_p(T) &= N_{CO_2}[AL + BL \times T + CL \ \ln(T)] \\ &\quad + N_{H_2O}[AL + BL \times T + CL \ \ln(T)] \\ &\quad + N_{N_2}[AL + BL \times T + CL \ \ln(T)]. \end{aligned}$$

For an initial temperature of 400 K, i.e. $T_r = 400$K,

$$\begin{aligned} H_p(T_r) &= 10[56835 + 66.27 \times 400 - 11634 \ln(400)] \\ &\quad + 11[88923 + 49.36 \times 400 - 7940.8 \ln(400)] \\ &\quad + 58.28[31317 + 37.46 \times 400 - 4559.3 \ln(400)] \\ &= 1914767 \text{ kJ}. \end{aligned}$$

Let us assume the flame temperature to be $T = 3000$ K. For temperatures between 1600 and 6000 K

$$\begin{aligned} H_p(T) &= N_{CO_2}[AH + BH \times T + CH \ln(T)]_{CO_2} \\ &\quad + N_{H_2O}[AH + BH \times T + CH \ln(T)]_{H_2O} \\ &\quad + N_{N_2}[AH + BH \times T + CH \ln(T)]_{N_2} \\ &= 10[93048 + 68.58 \times 3000 - 16979 \ln(3000)] \\ &\quad + 11[154670 + 60.43 \times 3000 - 19212 \ln(3000)] \\ &\quad + 58.28[44639 + 39.32 \times 3000 - 6753.4 \ln(3000)] \\ &= 9957095.0 \text{ kJ}. \end{aligned}$$

$$\overline{C_p}(T) = B + C/T \text{ (kJ/kmol K)}$$

$$\text{where,} \quad B = BL \text{ for } 400 \le T \le 1600 \text{ K,}$$

$$\quad\quad = BH \text{ for } 1600 \le T \le 6000 \text{ K.}$$

For the assumed value of $T = 3000$ K

$$\begin{aligned} C_p(T) &= N_{CO_2}(BH + CH/T)_{CO_2} + N_{H_2O}(BH + CH/T)_{H_2O} \\ &\quad + N_{N_2}(BH + CH/T)_{N_2} \end{aligned}$$

$$
\begin{aligned}
&= 10 \times (68.58 + 16979/3000) + 11 \times (60.43 - 19212/3000) \\
&\quad + 58.28 \times (39.32 - 6753.4/3000) \\
&= 3383.86 \text{ kJ/kmol K.} \\
T_{\text{new}} &= T - [H_{\text{p}}(T) - H_{\text{p}}(T_{\text{r}}) - QP]/C_p(T) \\
&= 3000 - [9957095.5 - 1914767 - 6261300]/3383.86 \\
&= 2473.67 \text{ K.}
\end{aligned}
$$

This T_{new} is compared with the assumed value of T, i.e. 3000 K. If their difference is less than say ± 5, T_{new} is taken as the adiabatic flame temperature. Otherwise, the process is repeated with new value of T_{new} (i.e. $T = T_{\text{new}}$) till convergence. Thus,

$$
\begin{aligned}
T = T_{\text{new}} &= 2473.67 \text{ K,} \\
H_{\text{p}}(T) &= 8189598.1 \text{ kJ,} \\
C_p(T) &= 3328.92, \text{ kJ/kmol K,} \\
T_{\text{new}} &= 2469.6 \text{ K.}
\end{aligned}
$$

As this T_{new} value is within ± 5 of the previous T_{new}, it is the adiabatic flame temperature of $C_{10}H_{22}$. Thus,

Adiabatic flame temperature = 2469.6 K.

Exercise

1. Write a computer program to calculate the adiabatic flame temperature of any fuel for any given input conditions.
2. Using the above program calculate the adiabatic flame temperature for the fuels C_8H_{18} and $C_{10}H_{22}$ from Y_{min} to Y_{max}, where $Y_{\text{max}} = 1.8\ Y_{\text{cc}}$ under constant-volume and constant-pressure combustion. Draw a graph of adiabatic flame temperature versus Y and discuss.

4

ISENTROPIC CHANGES OF STATE

4.1 Introduction

Many of the combustion engines involve a compression process and all of them involve an expansion process. The working fluid is a mixture of gases. The main question is how to calculate the temperature of the gases at the end of the process of compression or expansion. In the piston engine, in order to calculate the work done by or on the gases, these final temperatures must be known.

Ideally speaking, the compression and expansion processes should take place rapidly, with negligible heat transfer. Hence, compression and expansion calculations can be made on the assumption of isentropic behaviour.

Where the process is not isentropic, e.g. in compressors and turbines, the isentropic temperature computation is still required, since efficiencies are based on isentropic performance.

The relation between pressure, p_1, volume, V_1, and the temperature, T_1, for an ideal gas or a mixture of ideal gases at the same entropy is given by

$$\frac{T_2}{T_1} = \left(\frac{p_2}{p_1}\right)^{(k-1)/k} = \left(\frac{V_1}{V_2}\right)^{k-1} \tag{4.1}$$

These expressions are derived on the assumption that k is constant. Actually, C_p and C_v increase with temperature, while k decreases. Since C_p and C_v differ by a constant amount, the change in k with temperature is not very predominant. However, the application of eq.(4.1) may lead to an error in the calculation of the final temperature. The error is large for expansions from a higher temperature than for compressions from a lower temperature. Hence, it is worthwhile to focus our attention on the expansion process.

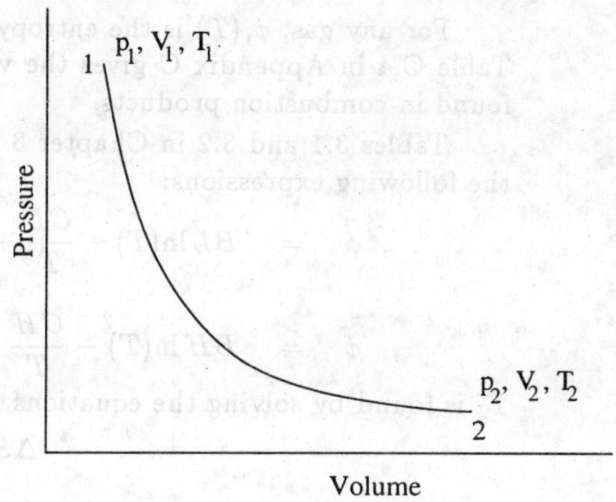

Fig.4.1 *Illustration of an expansion process*

Referring to Fig.4.1, let p_1 and T_1 denote the initial state of a mixture of gases. We wish to determine the temperature, T_2, when the mixture expands isentropically to p_2. We can proceed in three ways.

(i) We can apply eq.(4.1), find T_2 and let it go at that.

(ii) We can modify the error of the first method by finding an average value of k. For example, with k_1 found at T_1, we find T_2 and the corresponding value of k_2. Now we can take an average between k_1 and k_2, which should lead to a better approximation for T_2. This can be repeated until two successive values of T_2 differ by only a small amount, whatever amount we choose to call small. But the main question is how to find the average. Since k_1 is fixed for a fixed temperature T_1 while k_2 varies with each new value of T_2, what average shall we take? An arithmetic average like $(k_1 + k_2)/2$ or a geometric average $\sqrt{k_1 \cdot k_2}$, or whatelse? There is no apparent logic to guide us.

(iii) We can solve for this T_2 accurately by determining the value that equates the initial and final entropies of the gas mixture. The total entropy $S(p,T)$ of a mixture of ideal gases is given by

$$S(p,T) \quad = \quad \sum n_i \phi_i(T) - NR\ln(p), \tag{4.2}$$

where n_i denotes the mole numbers of the species, N the total mole number, R the universal gas constant and ϕ_i a function of temperature.

$$\phi_i \quad = \quad \int_0^T \left(\frac{C_{p_i}}{T}\right) dT + \phi_i(0), \tag{4.3}$$

where $\phi_i(0)$ is an integration constant.

For any gas, $\phi_i(T)$ is the entropy per mole at temperature T and 1 atm. Table C.4 in Appendix C gives the values of ϕ for gases that are commonly found in combustion products.

Tables 3.1 and 3.2 in Chapter 3 give the coefficients that can be used in the following expressions:

$$\left.\begin{aligned} \phi &= BL\ln(T) - \frac{CL}{T} + DL \qquad 400 \le T \le 1600, \\ \phi &= BH\ln(T) - \frac{CH}{T} + DH \qquad 1600 \le T \le 6000 \end{aligned}\right\}. \tag{4.4}$$

T_2 is found by solving the equations

$$\Delta S = 0,$$

$$S_2 - S_1 = 0,$$

that is,

$$S_2(p_2, T_2) - S_1(p_1, T_1) = 0, \tag{4.5}$$

which can be expanded to

$$\Delta S = \sum n_i\left[\phi_i(T_2) - \phi_i(T_1)\right] - NR\ln\left(\frac{p_2}{p_1}\right) = 0. \tag{4.6}$$

For the solution of the above equation, the Newton–Raphson iterative method may be used. To write the recursion expression, we need the derivative of ΔS with respect to T_2. The derivative can be written as

$$\frac{d}{dT_2}(S_2 - S_1) = \frac{C_p(T_2)}{T_2}, \tag{4.7}$$

where $C_p = \sum n_i C_{p_i}$.

The recursion equation would then appear as

$$T_{2\text{new}} = T_2\left(1 - \frac{S_2(p_2, T_2) - S_1(p_1, T_1)}{C_p(T_2)}\right). \tag{4.8}$$

However, some care must be exercised because the calculation will stop when $T_{2\text{new}}$ turns up negative as a result of the logarithm function in eq.(4.4). Figure 4.2 illustrates the problem. The slope of ΔS plotted against T_2 will decrease as shown because T_2 increases faster than C_p.

The limiting value for the initial guess for T_2 is as shown in the figure. The calculation will stop if the iteration begins with a larger value. Since it is not possible to know the limiting value at the outset, we may choose any T_2 to begin with the iteration and then decrease T_2 by a fixed amount until a positive $T_{2\text{new}}$ is obtained from the recursion statement. Thereafter, $T_{2\text{new}}$ will remain positive.

For the case of isentropic expansion to some specified volume, V_2, the same basic method of iterations can be employed p_2, being fixed by

$$p_2 = p_1\frac{V_1}{V_2}\frac{T_2}{T_1} \tag{4.9}$$

Thus, the computation of T_2 will help to obtain the value of p_2 also.

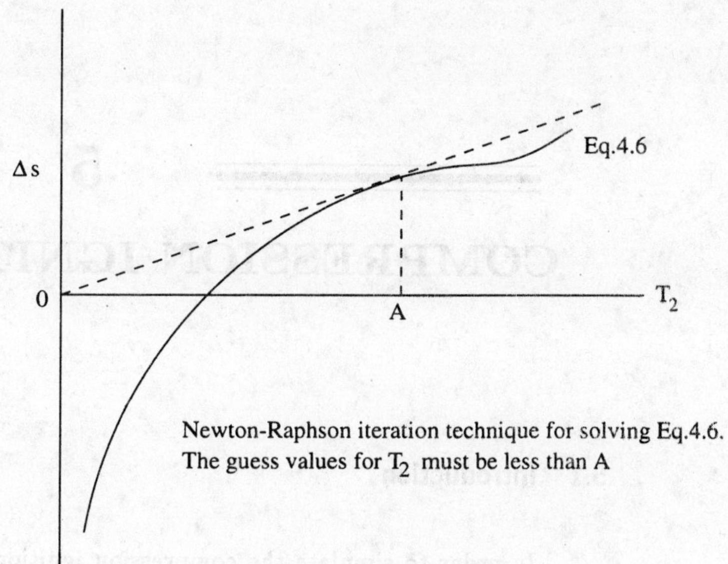

Fig.4.2 ***Newton–Raphson iteration technique***

4.2 Summary

The last two chapters along with this chapter provided the necessary background theory required to start the simulation process. However, the fundamentals of working principles and the nomenclatures associated with the compression ignition engine terminology will help the reader in understanding the simulation process. Hence, the next chapter is devoted to explain some important details (many of the readers may know these things already) about the compression ignition engine, so that even a beginner can learn simulation without much difficulty.

Exercise

Write a computer program to estimate the final temperature during a compression or expansion process with initial conditions known, using the three methods described in this chapter.

5

COMPRESSION IGNITION ENGINES

5.1 Introduction

In order to simulate the compression ignition (CI) engine on a digital computer, first of all it is necessary to know the various processes of the CI engine, and its working principle as well as the nomenclature associated with it. In this chapter we will review briefly the working principle of a four-stroke CI engine.

5.2 Some basic details and nomenclature

Let us first define a cycle. A *cycle* is a complete sequence of events starting from one state and returning to the same state in the same way. For example, it may be an interval or a period of time occupied by one round or course of events repeating in the same order in a series, such as the cycle of seasons, with spring, summer, autumn and winter following each other and then recurring.

Similarly, an *IC engine cycle* is a series of events that an internal combustion engine undergoes while it is operating and delivering power. Since these events occur in a certain sequence, they are said to be timed.

As already stated, our interest lies in reviewing the working principle of a four-stroke CI engine. The compression ignition engine was originally developed by Rudolf Diesel in Germany in 1892. Most of the reciprocating engines operate on a four-stroke five-event cycle. There are four strokes of the piston, two up and two down, for each engine operating cycle. The basic power-developing components of a typical CI engine are shown in Fig.5.1. They are:

(i)	the cylinder,	(iii)	the connecting rod,
(ii)	the piston,	(iv)	the crankshaft.

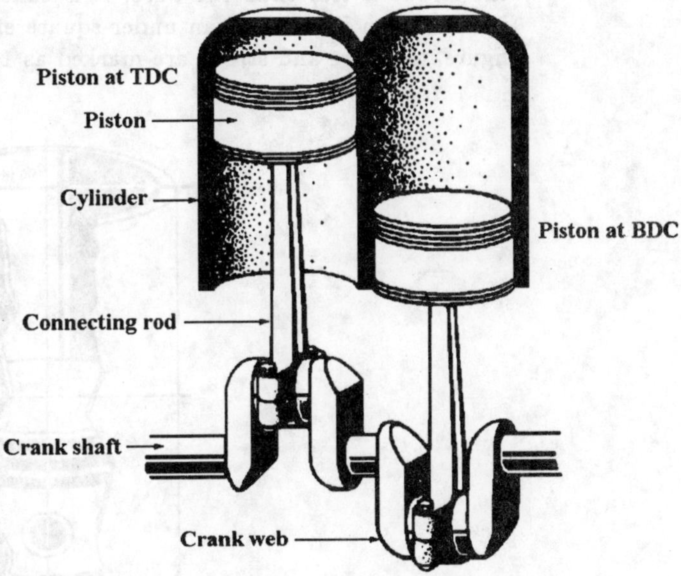

Fig.5.1 *Basic power-developing components of a CI engine*

The cylinder has a smooth surface so that the piston, with the aid of piston rings and a lubricant, can create a seal such that no gas can escape between the piston and the cylinder walls. The piston is connected to the crankshaft by means of a connecting rod so that the reciprocating motion is converted to rotary motion by means of the connecting rod and crank assembly.

The position of the working piston and the moving parts, which are mechanically connected to the piston, at the moment when the direction of its motion is reversed at either of the end points of the stroke, is called the dead centre. There are two dead centres, viz., top dead centre (TDC) and bottom dead centre (BDC). The limit of travel to which the piston can move, is called TDC and the limit to which it moves in the opposite direction is called BDC. For each revolution of the crankshaft there are two strokes of the piston, one up and one down, assuming that the cylinder is in a vertical position. In a four-stroke CI engine, one cycle is completed in two revolutions of the crankshaft.

Figure 5.2 illustrates the bore and stroke of the engine. The nominal inner diameter of the cylinder is called the *bore*, that is designated as B and is expressed in mm. The nominal distance through which a working piston moves between two successive reversals of its direction of motion is called the *stroke* and is designated as S and expressed in mm.

An engine having a bore equal to the stroke is called a square engine. If the stroke is less than the bore, it is called an over-square engine and if it is more then it is called an under-square engine. It can be seen that, in the figure, the bore and stroke are marked as 100 mm.

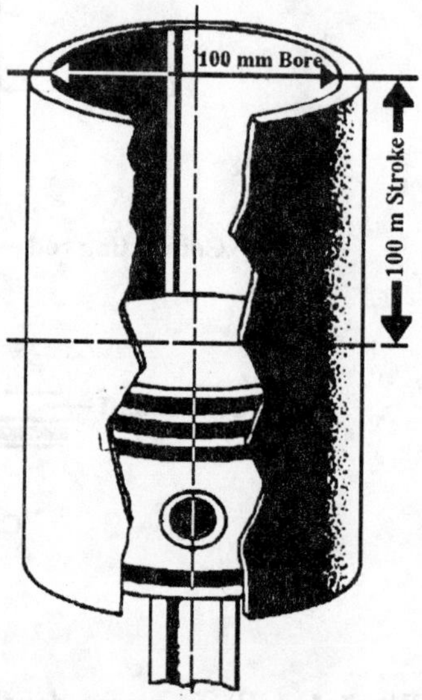

Fig.5.2 *Illustration of bore and stroke*

It is important to understand the positions of TDC and BDC, as these positions of the piston are used in setting the injection as well as valve timings and determining the valve overlap.

Top dead centre may also be defined as the point when the piston is at a maximum distance from the centre line of the crankshaft. Bottom dead centre may also be defined as the point where the piston is at a minimum distance from the centre line of the crankshaft. Figure 5.3 illustrates the piston position at top dead centre and at bottom dead centre.

Displacement volume is the nominal volume swept by the working piston when travelling from one dead centre to the other. It is designated as V_{disp} and normally expressed in cc. It is calculated as the product of the piston area and stroke.

$$V_{\text{disp}} = \frac{\pi}{4} B^2 S. \tag{5.1}$$

Clearance volume is the nominal volume of the space above the piston when it is at TDC. It is designated as V_{tdc} and expressed in cc.

Cylinder volume or the *total volume* is the space above the piston when the piston is at BDC. It is designated as V_{bdc} and usually expressed in cc.

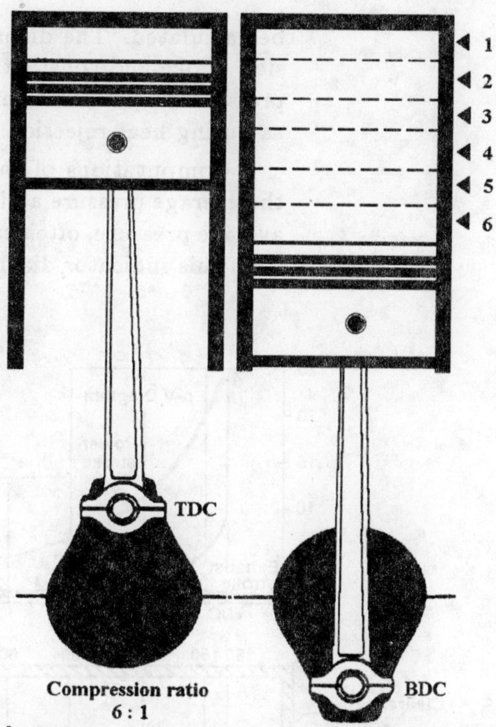

Fig.5.3 *Top and bottom dead centre*

Compression ratio, r, is the ratio of cylinder volume to clearance volume:

$$r = \frac{V_{\mathrm{bdc}}}{V_{\mathrm{tdc}}}. \quad (5.2)$$

Compression ratio is an important parameter which determines the type and efficiency of the engine. Further, it controls the maximum power that can be developed by the engine, provided other factors remain the same. The maximum power increases with increase in compression ratio. However, for CI engines the limit of the compression ratio is decided by its power to weight ratio since, with increase in compression the engines have to be sturdy. Increasing the compression ratio of an engine increases its thermal efficiency and lowers specific fuel consumption. It will be seen that the efficiency and power output of CI engines not only depends upon the compression ratio but also on a ratio called the cut-off ratio (see Chapter 6).

5.3 Cylinder pressure indicator diagram

A typical cylinder pressure indicator diagram is shown in Fig.5.4 for full load operation under ideal conditions. From Fig.5.4, the indicated power can be calculated. The diagram illustrates the pressure rise during the compression stroke and constant pressure during heat addition. Further, it shows the pressure drop with the expansion of the gases during the power stroke as well as during heat rejection.

Computations of the indicated power are somewhat simplified by using the average pressure acting on the piston throughout the working stroke. This average pressure, often called the mean effective pressure, is normally obtained from this indicator diagram.

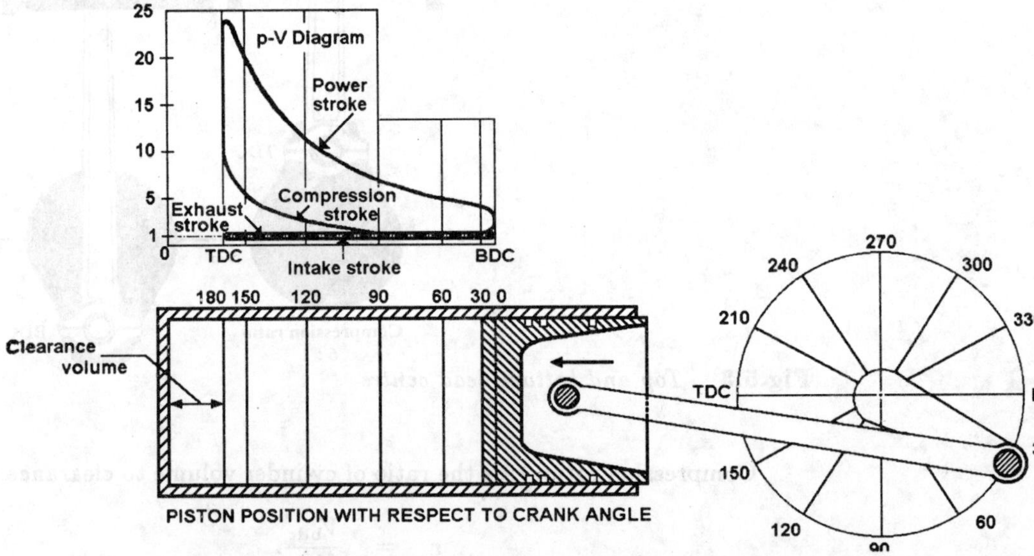

Fig.5.4 *Pressure–volume indicator diagram*

5.4 Indicated power

Indicated power is defined as the total power converted by the engine from heat energy to mechanical energy. It is usually abbreviated as *ip*.

If the characteristics of an engine are known, the indicated power rating can be easily calculated. The total force acting on the piston in each cylinder is the product of the indicated mean effective pressure (N/m^2) and area, A, of the piston head in m^2.

The product of the total force and the distance through which it acts in one second gives the work done per second. This product multiplied by the number of cylinders on operation gives the work done by the entire engine, per second, in Watts.

Indicated power is then given by

$$ip = \frac{P_{im} S A n K}{60000} \quad (5.3)$$

where
A = area of the piston in m^2
K = number of cylinders
n = number of working strokes per minute (rpm/2) per cylinder
P_{im} = indicated mean effective pressure in N/m^2
S = length of the stroke in m

5.5 Brake power

Brake power, bp, is the actual power delivered by an engine at the crankshaft. It is the difference between the indicated power, ip, and the friction power, fp. Friction power is that part of the total power necessary to overcome the friction of the moving parts in the engine and its accessories. The relationship between them may be expressed as

$$bp = ip - fp. \quad (5.4)$$

It may also be stated that bp is that part of the total power developed by the engine which can be used to perform work.

5.6 Working principle

In a four-stroke cycle engine, the cycle of operation is completed in four strokes of the piston, such as suction, compression, expansion and exhaust. Each stroke consists of one revolution of the crankshaft or 180° of crank rotation and hence a cycle consists of 720° of crank rotation.

The various strokes are illustrated in Fig.5.5 and the corresponding ideal cycle p–V diagram is shown in Fig.5.6.

The working principle of the engine is described below.

5.6.1 Suction stroke

The suction stroke is represented by 0→1 in Fig.5.6. It starts when the piston is at TDC, and about to move downwards. The inlet valve is in the open position and the exhaust valve is in the closed position [Fig.5.5(a)]. During this stroke, due to the sucking action of the piston, air from the atmosphere is drawn into the cylinder. At the end of the suction stroke, the inlet valve closes.

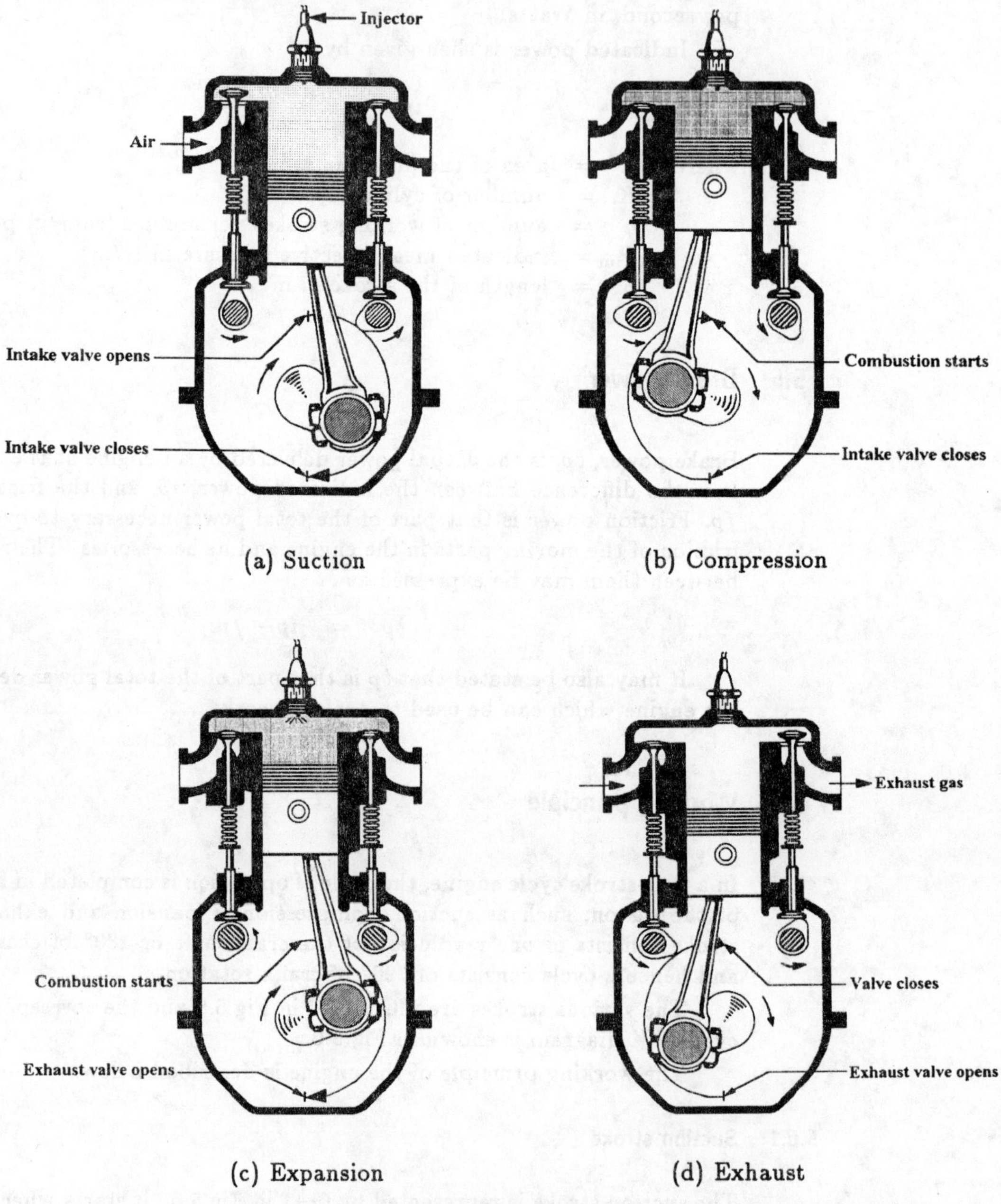

(a) Suction (b) Compression

(c) Expansion (d) Exhaust

Fig.5.5 *Various strokes in CI engine*

5.6.2 Compression stroke

The compression stroke is represented by 1→2 in Fig.5.6. The air taken into the cylinder during the suction stroke, along with the products of combustion of the previous cycle, is compressed by the return stroke of the piston 1→2. During the compression stroke, both inlet and exhaust valves remain closed [Fig.5.5(b)]. This air is compressed into the clearance volume at the end of the stroke. However, just before the end of the compression stroke, the fuel is injected with the help of an injector. Even though combustion ought to start immediately, in actual engines, it starts after a very small interval of time called the delay period.

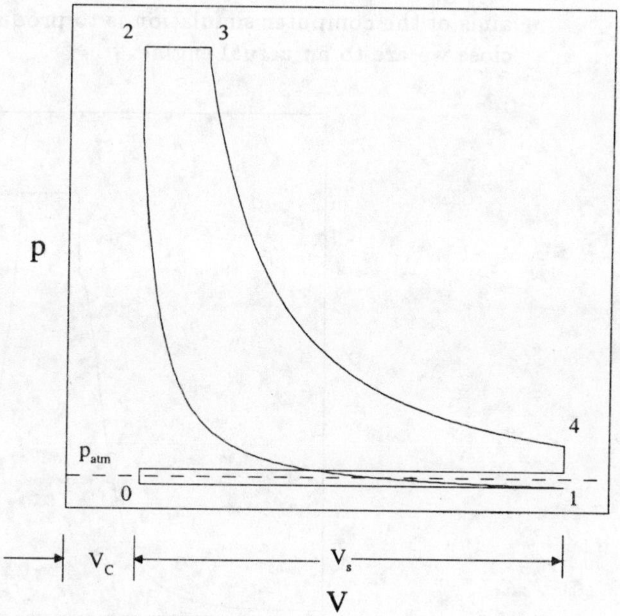

Fig.5.6 *Ideal p–V diagram*

During the combustion process, the chemical energy of the fuel is released in the form of heat energy, producing a temperature raise of about 1800 K and the pressure will remain constant (represented by 2→3 in Fig.5.6).

5.6.3 Expansion stroke

The expansion stroke is represented by 3→4 in Fig.5.6. The burning gases force the piston towards bottom dead centre. During this stroke, both inlet and exhaust valves remain closed [see Fig.5.5(c)]. Thus, power is obtained only during this stroke. Both pressure and temperature decrease during expansion.

5.6.4 Exhaust stroke

The exhaust stroke is represented by 4→0 in Fig.5.6. At the end of expansion stroke, the exhaust valve opens and the inlet valve remains closed [Fig.5.5(d)]. The piston moves from BDC to TDC and expels the burnt gases from the cylinder through the exhaust valve. The exhaust valve closes at the end of the exhaust stroke and some residual gases remain in the cylinder. In a multicylinder engine, each cylinder of the four-stroke engine completes the above four operations in two engine revolutions. When an engine executes these four strokes, during the crank rotation of 720° the pressure varies considerably. The variation of the pressure with respect to crank angle (p-θ) is illustrated in Fig.5.7 for a CI engine working on an ideal Diesel cycle. One of the main aims of the computer simulation is to produce the variation p–θ, and see how close we are to an actual engine.

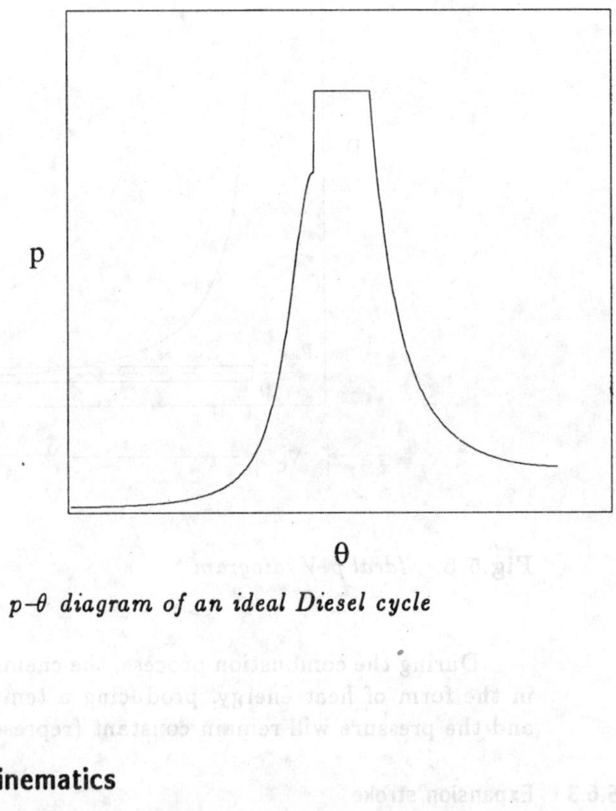

Fig.5.7 *p–θ diagram of an ideal Diesel cycle*

5.7 Engine kinematics

Four-stroke internal combustion engines are currently produced in two configurations, reciprocating piston and rotary.

The basic geometry of a reciprocating piston engine is shown in Fig.5.8. It is described in terms of cylinder bore (diameter) B, length of stroke S, length

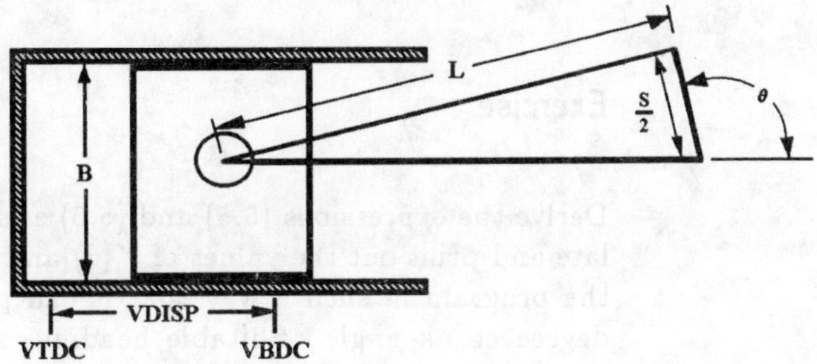

Fig.5.8 *Geometry of the reciprocating piston engine*

of connecting rod L and compression ratio r. The displacement volume V_{disp} is swept out as the piston moves from BDC to TDC.
Now,

$$V_{\text{disp}} = V_{\text{bdc}} - V_{\text{tdc}} = \frac{\pi}{4}B^2 S. \tag{5.5}$$

Since

$$r = \frac{V_{\text{bdc}}}{V_{\text{tdc}}},$$

we may write

$$V_{\text{bdc}} = \left[\frac{r}{r-1}\right] \times V_{\text{disp}}, \tag{5.6}$$

$$V_{\text{tdc}} = \left[\frac{1}{r-1}\right] \times V_{\text{disp}}. \tag{5.7}$$

With θ denoting the angular displacement of the crank from BDC, the volume $V(\theta)$ at any crank angle is represented by

$$V(\theta) = V_{\text{disp}} \times \left[\frac{r}{r-1} - \frac{1-\cos\theta}{2} + \frac{L}{S} - \frac{1}{2}\sqrt{\left(\frac{2L}{S}\right)^2 - \sin^2\theta}\right] \tag{5.8}$$

and

$$V'(\theta) = \frac{dV}{d\theta} = \frac{V_{\text{disp}}}{2} \times \left[\frac{1}{2}\frac{\sin 2\theta}{\sqrt{(2L/S)^2 - \sin^2\theta}} - \sin\theta\right] \tag{5.9}$$

Displacement volume is an important measure of engine design as it is directly related to theoretical work output in an ideal engine cycle. Note that in the above expression, $\theta = 0$ when the piston is at BDC during the start of compression stroke.

Exercise

Derive the expressions (5.5) and (5.6) and write a computer program to calculate and print out the values of $V(\theta)$ and $V'(\theta)$ at any crank angle θ. Develop the program in such a way that it can print out 720 values in steps of each degree crank angle. Suitable headings such as suction stroke, compression stroke, etc., may also be made to print at appropriate places.

6

CI ENGINE SIMULATION WITH AIR AS WORKING MEDIUM

6.1 Introduction

Many work-producing devices, e.g. internal combustion engines, always utilize a gaseous working fluid. Most engineering students are familiar with compression ignition automotive engines used in trucks, buses and lorries. In these engines there is a change in the composition of the working fluid because during combustion, the reactant — which is a fuel–air mixture — changes its composition to form the product of combustion. Combustion takes place inside the system, and for this reason these engines are called internal combustion engines.

Since the working fluid does not go through a thermodynamic cycle in the engine even though the engine operates in a mechanical cycle, internal combustion engines operate on the so-called open cycle. Hence, sometimes they are called *open Diesel cycle engines* and are commonly used in automobiles. Compared to SI engines, CI engines are more efficient due to a higher compression ratio and constant pressure heat addition.

In order to analyze internal combustion engines, it is advantageous to devise closed cycles that approximate open cycles. One such approach is ideal cycle simulation (ICS) with air as the working medium. Ideal cycle simulation is based on the following assumptions:

(i) The working fluid throughout the cycle is a fixed mass of air.

(ii) The working medium is assumed to be an ideal gas.

(iii) There is no intake or exhaust process.

(iv) The combustion process is replaced by a heat addition process from an external source.

(v) The heat addition takes place at constant pressure.

(vi) The cycle is completed by heat rejection to the surroundings at constant volume (in contrast to the exhaust and intake processes of the actual engine).

(vii) All processes are internally reversible.

(viii) There is no heat transfer to the surroundings.

(ix) There is no friction involved.

(x) The working medium has constant specific heats (C_p and C_v).

6.2 Ideal Diesel cycle

The main idea of CI engine simulation using ideal Diesel cycle is to enable the reader to qualitatively examine the influence of the different variables on its performance. The results obtained from ideal cycle simulation, such as pressures, temperatures, efficiency and mean effective pressure, will differ a great deal from those pertaining to the actual engine. The emphasis, therefore, in our consideration of the simulation of an ideal cycle will be primarily on the qualitative aspects.

Figure 6.1 illustrates an ideal Diesel cycle on the *p-V* diagram.

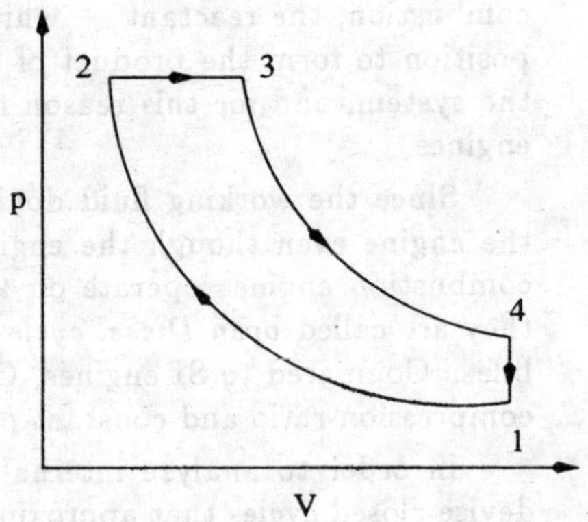

Fig.6.1 *p-V diagram of an ideal Diesel cycle*

We will assume a compression ratio (r) of 16:1, a cut-off ratio ($r_c = V_3/V_2$) of 4 and a specific heat ratio (k) of 1.4.

Isentropic compression of air occurs between 1 and 2 (Fig.6.1) as the piston moves from BDC to TDC. Heat is then added at constant pressure (process 2→3), heat addition is started when the piston is at the TDC. Because of heat addition, the temperature rises. Process 3→4 represents isentropic expansion as the piston moves from TDC to BDC; and process 4→1 represents instantaneous heat rejection at constant pressure when the piston is at BDC.

6.3 Simulation with air as the working medium

Our interest in this simulation is to calculate p, V and T at points 1 to 4 (Fig.6.1), and also the work output and thermal efficiency. Assuming a unit quantity of air, we have

$$\text{Heat added, } q_a = C_p(T_3 - T_2),$$

$$\text{Heat rejected, } q_r = C_p(T_4 - T_1).$$

Therefore, the net work output per unit quantity of air is

$$w_{net} = C_p(T_3 - T_2) - C_p(T_4 - T_1).$$

Thus the thermal efficiency η_{th} is

$$\eta_{th} = \frac{q_a - q_r}{q_a} = 1 - \frac{q_r}{q_a}$$

$$= 1 - \frac{C_v(T_4 - T_1)}{C_p(T_3 - T_2)}$$

$$= 1 - \frac{1}{\gamma}\left(\frac{T_4 - T_1}{T_3 - T_2}\right)$$

Considering the process 1→2

$$T_2 = T_1\left(\frac{V_1}{V_2}\right)^{(\gamma-1)} = T_1 r^{(\gamma-1)} \tag{6.1}$$

Considering the constant pressure process 2→3, we have

$$\frac{V_2}{T_2} = \frac{V_3}{T_3}$$

$$\frac{T_3}{T_2} = \frac{V_3}{V_2} = r_c \text{ (say)}$$

$$T_3 = T_2 r_c \tag{6.2}$$

From eqs.(6.1) and (6.2), we have

$$T_3 = T_1 r^{(\gamma-1)} r_c \tag{6.3}$$

Considering the process 3→4, we have

$$T_4 = T_3\left(\frac{V_3}{V_4}\right)^{(\gamma-1)} \tag{6.4}$$

$$= T_3\left(\frac{V_3}{V_2}\times\frac{V_2}{V_4}\right)^{(\gamma-1)}$$

$$= T_3\left(\frac{r_c}{r}\right)^{(\gamma-1)} \tag{6.5}$$

From eqs.(6.3) and (6.5), we have

$$T_4 = T_1 r^{(\gamma-1)} r_c \left(\frac{r_c}{r}\right)^{(\gamma-1)} = T_1 r_c^{\gamma}$$

$$\eta_{Diesel} = 1 - \frac{1}{\gamma}\left[\frac{T_1(r_c^{\gamma}-1)}{T_1\left(r^{(\gamma-1)}r_c - r^{(\gamma-1)}\right)}\right]$$

$$= 1 - \frac{1}{\gamma}\left[\frac{(r_c^{\gamma}-1)}{r^{(\gamma-1)}r_c - r^{(\gamma-1)}}\right]$$

$$= 1 - \frac{1}{r^{(\gamma-1)}}\left[\frac{r_c^{\gamma}-1}{\gamma(r_c-1)}\right] \tag{6.6}$$

where r is the compression ratio and r_c is the cut-off ratio, given by,

$$r = \frac{V_1}{V_2}; \quad r_c = \frac{V_3}{V_2}.$$

Figure 6.2 shows the effect of r on the efficiency for various cut-off ratios. The important point to note is that the efficiency of the ideal Diesel cycle is a function not only of the compression ratio but also of the cut-off ratio. Even though efficiency increases with the compression ratio it decreases with an increase in the cut-off ratio. This is due to the fact that the expansion ratio decreases with an increase in the cut-off ratio. It is also true of an actual compression ignition engine that the efficiency can be increased by increasing the compression ratio. The trend towards higher compression ratios is prompted by the effort to obtain higher thermal efficiency. However, in the actual engine there is an increase in weight of the engine as the compression ratio is increased. Therefore, the maximum compression ratio that can be used is fixed from the point of optimum weight to power ratio.

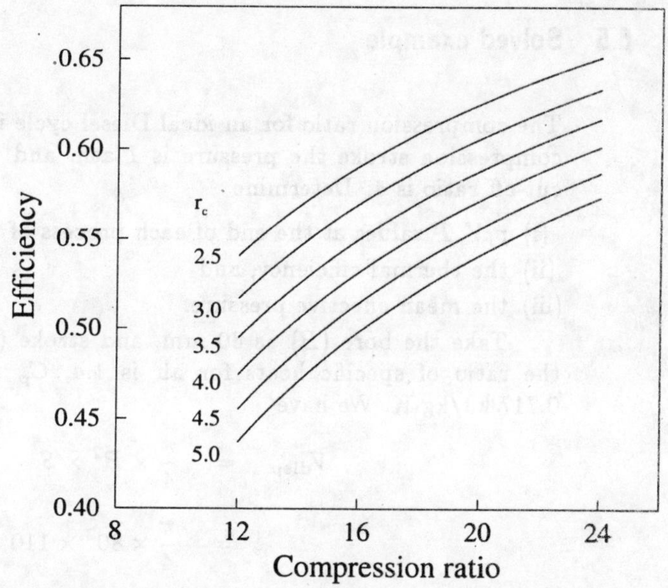

Fig.6.2 *Effect of compression ratio and cut-off ratio on efficiency*

6.4 Deviation between actual and ideal cycle

Some of the most important ways in which the actual cycle compression ignition engine deviates from the ideal cycle are as follows :

(i) The working medium is not air and the specific heats of the actual gases increase with temperature.

(ii) The combustion process replaces the heat transfer process at high temperatures and the combustion may be incomplete.

(iii) Each mechanical cycle of the engine involves an inlet and exhaust process and, due to the pressure drop through the valves, a certain amount of work is required to charge the cylinder with fuel-air mixture and also to drive out the products of combustion.

(iv) There will be considerable heat transfer between the gases in the cylinder and the cylinder walls.

(v) There will be irreversibilities associated with the pressure and temperature gradient.

Thus, we see that the simulation of CI engine processes through an ideal cycle will give the highest pressure and temperature values which are very different from those for the actual engine. To move a step closer to an actual engine, let us incorporate the first two points in our analysis. This analysis is referred to as simulation of CI engine processes using fuel-air mixture as the working medium. Before that we will work out a simple example. The reader is advised to write a computer program for this worked-out example so that the results can be checked.

6.5 Solved example

The compression ratio for an ideal Diesel cycle is 16. At the beginning of the compression stroke the pressure is 1 atm and the temperature 300 K. The cut-off ratio is 4. Determine

(i) p, V, T values at the end of each process of the cycle,
(ii) the thermal efficiency, and
(iii) the mean effective pressure.

Take the bore (B) as 80 mm, and stroke (S) of the engine as 110 mm; the ratio of specific heats for air is 1.4, C_p is 1.004 kJ/kg K and C_v is 0.717 kJ/kg K. We have

$$V_{\text{disp}} = \frac{\pi}{4} \times B^2 \times S$$

$$= \frac{\pi}{4} \times 80^2 \times 110 \times 10^{-3}$$

$$= 552.9 \text{ cc},$$

$$V_{\text{bdc}} = \frac{r}{r-1} \times V_{\text{disp}}$$

$$= \frac{16}{16-1} \times 552.9$$

$$= 589.8 \text{ cc},$$

$$V_{\text{tdc}} = V_{\text{bdc}} - V_{\text{disp}}$$

$$= 36.9 \text{ cc}.$$

Now p, V, T values at point 1 (before compression) are:

$$p_1 = 1 \text{ atm}; \quad T_1 = 300 \text{ K}; \quad V_1 = V_{\text{bdc}} = 589.8 \text{ cc}.$$

At point 2 (at the end of compression):

$$p_2 = p_1 r^k = 1 \times 16^{1.4} = 48.5 \text{ atm},$$

$$T_2 = T_1 r^{(k-1)}$$

$$= 300 \times 16^{(1.4-1)} = 909.4 \text{ K},$$

$$V_2 = V_{\text{tdc}} = 36.9 \text{ cc}.$$

At point 3 (at the end of heat transfer):

$$p_3 = p_2 = 48.5 \text{ atm},$$

$$T_3 = r_c \times T_2$$

$$= 4 \times 909.4 = 3637.6 \text{ K},$$

$$V_3 = r_c \times V_2 = 4 \times 36.9$$

$$= 147.6 \text{ cc.}$$

At point 4 (end of expansion):

$$p_4 = p_3 \left(\frac{V_3}{V_4}\right)^k$$

$$= 48.5 \times \left(\frac{147.6}{589.8}\right)^{1.4}$$

$$= 7 \text{ atm.}$$

$$T_4 = T_3 \left(\frac{V_3}{V_4}\right)^{k-1}$$

$$= 3637.6 \times \left(\frac{147.6}{589.8}\right)^{0.4}$$

$$= 2090.1 \text{ K},$$

$$V_4 = V_{\text{bdc}} = 589.8 \text{ cc.}$$

Assuming unit mass of air

$$\text{expansion work, } W_{\text{exp}} = C_v(T_3 - T_4)$$

$$= 0.717 \times (3637.6 - 2090.1)$$

$$= 1109.6 \text{ kJ/kg},$$

$$\text{combustion work, } W_{\text{comb}} = R \times (T_3 - T_2)$$

$$= 0.287 \times (3637.6 - 909.4)$$

$$= 783 \text{ kJ/kg}$$

$$\text{compression work, } W_{\text{comp}} = C_v(T_2 - T_1)$$

$$= 0.717 \times (909.4 - 300)$$

$$= 436.939 \text{ kJ/kg},$$

$$\text{Heat added, } H_{\text{add}} = C_p(T_3 - T_2)$$

$$= 1.004 \times (3637.6 - 909.4)$$

$$= 2739.1 \text{ kJ/kg},$$

Therefore,

$$\text{net work done, } W_{\text{net}} = W_{\text{exp}} + W_{\text{comb}} - W_{\text{comp}}$$

$$= 1109.6 + 783 - 436.9$$

$$= 1455.7 \text{ kJ/kg},$$

$$\text{thermal efficiency} = \frac{W_{\text{net}}}{H_{\text{add}}}$$

$$= \frac{1455.7}{2739.1} = 53.1\%,$$

$$\text{mean effective pressure} = \left(\frac{W_{\text{net}}}{V_{\text{disp}}}\right)\left(\frac{p_1V_1}{RT_1}\right)\left(\frac{10^6 \times 10^3}{101325}\right)$$

$$= \frac{1455.7}{552.9} \times \frac{101325 \times 589.8 \times 10^{-6}}{287 \times 300} \times \frac{10^6 \times 10^3}{101325}$$

$$= 18.29 \text{ bar.}$$

Note: In this example, the cut-off ratio is assumed as 4 which is a little too large. Hence, the efficiency is only 53.1%. Normally, it will be between 2 and 3. This illustrates that the cut-off ratio is also a deciding factor in a Diesel cycle.

Exercise

Write a program to simulate CI engine processes using an ideal Diesel cycle. Generate the required data at each degree crank angle to draw the p-θ and p-V diagrams. Print out the efficiency as a function of the compression ratio and cut-off ratio.

7

CI ENGINE SIMULATION WITH ADIABATIC COMBUSTION

7.1 Introduction

In the last chapter we discussed CI engine simulation with air as the working medium. In this chapter we will consider fuel-air mixture as the working medium and also include the intake process with some simplifying assumptions. Further, we will incorporate the constant-pressure adiabatic combustion calculations, in order to simulate the combustion process. We will call this analysis fuel-air cycle simulation (FCS).

Figure 7.1 illustrates a typical cycle, showing all the processes, including the intake and exhaust stroke. It should be noted that, in this simulation, the intake process is rather bit over-simplified. We will consider the intake and exhaust process in greater detail in Chapter 9.

7.2 Engine details

The simulation that follows in this chapter and in the rest of the book will examine the performance characteristics of a piston-cylinder engine. The details of the engine under consideration for the simulation are given in Table 7.1.

The main aim of the simulation using adiabatic combustion calculations is to evaluate the power output and thermal efficiency for a given engine speed, ambient air temperature, fuel and fuel-air ratio. In this chapter we will simulate CI engine for naturally aspirated and supercharged conditions. It is hoped that this will make the reader understand and appreciate the effect of intake process and air-fuel ratio on engine performance, which were not included in the ideal cycle simulation.

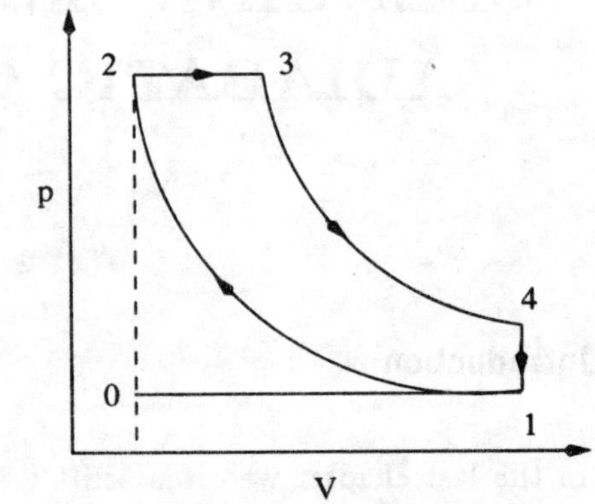

Fig.7.1 *Diesel cycle at naturally aspirated condition*

Table 7.1 Details of the engine for simulation

B	Bore	80.0 mm
S	Stroke	110.0 mm
L	Connecting rod length	230.0 mm
r	Compression ratio	16.5
V_{disp}	Displacement volume	552.9 cc
V_{tdc}	Volume at TDC	35.7 cc
V_{bdc}	Volume at BDC	588.6 cc

7.3 Naturally aspirated operation

Maximum power of the compression-ignition engine will be obtained when it is run at full load and at this condition, we have,

$$p_1 = p_5 = p_a = \text{ambient pressure} = 1\ \text{atm(say)}$$

$$V_1 = V_{\text{bdc}}.$$

Let T_a = ambient air temperature and
T_m = intake manifold temperature:

There will be no temperature drop in the intake manifold as the fuel is injected into the cylinder. Therefore,

$$T_m = T_a. \tag{7.1}$$

Let us now define certain terms that are used quite often in the simulation.

N_{mo} kilomoles of air plus fuel vapour in a mixture containing 1 kmol of fuel.

N_{po} kilomoles of products formed from the combustion of N_{mo}.

N_{a} kilomoles of air taken in during suction.

N_{f} kilomoles of fuel injected.

N_{x} kilomoles of residual exhaust from the previous cycle in the engine during the compression stroke.

N_{p} kilomoles of products formed from the combustion of $N_{\mathrm{a}} + N_{\mathrm{x}} + N_{\mathrm{f}}$.

C_{pa} specific heat of air.

C_{pf} specific heat of fuel.

A/F air-fuel ratio.

7.3.1 Isentropic compression process 1→2

Let us consider the engine cycle (Fig.7.1) and start from point 1. Initially, we have to assume the values of N_{x} and T_1, both depending on the previous cycle, which in turn, depends on the cycle before that, and so on. To start with, let us assume

$$N_{\mathrm{x}} = 0 \quad \text{and} \quad T_1 = T_a; \tag{7.2}$$

$$N_{\mathrm{a}} = \frac{p_1 V_{\mathrm{bdc}}}{RT_1}. \tag{7.3}$$

At the beginning of the compression process, there are $N_{\mathrm{a}} + N_{\mathrm{x}}$ moles of the working fluid.

Let C_{pr} be the constant-pressure heat capacity (kJ/kmol K) for the reactant $N_{\mathrm{a}} + N_{\mathrm{x}}$.

Then the polytropic index for compression ($k = C_p/C_v$) can be written as

$$k_{\mathrm{r}} = \frac{C_{\mathrm{pr}}}{(C_{\mathrm{pr}} - R)} \tag{7.4}$$

where $R = 8.314$ (kJ kmol^{-1} K^{-1}). Since we know T_1 as well as r, we get

$$T_2 = T_1 r^{k_r - 1}, \tag{7.5}$$

$$p_2 = p_1 r^{k_r}, \tag{7.6}$$

$$V_2 = V_{tdc}. \tag{7.7}$$

7.3.2 Adiabatic combustion process 2→3

Let us assume that the combustion takes place adiabatically and at constant pressure. Since there is no heat transfer, the energy equation can be written as

enthalpy of the reactant = enthalpy of the product, i.e.

$$H_r(T_2) + H_f(T_f) = H_p(T_3) \tag{7.8}$$

where the suffixes r, f and p denote the $N_a + N_x$ moles of reactants, fuel and the products of combustion.

The solution of eq.(7.8) will be taken up shortly. By solving eq.(7.8) we will get the value of T_3. Since, the process is at constant pressure, we can write

$$p_3 = p_2, \tag{7.9}$$

Knowing p_3 and T_3, we can calculate

$$V_3 = N_p R \left(\frac{T_3}{p_3} \right). \tag{7.10}$$

Now let us consider the combustion process 2→3 in detail. For a constant-pressure adiabatic combustion, we can write [refer to eq.(3.43)]

$$Q_p = \sum \{ N_i \left[\bar{h}_i(T_3) - \bar{h}_i(T_2) \right] \} \tag{7.11}$$

Equation (7.11) can be conveniently solved using the Newton-Raphson iteration technique, once we know the values of the product gas mole numbers, N_i in eq.(7.11). We will evaluate these mole numbers in terms of the actual values for the engine under consideration.

For CI engines normally diesel, $C_{10}H_{22}$, is the fuel used. Hence, the various products moles are set as

$$N_1 = CO; \quad N_2 = CO_2; \quad N_3 = H_2O; \quad N_4 = N_2; \quad N_5 = O_2.$$

Let Y represent moles of O_2 per mole of $C_{10}H_{22}$, then the reactant fuel-air mixture is

$$C_{10}H_{22} + Y\,O_2 + 3.76\,Y\,N_2 \tag{7.12}$$

We have

$$N_{\rm mo} = 1 + 4.76\,Y \tag{7.13}$$

$$\left.\begin{aligned} N_{\rm po} &= 17 + 3.76\,Y, \quad \text{for } 10.5 \le Y \le 15.5 \\ &= 4.5 + 4.76\,Y, \quad \text{for } Y \ge 15.5 \end{aligned}\right\} \tag{7.14}$$

From Table 2.3 in Chapter 2, the value of $H_{\rm rp}$ can be obtained, which is close to −6,796,000 kJ/kmol of $C_{10}H_{22}$ vapour.

Now the mole numbers and the value of Q_p required in eq.(7.11) can be written as follows:

$$\left.\begin{array}{ll} \underline{10.5 \le Y \le 15.5} & \underline{Y \ge 15.5} \\ N_1 = 2(15.5 - Y)S_f & N_1 = 0 \\ N_2 = (2Y - 21)S_f & N_2 = 10S_f \\ N_3 = 11S_f & N_3 = 11S_f \\ N_4 = 3.76Y\,S_f & N_4 = 3.76Y\,S_f \\ N_5 = 0 & N_5 = (Y - 15.5)S_f \end{array}\right\} \tag{7.15}$$

$$Q_p = -(H_{\rm rp} + N_{\rm CO} \times 282800)\frac{N_{\rm m}}{N_{\rm mo}}$$

where

$$S_f = \frac{N_{\rm a}}{N_{\rm mo}} + \frac{N_{\rm x}}{N_{\rm po}}. \tag{7.16}$$

The value of Y fixes $N_{\rm mo}$ and $N_{\rm po}$ by eqs.(7.13) and (7.14), respectively. The scale factor, S_f, reduces the mole numbers to a proper size to fit the engine, once $N_{\rm a}$ and $N_{\rm x}$ are known, or assumed in the case of $N_{\rm x}$, for the first cycle.

By substituting these values of N_is in eq.(7.11) and evaluating h_is using the thermodynamic function given in Appendix C and solving eq.(7.11), by means of the method already explained in Chapter 3, the adiabatic flame temperature, T_3, can be calculated. V_3 can then be evaluated using eq.(7.10).

7.3.3 Isentropic expansion process 3→4

Having calculated the values of T_3, p_3 and V_3, we can now proceed to calculate the values of T_4 and p_4 during the expansion process 3→4. Now,

$$T_4 = \frac{T_3}{r^{(k_p-1)}}, \tag{7.17}$$

$$p_4 = \frac{p_3}{r^{k_p}}, \tag{7.18}$$

where

$$k_p = \frac{C_{pp}}{(C_{pp} - R)}, \tag{7.19}$$

$$V_4 = V_{bdc}. \tag{7.20}$$

7.3.4 Exhaust and intake processes 1→5 and 5→1

At point 4, we assume that the exhaust valve opens and the pressure drops to ambient, and that the temperature of the exhaust drops to

$$T_5 = T_4 \left(\frac{p_1}{p_4}\right)^{(k_p-1)/k_p} \tag{7.21}$$

As the piston moves from BDC to TDC, most of the exhaust gases are pushed out, and what remains in the engine at TDC is

$$N_x = \frac{p_1 V_{tdc}}{RT_5} \tag{7.22}$$

The exhaust valve now closes and the intake valve opens. The piston moves slowly to BDC position, during which time N_a moles of air are drawn into the working space; after mixing with N_x, the resulting temperature will be T_1. Note that N_a is not given by eq.(7.3). N_a and T_1 are to be found by analyzing the intake process shown in Fig.7.2 and setting up the energy equation.

Let us assume that the air that will be drawn into the engine during the intake stroke initially occupies a volume V_a in the intake manifold. A control mass is placed around $N_a + N_x$, as shown in Fig.7.2. The initial energy in the control mass is

$$N_x u_p(T_5) + N_a u_a(T_a) \tag{7.23}$$

As the piston moves through the length of the stroke, an amount of work equal to

$$p_1(V_{bdc} - V_{tdc}) \tag{7.24}$$

will be done by the gases in the working space, while work amounting to

$$p_1 V_a \tag{7.25}$$

is done on the control mass by the air behind N_a. At BDC, the energy in the control mass is

$$N_x u_p(T_1) + N_a u_a(T_1) \tag{7.26}$$

Now we can combine eqs.(7.23) to (7.26) to form the energy equation as

$$\begin{aligned} & N_x u_p(T_5) + N_a u_a(T_a) - p_1(V_{bdc} - V_{tdc}) + p_1 V_a \\ = \; & N_x u_p(T_1) + N_a u_a(T_1) \end{aligned} \tag{7.27}$$

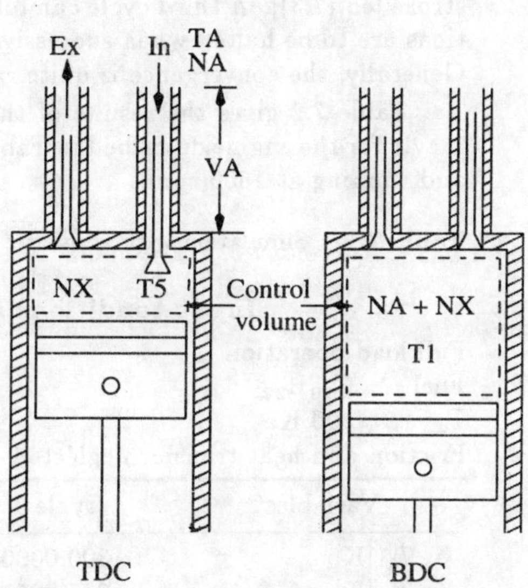

Fig.7.2 *Intake stroke in piston-cylinder engine*

and by grouping the U and pV terms, we get

$$N_x h_p(T_5) + N_a h_a(T_a) = N_x h_p(T_1) + N_a h_a(T_1). \tag{7.28}$$

Replacing enthalpy terms by $C_p T$ products and noting that

$$N_a = \frac{p_1 V_{bdc}}{RT_1} - N_x, \tag{7.29}$$

the energy equation reduces to

$$\left(\frac{C_{pp}}{C_{pa}} - 1\right)\frac{T_1^2}{T_a T_5} + \left(r + \frac{T_a}{T_5} - \frac{C_{pp}}{C_{pa}}\right)\frac{T_1}{T_a} - r = 0, \tag{7.30}$$

where C_{pa} is the constant-pressure heat capacity of air in kJ kmol^{-1} K^{-1}.

Equation (7.30) can be solved for T_1. However, if the difference between C_{pp} and C_{pa} is ignored, eq.(7.30) reduces to

$$T_1 = \frac{rT_a}{r - 1 + (T_a/T_5)}. \tag{7.31}$$

To return to the chain of calculations, with the new values for T_1 [eq.(7.31)], N_a [eq.(7.29)] and N_x [eq.(7.22)], a new value for C_{pr} is calculated and the computations proceed through a second cycle beginning with the compression stroke [eq.(7.3)]. A third cycle can follow the second and so on. The computations are to be halted when successive cycles produce almost the same values. Generally, the convergence is quite rapid.

Table 7.2 gives the results of the computation (with four decimal accuracy!) for the engine described in Table 7.1 in the naturally aspirated condition and running at 1500 rpm.

Table 7.2 Simulation with adiabatic combustion

Input conditions and predicted results

Full load operation		Chemically correct mixture	
Fuel	$C_{10}H_{22}$	Speed	1500 rpm
T_a	300 K	p_1	1 atm
Friction and heat transfer neglected		r	16.5

Variables	Cycle 1	Cycle 2	Cycle 3
T_1 [K]	300.0000	314.8110	314.8340
T_2 [K]	915.2251	959.8059	960.0320
T_3 [K]	2883.6899	2897.3770	2897.6672
T_4 [K]	1962.9824	1981.2449	1981.3900
T_5 [K]	1340.9672	1347.8854	1347.9858
p_2 [atm]	50.3374	50.3057	50.3139
p_3 [atm]	50.3374	50.3057	50.3139
p_4 [atm]	7.0310	7.1860	7.1861
r_c	3.3857	3.4468	3.4464
k_r	1.3979	1.3977	1.3977
k_p	1.2428	1.2427	1.2427
$N_a/(N_a + N_x)$	0.9864	0.9858	0.9858
P [kW]	11.5018	11.5327	11.7227
p_{imef} [atm]	16.4239	16.4681	16.7393
η_{th} [%]	45.3490	45.4710	46.2199

7.4 Work output and efficiency calculations

Having calculated p, V, T values at the salient points in the cycle, we can now calculate the work output and efficiency of the cycle.

Net work output of the cycle

$$W_{net} = W_{exp} + W_{comb} - W_{comp}, \tag{7.32}$$

$$W_{exp} = U_p(T_3) - U_p(T_4), \tag{7.33}$$

$$W_{comp} = (N_a + N_x)(C_{pr} - R)(T_2 - T_1). \tag{7.34}$$

From eqs.(7.22) and (7.29), it follows that

$$\frac{N_a}{N_a + N_x} = 1 - \frac{1}{r}\frac{T_1}{T_5}. \tag{7.35}$$

The thermal efficiency, η_{th}, is calculated from

$$\eta_{th} = \frac{W_{net}}{H_{rp}}\frac{N_{mo}}{N_a}. \tag{7.36}$$

The mean effective pressure, p_{mef}, is defined as the hypothetical pressure which, if acting throughout the power stroke, would produce the calculated work of that stroke, i.e.

$$W_{net} = p_{mef}\frac{\pi}{4}B^2 S, \tag{7.37}$$

so that

$$p_{mef} = \frac{W_{net}}{V_{disp}}. \tag{7.38}$$

Another way of examining the ratio of net work (or power) to displacement volume is to start with

$$W_{net} = W_{exp} + W_{comb} - W_{comp}, \tag{7.39}$$

which can be written as

$$W_{net} = N_p\{u_p(T_3) - u_p(T_4)\} + N_p R(T_3 - T_2) - N_r\{u_r(T_2) - u_r(T_1)\} \tag{7.40}$$

where N_p and N_r denote the moles of products and reactants, respectively. Now

$$N_r = \frac{p_1 V_{bdc}}{RT_1} \quad \text{and} \quad V_{bdc} = \frac{r}{r-1}V_{disp}.$$

Hence,

$$\frac{W_{net}}{V_{disp}} = \left(\frac{r}{r-1}\frac{p_1}{R\,T_1}\right) \times$$

$$\left[\frac{N_p}{N_r}\{u_p(T_3) - u_p(T_4)\} - \{u_r(T_2) - u_r(T_1)\} + N_p R(T_3 - T_2)\right] \tag{7.41}$$

In Table 7.3, calculations are shown for a 553 cc displacement volume engine. The mention of displacement volume has no meaning, or rather adds no meaning. All 16.5 compression ratio engines will exhibit the values shown in Table 7.2. For that matter, all 16.5 compression ratio engines operating on chemically correct diesel-air mixture will produce 21.21 kW/litre running at 1500 rpm under naturally aspirated condition with 300 K intake manifold

Table 7.3 Effect of r on various engine parameters (results from the converged cycle)

Input conditions and predicted results

Full load operation		Chemically correct mixture	
Fuel	$C_{10}H_{22}$	Speed	1500 rpm
T_a	300 K	p_1	1 atm
Friction and heat transfer neglected			

r	12.0000	14.0000	16.5000	18.0000	20.0000
T_1 [K]	321.1268	317.7875	314.8340	313.4828	312.0170
T_2 [K]	862.0258	907.3971	960.0320	989.7369	1027.4467
T_3 [K]	2812.5854	2852.2996	2897.6672	2923.0403	2955.3616
T_4 [K]	2127.7612	2054.3193	1981.3900	1944.9009	1902.8473
T_5 [K]	1425.1483	1386.5930	1347.9858	1328.5470	1306.0485
p_2 [atm]	32.2125	39.9750	50.3139	56.8301	65.8584
p_3 [atm]	32.2125	39.9750	50.3139	56.8301	65.8584
p_4 [atm]	7.7457	7.4640	7.1861	7.0476	6.8885
r_c	3.8142	3.6294	3.4464	3.3549	3.2490
k_r	1.3974	1.3976	1.3977	1.3978	1.3978
k_p	1.2434	1.2431	1.2427	1.2425	1.2423
$N_a/(N_a + N_x)$	0.9812	0.9836	0.9858	0.9869	0.9881
P [kW]	10.2394	10.9807	11.7227	12.0982	12.5400
p_{imef} [atm]	14.6213	15.6799	16.7393	17.2755	17.9065
η_{th} [%]	39.3949	42.7958	46.2199	47.9568	50.0008

temperature and with $r_c = 3.44$. However, it may be noted that diesel engines normally operate on lean mixtures and rarely on chemically correct mixtures.

The important feature in eq.(7.41) is the fact that the compression ratio, pressure, temperature and mole ratio quantities that appear on the right-hand side are intensive parameters; that is, the size of the engine does not influence them.

Also, eq.(7.41) does not indicate how net work or power multiplied by half the rpm, changes as r, p_1 or T_1 are changed. To examine these effects, the cycle calculations must be carried through. Table 7.3 reveals the effect of compression ratio on engine performance. As the compression ratio increases, the amount of residual exhaust gas in the clearance volume of the engine decreases, as does T_1, the cylinder temperature, at the start of compression. These two factors combine to produce an increase in power and thermal efficiency as the compression ratio increases. It may also be noted that with the increase in compression ratio, the cut-off ratio decreases due to increase in T_2.

Table 7.4 illustrates the influence of equivalence ratio on the operating variables. Fuel-air ratio is indicated by Y moles of oxygen per mole of $C_{10}H_{22}$, for which the chemically correct value is $Y_{cc} = 15.5$.

Table 7.4 Effect of equivalence ratio on various engine parameters neglecting the effect of fuel vaporization (results from the converged cycle)

Input conditions and predicted results

Full load operation		Chemically correct mixture	
Fuel	$C_{10}H_{22}$	Speed	1500 rpm
T_m	300 K	p_1	1 atm
Y_{cc}	15.5	r	16.5
Friction and heat transfer neglected			

Y_{cc}/Y	1.0000	0.8860	0.7950	0.7210	0.6600
RAF	1.0000	1.1290	1.2508	1.3870	1.5160
Y	15.5000	17.5000	19.5000	21.5000	23.5000
T_1 [K]	314.8340	314.4977	314.1844	313.8915	313.6172
T_2 [K]	960.0320	959.5187	959.0402	958.5934	958.1749
T_3 [K]	2897.6672	2731.2021	2593.5796	2477.8313	2379.0757
T_4 [K]	1981.3900	1821.6040	1691.8729	1584.4867	1494.1532
T_5 [K]	1347.9858	1253.3303	1176.2166	1112.1477	1058.0471
p_2 [atm]	50.3139	50.3408	50.3658	50.3894	50.4114
p_3 [atm]	50.3139	50.3408	50.3658	50.3894	50.4114
p_4 [atm]	7.1861	6.5610	6.0609	5.6518	5.3110
r_c	3.4464	3.2243	3.0438	2.8941	2.7679
k_r	1.3977	1.3979	1.3981	1.3982	1.3984
k_p	1.2427	1.2481	1.2527	1.2569	1.2605
$N_a/(N_a + N_x)$	0.9858	0.9848	0.9838	0.9829	0.9820
P [kW]	11.7227	10.8348	10.0870	9.5004	8.9375
p_{imef} [atm]	16.7393	15.4715	14.4036	13.5661	12.7623
η_{th} [%]	46.2199	48.2299	50.0316	51.9543	53.4217

It is seen that the peak temperature and power are produced by the chemically correct mixture. The thermal efficiency tends to increase with the leaner mixture while the power tends to decrease with the leaner mixture.

7.5 Supercharged operation

Diesel engines are normally supercharged in order to increase the power output. This is achieved by installing a compressor in the intake system, thereby increasing the density of air at the start of the compression stroke. Usually, the compressor is placed in the inlet manifold pipe. Because of the supercharger both intake pressure and temperature increase. These two factors may improve the fuel vaporization when the fuel is injected.

Supercharged cycles can be simulated easily in a single iteration in a computer. It is entirely reasonable to assume that all the exhaust gases are swept out of the working space with the intake manifold pressure increased above ambient pressure in the exhaust manifold. This happens during the period of valve overlap, i.e. the time interval during which both the valves are open. However, if the period of overlap is excessive, fresh air inducted may be swept into the exhaust systems. This will reduce the availability of oxygen for combustion.

Power is required to drive the compressor and may be obtained by a direct mechanical drive from the crank shaft, or by installing a turbine driven by the exhaust gases. Let us examine both cases.

Figure 7.3 illustrates the pressure-volume trace during exhaust and intake strokes, for a gear-driven compressor arrangement shown in Fig.7.4.

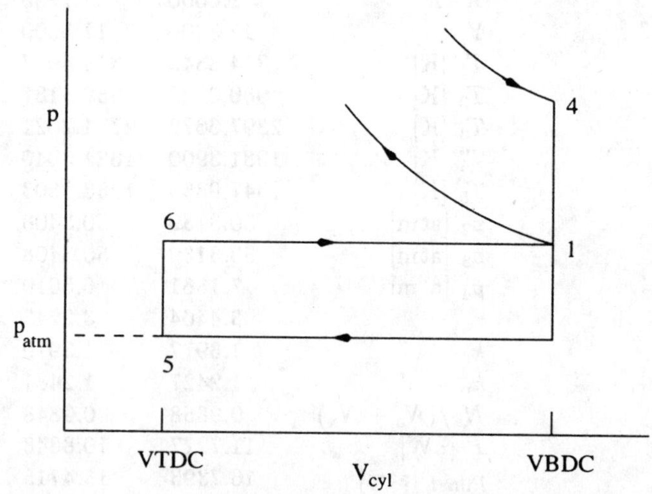

Fig.7.3 *The exhaust-intake loop for a gear-driven supercharger*

Consider Fig.7.3. If T_a denotes the temperature of the air before the compressor, the exit temperature from the compressor, T_1, is given by

$$T_1 = T_a \left[\frac{1}{\eta_{\text{comp}}} \left\{ \left(\frac{p_1}{p_a} \right)^{(k_r - 1)/k_r} - 1 \right\} + 1 \right], \tag{7.42}$$

where η_{comp} is the isentropic efficiency of the compressor.

Work required to drive the compressor, W_{spch}, is given by

$$W_{\text{spch}} = N_{\text{a}} C_{\text{pr}} (T_1 - T_a) \tag{7.43}$$

where N_{a} denotes the moles of air compressed during the compression stroke, and is given by

$$N_{\text{a}} = \frac{p_1 V_{\text{bdc}}}{R T_1}. \tag{7.44}$$

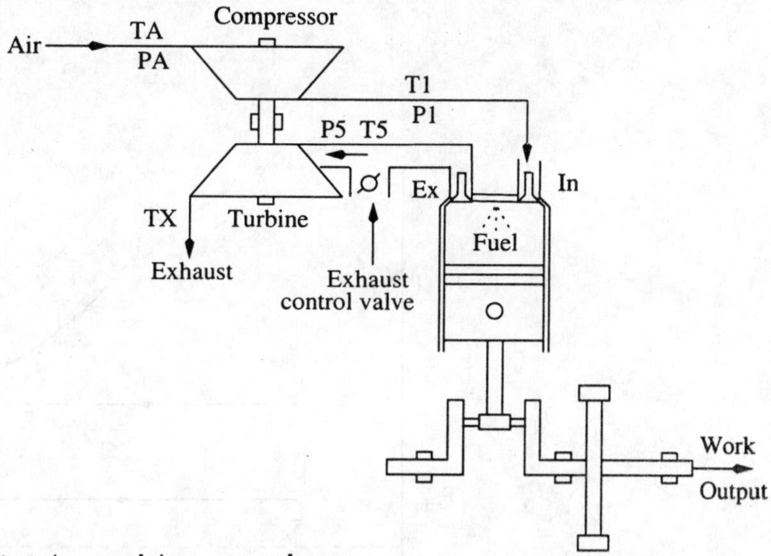

Fig.7.4 *A gear-driven supercharger*

For the calculation of the net work output of the cycle, W_{spch} should also be included, along with W_{loop}, the work associated with the exhaust-intake loop (Fig.7.3). If we define W_{loop} as

$$W_{loop} = (p_1 - p_5)V_{disp}, \tag{7.45}$$

then,

$$W_{net} = W_{exp} + W_{comb} - W_{comp} - W_{spch} + W_{loop} \tag{7.46}$$

Table 7.5 lists the output from the computer program, for a gear-driven supercharger. The power increase is around 16% for a 50% increase in manifold pressure. It may be seen that the improvement in power output is not high (only 16% for a 50% increase in p_1). This is due to the fact that we have assumed constant pressure adiabatic combustion. Actual diesel engines work on dual combustion (partly constant volume and partly constant pressure). If the analysis is modified to take into account the dual combustion, better results will be obtained. This is left to the reader. However, power output increases with increase in the degree of supercharging. It may be noted that the power increase depends on compressor efficiency. Here, we have assumed an isentropic compressor efficiency of 90%.

Figure 7.5 depicts the exhaust and intake strokes for a supercharger driven by an exhaust turbine. Figure 7.6 illustrates the details of an exhaust turbine supercharger. From Fig.7.5 it is clear that the exhaust stroke takes place at a pressure greater than the ambient pressure, as otherwise there would be no driving force to move the turbine wheel. Figure 7.6 includes an exhaust control valve upstream from the turbine.

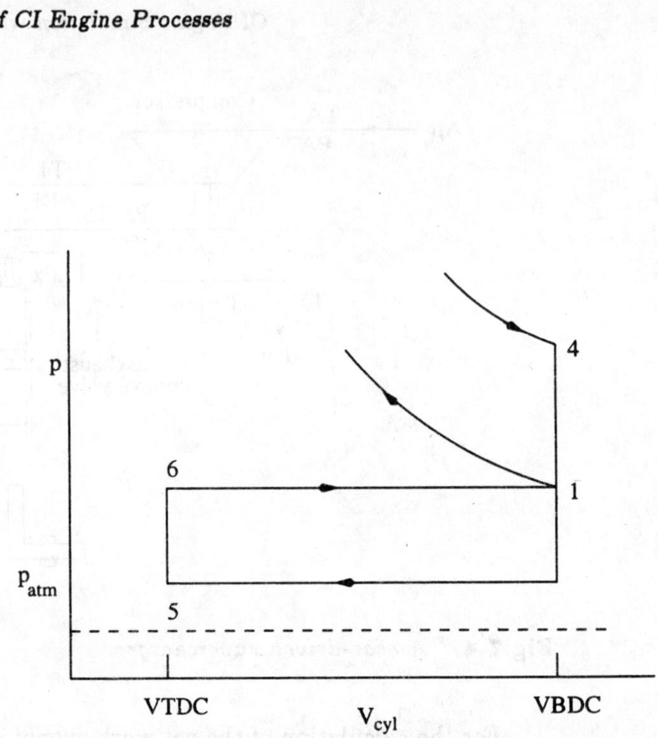

Fig.7.5 *The exhaust-intake loop for an exhaust turbine supercharger*

The position of the valve determines the fraction of the exhaust flow that passes through the turbine. Thus, the power output of the turbine is controllable. This feature is not available in a gear-driven supercharger. In the gear-driven supercharger, to control the power input to the compressor, a gear box would be required. This increases the complexity of the system.

The work required to drive the compressor is, as before,

$$N_a C_{pr}(T_1 - T_a),$$

while the work output of the turbine, assuming that all the exhaust passes through the turbine, is

$$W_{turb} = N_p C_{pp}(T_5 - T_x)\eta_{turb}, \tag{7.47}$$

where T_x is the outlet temperature in the turbine for isentropic expansion and η_{turb} is the turbine efficiency. With p_a denoting ambient pressure, the turbine work output can be written in the form

$$W_{turb} = N_p C_{pp} T_4 \left(\frac{p_a}{p_4}\right)^{(k_p-1)/k_p} \times \left[\left(\frac{p_5}{p_4}\right)^{(k_p-1)/k_p} - 1\right]\eta_{turb}. \tag{7.48}$$

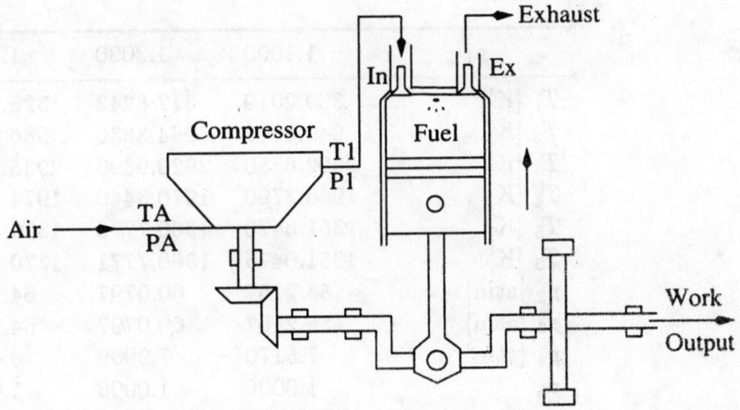

Fig.7.6 *An exhaust turbine supercharger*

The required exhaust manifold pressure, p_5, can be computed by equating compressor work input with the turbine work output:

$$\left(\frac{p_5}{p_a}\right)^{(k_p-1)/k_p} = 1 + \frac{N_a C_{pr}(T_1 - T_a)}{N_p C_{pp} T_4 \eta_{turb}} \left(\frac{p_4}{p_a}\right)^{(k_p-1)/k_p} \quad (7.49)$$

For an exhaust turbine system, net work is calculated from

$$W_{net} = W_{exp} + W_{comb} - W_{comp} + W_{loop},$$

where work done by the gases on the piston is given by

$$W_{loop} = (p_1 - p_5)V_{disp}, \quad (7.50)$$

as shown in Fig.7.5.

Table 7.6 gives the performance details of an exhaust driven supercharger engine, with all the exhaust products flowing through the turbine. The gain

Table 7.5 Effect of supercharging on various engine parameters (gear-driven supercharger)

Input conditions and predicted results

Full load operation		Chemically correct mixture	
Fuel	$C_{10}H_{22}$	Speed	1500 rpm
T_m	300 K	r	16.5
Friction and heat transfer neglected			

p_1	1.1000	1.2000	1.3000	1.4000	1.5000
T_1 [K]	309.2019	317.8242	325.9474	333.6359	340.9414
T_2 [K]	940.6669	964.3836	986.6198	1007.5700	1027.3920
T_3 [K]	2902.6280	2920.9390	2938.9660	2956.8630	2973.8840
T_4 [K]	1966.3790	1970.3440	1974.9880	1980.2970	1985.5200
T_5 [K]	1351.0470	1360.7770	1370.3310	1379.7920	1388.7940
T_6 [K]	1351.0475	1360.7771	1370.3314	1379.7920	1388.7936
p_2 [atm]	55.2167	60.0797	64.9276	69.7613	74.5816
p_3 [atm]	55.2167	60.0797	64.9276	69.7613	74.5816
p_4 [atm]	7.5170	7.9939	8.4642	8.9292	9.3866
p_5	1.0000	1.0000	1.0000	1.0000	1.0000
p_6	1.1000	1.2000	1.3000	1.4000	1.5000
r_c	3.3157	3.2546	3.2009	3.1534	3.1104
k_r	1.3969	1.3960	1.3951	1.3943	1.3935
k_p	1.2427	1.2425	1.2424	1.2422	1.2421
$N_a/(N_a + N_x)$	1.0000	1.0000	1.0000	1.0000	1.0000
P [kW]	12.3116	13.0984	13.8667	14.6195	15.3540
p_{imef} [atm]	17.5802	18.7038	19.8009	20.8757	21.9246
η_{th}	45.4824	45.5938	45.6939	45.7885	45.8660

in power output is nearly the same for the two systems when all the exhaust flows through the turbine.

However, Table 7.6 does not represent a true example of an exhaust turbine system because it has been calculated on the assumption of full exhaust flow through the turbine. There is the tacit assumption that the resistance the turbine offers to gas flow can be altered by some means, thereby altering pressure p_5 upstream from the turbine. In theory this could be accomplished by changing the blade setting; however, in practice this would be difficult to do. What can be done is illustrated in Fig.7.6. The exhaust control valve determines the quantity of exhaust passing through the turbine, with the remaining diverted directly to the atmosphere.

If a fraction f of the exhaust passes through the turbine, the equation for turbine work output is now given by

$$W_{\text{turb}} = f N_p C_{pp} (T_5 - T_x) \eta_{\text{turb}}. \tag{7.51}$$

Table 7.6 Effect of supercharging on various engine parameters (exhaust driven supercharger)

Input conditions and predicted results

Full load operation		Chemically correct mixture	
Fuel	$C_{10}H_{22}$	Speed	1500 rpm
T_m	300 K	r	16.5
Friction and heat transfer neglected			

p_1	1.1000	1.2000	1.3000	1.4000	1.5000
T_1 [K]	309.2019	317.8242	325.9474	333.6359	340.9414
T_2 [K]	940.6669	964.3836	986.6198	1007.5700	1027.3920
T_3 [K]	2902.6280	2920.9390	2938.9660	2956.8630	2973.8840
T_4 [K]	1966.3790	1970.3440	1974.9880	1980.2970	1985.5200
T_5 [K]	1332.6730	1325.8850	1320.4380	1316.1500	1312.4820
T_6 [K]	1351.0476	1360.7771	1370.3314	1379.7920	1388.7936
p_2 [atm]	55.2167	60.0797	64.9276	69.7613	74.5816
p_3 [atm]	55.2167	60.0797	64.9276	69.7613	74.5816
p_4 [atm]	7.5170	7.9939	8.4642	8.9292	9.3866
p_5	1.0255	1.0505	1.0749	1.0989	1.1225
p_6	1.1000	1.2000	1.3000	1.4000	1.5000
r_c	3.3157	3.2546	3.2009	3.1534	3.1104
k_r	1.3969	1.3960	1.3951	1.3943	1.3935
k_p	1.2427	1.2425	1.2424	1.2422	1.2421
$N_a/(N_a + N_x)$	1.0000	1.0000	1.0000	1.0000	1.0000
P [kW]	12.3796	13.2400	14.0866	14.9223	15.7437
p_{imef} [atm]	17.6773	18.9059	20.1149	21.3081	22.4812
η_{th}	45.7337	46.0864	46.4186	46.7369	47.0303

Then in eq.(7.49), for p_5, f will appear in the denominator of the second part of the expression, with a resulting increase in p_5. The net effect on power is to decrease W_{loop} (Fig.7.5), thereby decreasing the power output.

The inclusion of the factor, f in the calculations does not present any computational difficulty, rather the problem is one of knowing how a real turbine operates in conjunction with an exhaust control valve, which can be positioned as we please. The value for f is fixed in accordance with the relative flow resistances of the turbine and the control valve, and we have a problem in fluid mechanics dealing with divided flow.

Note that with increase in p_5, which will occur with decreasing f values, not only will W_{loop} be reduced, but also when carried to the point where p_5 exceeds p_1, the intake manifold pressure, the engine will no longer scavenge residual exhaust gases completely. One of the desirable features of supercharged engines is then lost. All this means that the turbine must be matched to the engines and, to solve the problem properly, power calculations require a

detailed knowledge of turbine characteristics as well as exhaust control valve geometry.

Exercise

1. **Develop a computer program to simulate an CI engine at naturally aspirated and supercharged conditions. Develop also the post-processor for parametric studies.**
2. **Diesel engines normally operate on a dual combustion cycle. Modify the above program to take into account the constant volume and constant pressure adiabatic combustion. Then, compare your results with normal diesel cycle simulation.**

8

CI ENGINE SIMULATION WITH PROGRESSIVE COMBUSTION

8.1 Introduction

In Chapter 7, the CI engine simulation was carried out for naturally aspirated and supercharged conditions, taking into account the concept of adiabatic combustion. The main assumption in that analysis was about the heat release which is assumed to be at constant-pressure. In actual engines this is not the case and it will have a significant effect on the performance of the engine.

Figure 8.1 compares the measured and calculated power output for a single cylinder reciprocating engine at naturally aspirated conditions at full load. It is seen that peak power occurs around 1500 rpm. If Ideal Cycle Simulation (ICS) is carried out with adiabatic combustion for the same engine, the output versus speed plot will be as shown in Fig.8.1, a straight line passing through the origin.

Our immediate concern is not with the difference in values between the two curves; the calculated power is expected to exceed the measured performance. The shape of the measured power curve is the feature of interest. All naturally aspirated engines exhibit a power peak with respect to speed. Hence, it is clear that adiabatic combustion analysis must be modified in a suitable way to achieve closer approximation in order to study the behaviour of actual engines.

Within the methods and tactics of thermodynamics, modifications can be attempted in the following three processes:

(i) the combustion process,

(ii) the gas exchange process, and

(iii) the heat transfer process.

We will take up the first modification in this chapter and will call it progressive combustion simulation (PCS).

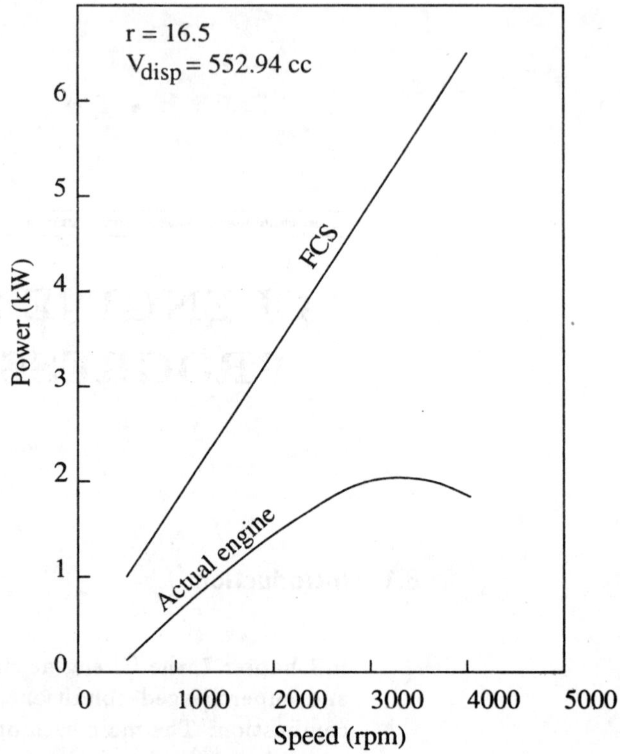

Fig.8.1 *Power output vs speed of an CI engine*

Combustion in an actual compression-ignition engine is not instantaneous. The injection starts well before TDC and combustion depends on many factors, the prominent ones being

(a) the amount of fuel injected
(b) delay period
(c) the engine speed,
(d) the injector location,
(e) combustion chamber size and geometry.

Thermodynamics suggests a way to deal with combustion that proceeds at some finite rate, although it sheds no light whatsoever on the central question of the rate itself. Progressive combustion is what we are going to discuss in this chapter.

In order to calculate the net work done by the gases between the start of ignition and the end of combustion, initially, we have to define these two events in the cycle in addition to the *p–V* trace during combustion.

First, it is necessary to find the volume, V, of the cylinder with respect to the crank angle, θ. The relation between V and θ is governed by the engine geometry and kinematics. This has already been dealt with in Chapter 5.

8.2 Progressive combustion

In real compression-ignition engines, the process of heat addition between points 2 and 3 of Fig.7.1 is to be replaced by a suitable rate of combustion equation. In an ideal CI engine, high compression ratios bring the air to high temperature at the end of compression stroke. Fuel injection begins immediately, and the quantity of fuel injected is adjusted with the piston movement to keep cylinder pressure constant. In this analysis combustion is assumed to begin as soon as injected fuel makes contact with hot air without any ignition delay and continues in that manner, with no need for a spark. However, it may be noted that this does not happen in an actual engine.

Hence, we want to examine CI engine combustion in greater detail, for reasons that will become evident shortly. In order to achieve, or to approximate, constant pressure during the combustion process, fuel must be injected and burned over a finite span of crankshaft rotation. Diesel combustion is also progressive and can be analysed in a similar way, to that of a spark-ignition engine.

If mass fraction, Δn, of fuel burns while the piston moves through a volume change amounting to ΔV, the resulting change in pressure, ΔP, can be given as

$$\Delta p = -pk\frac{\Delta V}{V} + (p_{3'} - p_2)\frac{V_{tdc}}{V}\Delta n \tag{8.1}$$

where k is the ratio of specific heats ($k = c_p/c_v$),
p_2 is the pressure at TDC, at end of the compression stroke, and
$p_{3'}$ is the pressure that would be reached if all the fuel burned instantaneously at TDC (i.e. at constant volume).

The first term in eq.(8.1) represents the pressure change due to piston movement and the second term is due to combustion.

When we set $\Delta p = 0$ in eq.(8.1), along with $p = p_2$, assume k to be constant during combustion. Equation (8.1) can be integrated and can be shown to be

$$n = \frac{V - V_{tdc}}{V_3 - V_{tdc}} \tag{8.2}$$

where V_3 is the volume at the instant when combustion is completed and can be determined from

$$V_3 = V_{tdc}\left(1 + \frac{p_{3'} - p_2}{kp_2}\right) \tag{8.3}$$

Equation 8.2 describes the manner in which fuel must be injected and then burned without any ignition delay if constant pressure is to be maintained. Thermodynamics makes no distinction between injection and burning, whereas in real engines, there could be a time lag between injection and burning.

Now we can examine the time rate of burning, represented by the ratio dn/dt, writing the quotient in the following form:

$$\frac{dn}{dt} = \frac{dn}{dV}\frac{dV}{d\theta}\frac{d\theta}{dt} = \frac{1}{V_3 - V_{tdc}} \cdot V'(\theta)\frac{d\theta}{dt} \tag{8.4}$$

Here, θ denotes engine crank angle, while $V'(\theta)$, rate of change of volume with θ, which represents the functional relation between engine volume and θ. The first term on the right-hand side of the eq.(8.4) comes from eq.(8.2); that is, we assume we are dealing with an engine designed for constant pressure combustion, starting at TDC. The total quantity of fuel to be burned fixes V_3, so the first term in eq.(8.4) may be treated as constant. According to eq.(8.4), the time rate of burning required to maintain constant pressure is proportional to engine speed and increases with θ as burning proceeds, since $V'(\theta)$ is a positive function. Figure 8.2 illustrates the meaning of eq.(8.4).

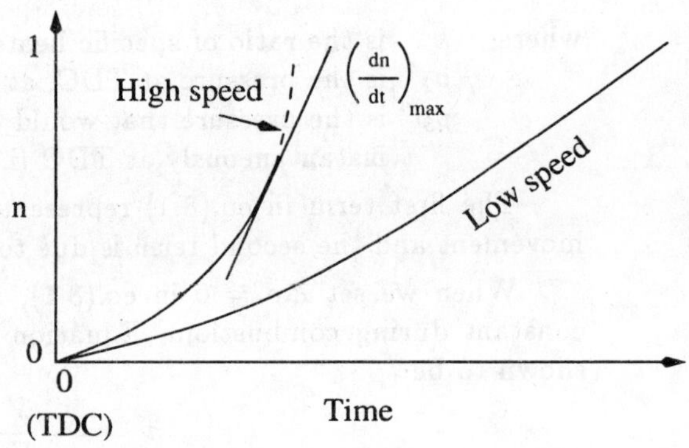

Fig.8.2 *Burning rate curves for a diesel engine*

In the figure, we have assumed what seems to be an altogether reasonable expectation, namely, that there is an upper limit to the allowable and achievable burning rate, in time, which cannot be exceeded. As indicated in Fig.8.2, it is entirely reasonable to assume that engine speed could be raised to a value such that the maximum allowable burning rate is reached before all the fuel has been injected and burned. If this condition is found to exist, then we assume that all subsequent burning would proceed at the maximum burning rate, not at the burning rate required for constant pressure combustion, as in eq.(8.4). We can expect, therefore, that if the maximum burning rate is reached, the balance of the combustion process will not maintain a constant pressure; instead, pressure will fall off and with it a decrease in work output for the cycle.

With the above background, the details of the progressive combustion in CI engines can now be outlined. We begin with known values for P_2 and T_2, conditions at the end of the compression stroke. The fuel-air ratio is known. We now compute $P_{3'}$, the pressure as if the combustion is at ***constant-volume*** at top dead centre, and then V_3, from eq.(8.3), the volume at the end of constant pressure combustion.

Suppose the maximum burning rate is known or some hypothetical value is agreed upon, we can find θ_3, the crank angle corresponding to V_3, and for the given speed, we can compute

$$\left(\frac{dn}{dt}\right)_{\theta=\theta_3}$$

from eq.(8.4). As indicated in Fig.8.2, the maximum required burning rate occurs at the end of combustion. We should compare it with the maximum allowable burning rate. If this rate is not exceeded, then we know the entire combustion process will proceed at constant pressure. We can calculate T_3 using the following equation:

$$T_3 = \frac{p_2 V_3}{N_p R} \tag{8.5}$$

The work done on the expansion stroke from

$$W_{exp} = p_2(V_3 - V_2) + \{U_p(T_3) - U_p(T_4)\} \tag{8.6}$$

On the other hand, if the burning rate calculation indicates that the maximum will be exceeded, then the combustion process must be followed in a step-wise fashion. Suppose we choose to carry on combustion in N steps, so that

$$\Delta\theta = \frac{\theta_3 - 180}{N}$$

$$\Delta V = V'(\theta)\Delta\theta$$

and as long as the maximum burning rate is not exceeded,

$$\Delta n = \frac{\Delta V}{V_3 - V_{tdc}} \tag{8.7}$$

Once the burning rate reaches the maximum allowable, in place of eq.(8.7)

$$\Delta n = \left(\frac{dn}{dt}\right)_{max} \Delta t \tag{8.8}$$

for all subsequent increments in time. The integration is completed (i.e. combustion is completed) when

$$\sum \Delta n = 1 \tag{8.9}$$

and the work of expansion is calculated from

$$W_{exp} = \sum\left(P + \frac{\Delta P}{2}\right)\Delta V + \{U_p(T_3) - U_p(T_4)\} \tag{8.10}$$

where the summation applies for the entire combustion process, and T_3 is the temperature at the end of combustion.

Figure 8.3 illustrates how the pressure-volume trace of the CI engine cycle is altered when the maximum allowable burning rate is reached. When the maximum allowable burning rate is large, say 450 s^{-1}, it is reached, in this case, just before the end of combustion; whereas a rate of 300 s^{-1} allowable burning rate is reached early in the combustion process, followed by a sharp decrease in pressure and in power output.

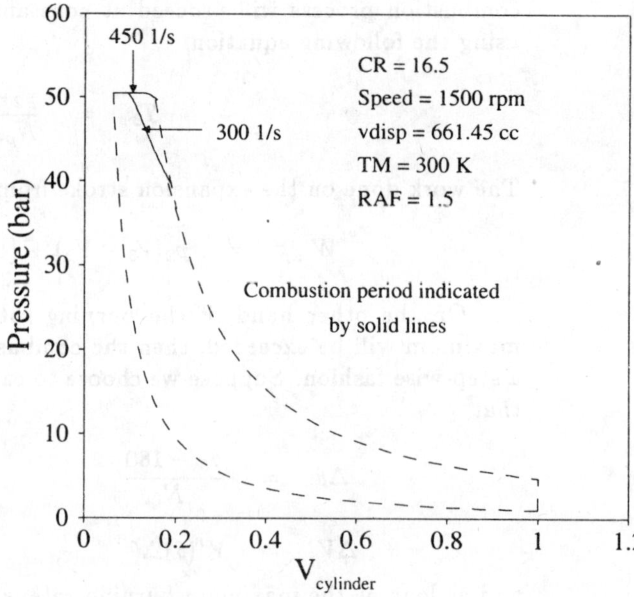

Fig.8.3 *Pressure-volume traces for two assumed maximum burning rates*

Figure 8.4(a) is another way of looking at the same calculations. Injection and combustion begins at TDC. As the maximum allowable burning rate increases, it is reached later and later in the combustion process; the total crankshaft span of rotation for combustion decreases and correspondingly power output also increases [Fig.8.4(b)].

Injection may be initiated at any crank angle of our choice. If θ_i denotes the crank angle at the start of injection, then in place of eq.(8.4).

$$\Delta n = \frac{V'(\theta - \theta_i)}{V_3 - V_{tdc}} \Delta\theta \tag{8.11}$$

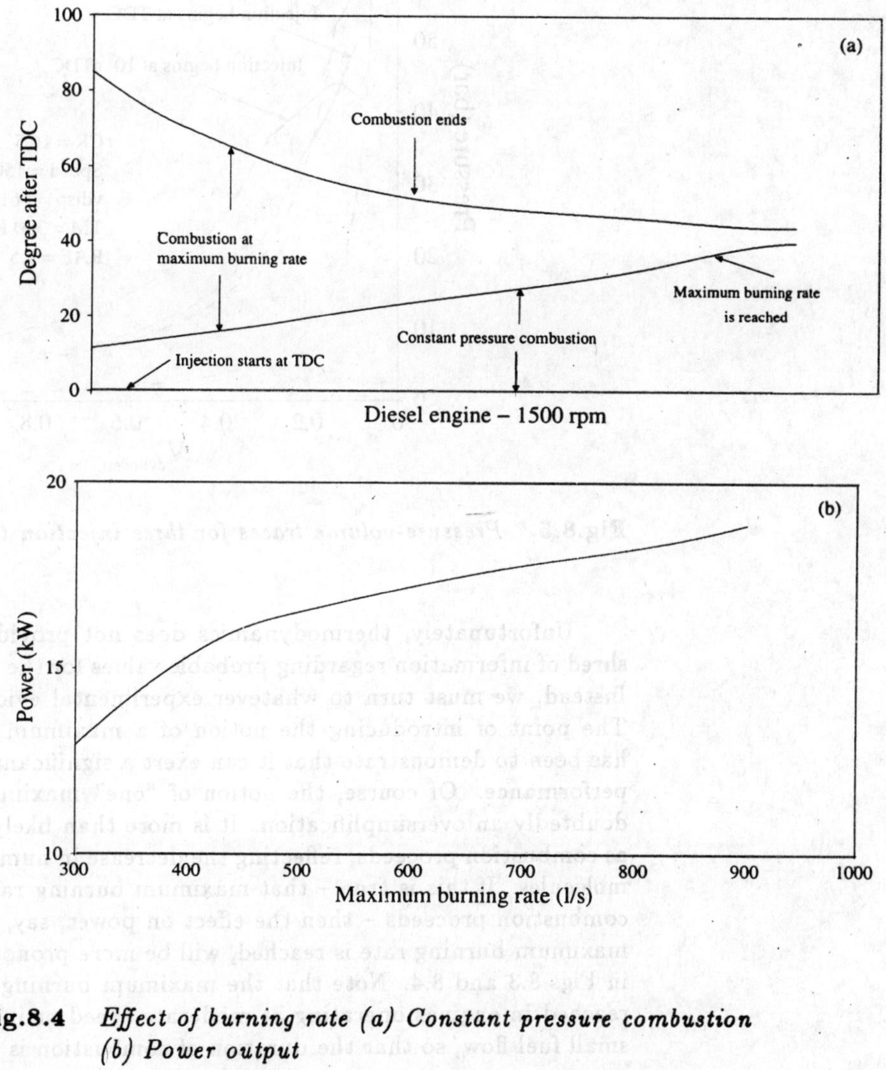

Fig.8.4 ***Effect of burning rate (a) Constant pressure combustion (b) Power output***

Figure 8.5 illustrates just how drastically the pressure-volume trace of the cycle can change as the start of the injection is changed. With early injection, 10° before TDC, there is a substantial gain in power but at the expense of an equally substantial increase in peak pressure. On the other hand, by delaying injection until 10° after TDC, peak pressure is reduced considerably, but so also is power. The sharp changes in the combustion curves with 10° before TDC, and TDC injection, indicate that the maximum allowable burning rate has been reached.

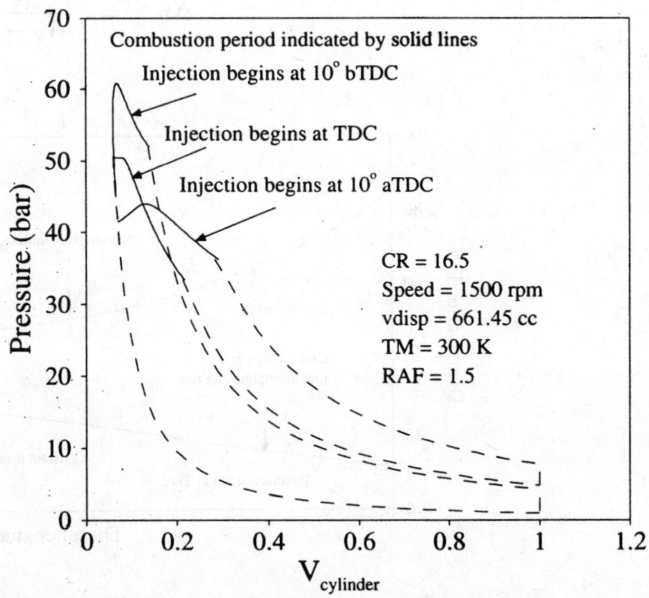

Fig.8.5 *Pressure-volume traces for three injection timings*

Unfortunately, thermodynamics does not provide us with the smallest shred of information regarding probable values for the maximum burning rate. Instead, we must turn to whatever experimental evidence may be available. The point of introducing the notion of a maximum allowable burning rate has been to demonstrate that it can exert a significant influence on CI engine performance. Of course, the notion of "one" maximum burning rate is undoubtedly an oversimplification. It is more than likely that its value changes as combustion proceeds, reflecting the decrease in numbers of available oxygen molecules. If this is true – that maximum burning rate decreases in value as combustion proceeds – then the effect on power, say, which results when the maximum burning rate is reached, will be more pronounced than is suggested in Figs.8.3 and 8.4. Note that the maximum burning rate is not likely to be reached in engines operating at moderate speed or in engines operating with small fuel flow, so that the duration of combustion is short, to begin with.

As a final comment, note that it is not necessary to equip CI engines with throttles in order to control power output. Instead, power can be controlled by fuel flow. The end of combustion is fixed by the amount of fuel injected which can be varied over a wide range of limits, down to something quite close to zero. The upper limit on fuel is generally set by the amount of smoke that can be tolerated in the engine exhaust. Presumably, the appearance of smoke suggests the presence of unburned carbon, indicating that the engine may be operating at the limit of maximum burning rate or at the limit of available oxygen, or both.

8.3 Combustion modelling

In the previous section we dealt with progressive nature of combustion. Some general observations about models of engine processes provide a context for the details that follow. In engines, the processes themselves are extremely complex. While much is known about these processes, they are not adequately understood at a fundamental level. At present, it is not possible to construct models that predict engine operation from the basic governing equations alone. Thus, the objectives of any model development effort should be clearly defined, and the structure and the detailed content of the model should be appropriate to these objectives. It is impractical to construct models that attempt to describe ***all*** important aspects of engine operation. Hence, limited objectives are appropriate.

Due to the complexity of engine processes and our inadequate understanding at a fundamental level, most engine models are incomplete. Empirical relations and *ad hoc* approximations are often needed to bridge gaps in our understanding of critical phenomena. Since models will continue to develop over a period with greater completeness, the emphasis in this chapter is on the basic relationships used in engine process models rather than the current status of these models.

The progressive combustion model we have discussed in the previous section is a little over-simplified. In the modern simulation techniques, various models like zero–, one–, two– and multi– zone/dimensional models are being attempted.

For the processes that govern engine performance and emissions, two basic types of models have been developed. These can be categorized as ***thermodynamic*** or ***fluid dynamic*** in nature, depending on whether the equations which give the model its predominant structure are based on energy conservation or on a full analysis of the fluid motion. Other labels given to thermodynamic energy-conservation-based models are: zero-dimensional (since in the absence of any flow modeling, geometric features of the fluid motion cannot be predicted), phenomenological (since additional detail beyond the energy conservation equations is added for each phenomenon in turn), and quasi-dimensional (where specific geometric features, e.g., the spark-ignition flame or the diesel fuel spray shapes, are added to the basic thermodynamic approach). Fluid-dynamic-based models are often called multi-dimensional models due to their inherent ability to provide detailed geometric information on the flow field, based on solution of the governing flow equations.

Finally, an important issue in an any overall engine model is balance in complexity and detail amongst the process sub-models. A model is no more accurate than its weakest link. Thus, critical phenomena should be described at comparable levels of sophistication to achieve better results.

8.4 Zero-dimensional combustion model

In this section we will discuss the zero-dimensional model. The software corresponding to both progressive combustion as well as zero-dimensional models have been incorporated in the computer program given in the Appendix. In the zero-dimensional model we also take into account the ignition delay.

This model is based on the first law of thermodynamics. The starting point of the thermodynamic calculation is chosen at the instant at which the inlet valve closes.

The energy equation for the closed cycle period can be written as

$$m\frac{du}{d\theta} = \frac{dQ_c}{d\theta} - \frac{dQ_h}{d\theta} - \frac{dW}{d\theta} \tag{8.12}$$

Equation 8.12 states that the rate of change of internal energy is due to three factors viz., rate of heat release $\frac{dQ_c}{d\theta}$, rate of heat transfer $\frac{dQ_h}{d\theta}$ and the rate of work transfer $\frac{dW}{d\theta}$.

Assuming that u is a function of temperature only, replacing the work transfer $\frac{dW}{d\theta}$ by $p\frac{dV}{d\theta}$ or $mRT\frac{dV}{d\theta}$ and writing the heat transfer rate in terms of heat transfer coefficient h, viz.,

$$\frac{dQ_h}{d\theta} = hA(T - T_w), \tag{8.13}$$

Equation 8.12 becomes

$$\frac{dT}{d\theta} - \frac{1}{mC_v}\frac{dQ_c}{d\theta} = \frac{hA(T - T_w)}{mC_v} - \frac{RT}{C_v}\frac{1}{V}\frac{dV}{d\theta} \tag{8.14}$$

Therefore,

$$\frac{dT}{d\theta} = f(T, \theta)$$

Thus, a differential equation of the first order, relating the temperature to the crank angle at every point is obtained, which can be solved numerically by Runge-Kutta method.

Knowing the temperature at every crank angle, the pressure at each crank angle can also be determined by the relation

$$p = \frac{mRT}{V}.$$

Since, in the zero-dimensional model we can also take into account the ignition delay, the ignition delay period is determined by integrating the Wolfer's relation (Wolfer, 1959), which is given by

$$\int_0^{t_{ign}} \frac{dt}{t(p,T)} = \frac{1}{C}\int_0^{t_{ign}} \frac{dt}{\{p(t)\}^{-q}\exp\left[E/RT(t)\right]} = 1 \qquad (8.15)$$

t is the time in seconds or in °CA. $P(t)$ and $T(t)$ are assumed to be quantities which vary during compression. In Wolfer's relation

$$C = 2272, \quad q = -1.19, \quad \frac{E}{R} = 4650.$$

The above values are to be fitted into eq.(8.15) to get the ignition delay.

8.5 Heat release and heat transfer models

In eq.(8.12), $\frac{dQ_c}{d\theta}$ is the heat release rate. As already commented, thermodynamics cannot shed any light in quantifying the rate. Hence, one has to look into experimental results or empirical equations. Many attempts have been made to characterize the heat release pattern in CI engines. One such attempt is by Wiebe (Heywood, 1988) and this is explained in the following section.

8.5.1 Wiebe heat release model

The Wiebe heat release pattern is based on the exponential rate of the chemical reactions. In this model, it is assumed that all the fuel is injected before the end of ignition delay period itself.

The fraction of heat released is expressed by the non-dimensional equation

$$x = 1 - \exp\left[-a\left(\frac{\theta-\theta_i}{\Delta\theta_c}\right)^{m+1}\right] \qquad (8.16)$$

By differentiating eq.(8.16), the rate of heat released $\frac{dx}{d\left(\frac{\theta-\theta_i}{\Delta\theta_c}\right)}$ can be expressed as

$$\dot{Q} = a(m+1)\left(\frac{\theta-\theta_i}{\Delta\theta_c}\right)^{m}\exp\left[-a\left(\frac{\theta-\theta_i}{\Delta\theta_c}\right)^{m+1}\right] \qquad (8.17)$$

Both eqs.(8.16) and (8.17) are non-dimensionalized equations. Equation 8.17 can be expressed in terms of KJ/°CA as follows:

$$\frac{dQ_c}{d\theta} = a(m+1)\left(\frac{Q_{av}}{\Delta\theta_c}\right)^m \left(\frac{\theta-\theta_i}{\Delta\theta_c}\right)^m \exp\left[-a\left(\frac{\theta-\theta_i}{\Delta\theta_c}\right)^{m+1}\right] \quad (8.18)$$

where

$\Delta\theta_c$ duration of combustion in °CA.

θ crank angle at any instant

θ_i crank angle at the start of combustion

Q_{av} heat released per cycle in KJ.

a This is the parameter which characterizes the completeness of combustion. Wiebe assumed $x_{\max} = 0.990$ and, hence, $a = 6.908$.

m It is the parameter characterizing the rate of combustion. The small values for m means a high rate at the beginning of combustion, while large values of m means a high rate by the end of combustion.

The plots of the function x and $dx/d\left(\frac{\theta}{\Delta\theta_c}\right)$ with $a = 6.908$ for several values of m are shown in Figs.8.6 and 8.7.

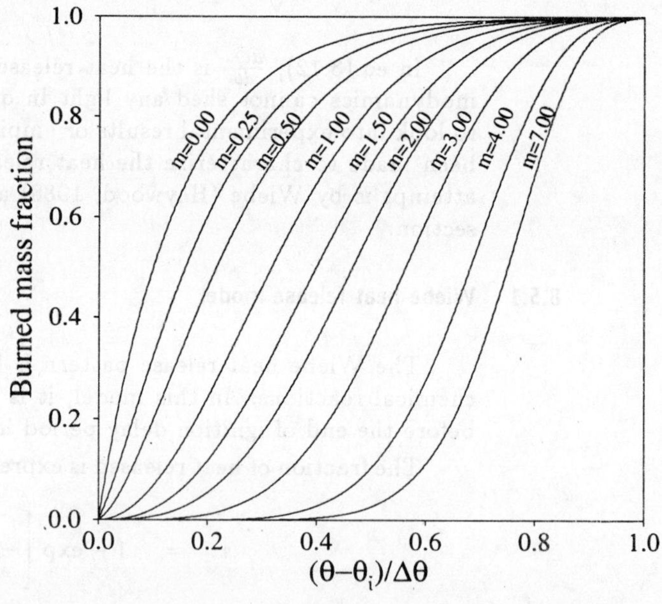

Fig.8.6 *Heat release as a function of relative duration of combustion*

The heat release rate depends upon overall equivalence ratio. Knowing the fuel-air ratio, we can fix the mass of air admitted. It should be noted that the above model cannot take care of premixed and diffusive combustion.

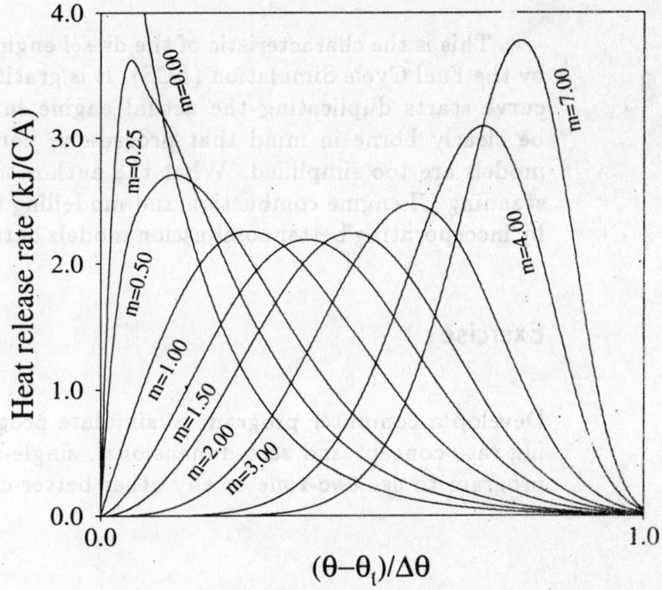

Fig.8.7 *Heat release rate as a function of relative duration of combustion*

However, this is better than the progressive combustion model since we can calculate the delay period in this model from the Wolfer's relation (Wolfer, 1959), viz. from eq.(8.15).

Figure 8.8 shows the variation of brake output with speed. It is seen that the power peak occurs at a speed of 2100 rpm. However, at 2300 rpm the power output falls as seen in Fig.8.8.

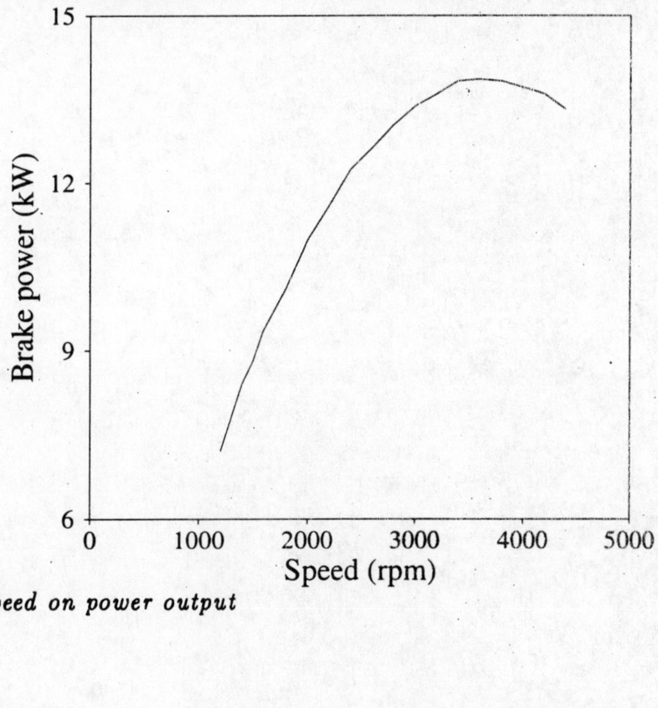

Fig.8.8 *Effect of speed on power output*

This is the characteristic of the diesel engine which could not be predicted by the Fuel Cycle Simulation (FCS). It is gratifying to note that the predicted curve starts duplicating the actual engine in the trend. However, it is to be clearly borne in mind that progressive combustion and zero-dimensional models are too simplified. What the author tries to establish is that, understanding CI engine combustion and modelling the same will be rewarding and by incorporating better combustion models bctter predictions can be obtained.

Exercise

Develop a computer program to simulate progressive combustion with burning rate concept and zero-dimensional, single-zone model. Extend the above program to use two-zone or any other better combustion model.

9

CI ENGINE SIMULATION WITH GAS EXCHANGE PROCESS

9.1 Introduction

In the last three chapters we have seen the step-by-step improvement in the predicted performance characteristics, starting from ideal cycle analysis to progressive combustion analysis. In this chapter, we will move closer to the actual engine by taking into account the following two processes:

(i) gas exchange process, and

(ii) heat transfer process.

Further, we will also take friction into account using empirical relations. We will call this analysis actual cycle simulation (ACS), as almost all the processes are taken into account.

9.2 Gas exchange process

The analysis of the exhaust and intake processes for full-load and part-load operations (Chapter 7) was based on the assumption that the piston moves very slowly during intake and exhaust stroke. However, it may be noted that in the actual engine, the piston moves at finite speeds, which can become large; when large, their motion exerts a controlling influence on engine performance.

In this chapter we will re-examine the intake and exhaust processes (gas exchange process) and develop new schemes for following the progress of events. Simulation of the gas exchange process is rather involved in comparison to other processes in the engine. However, the effort is well rewarded, for the calculated performance curve begins to duplicate real engine operation.

Figure 9.1 illustrates the gas exchange process; a control volume analysis fits the problem easily.

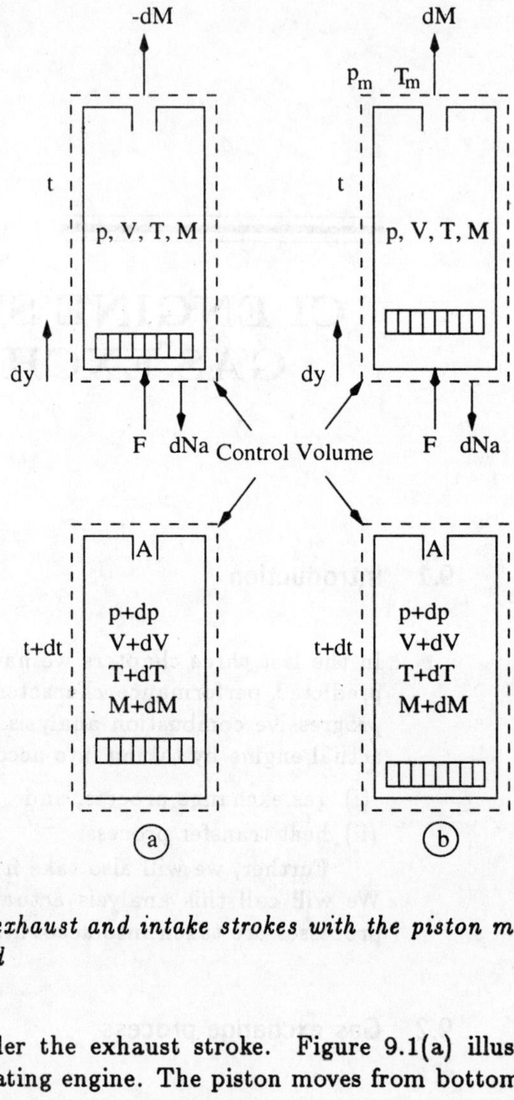

Fig.9.1 *Analysis of exhaust and intake strokes with the piston moving at a finite speed*

Let us first consider the exhaust stroke. Figure 9.1(a) illustrates the details for the reciprocating engine. The piston moves from bottom to top.

At some engine volume V_y, let the pressure, temperature and the mass of the exhaust gas be p_y, T_y and M_y, respectively, and let these values be known.

At time t, let p, V, T and M be the pressure, volume, temperature and mass of the exhaust gas, respectively, inside the cylinder.

At time $t + dt$, let these values change to $p + dp$, $V + dV$, $T + dT$ and $M + dM$.

Conservation of mass requires that mass $-dM$ leaves the cylinder in the interval dt. (As time passes, M decreases and, therefore, dM is negative.)

Let p_0 denote exhaust manifold and crank case pressure. At time t, the energy in the control volume is

$$MC_vT \qquad (i)$$

During the time interval dt, energy

$$-dMC_pT \tag{ii}$$

leaves the control volume, and the work done by force F enters the control volume:

$$\begin{aligned} Fdy &= (p - p_0)A_p dy \\ &= -(p - p_0)dV, \end{aligned} \tag{iii}$$

where A_p is the piston area and dy is positive as shown in Fig.9.1.

During time dt, let some air dN_a moles enter the control volume bringing in energy given by

$$\begin{aligned} h_a dN_a &= (U_a + p_0 v_a)dN_a \\ &= U_a dN_a - p_0 dV \end{aligned} \tag{iv}$$

Let us assume that no heat transfer occurs across the control volume boundary. The energy in the control volume at time $t + dt$ is

$$(M + dM)C_v(T + dT) + U_a dN_a \tag{v}$$

Now, according to the law of conservation of energy,

$$(i) - (ii) + (iii) + (iv) = (v).$$

Inserting each term and simplifying, reduces the equation to

$$-p\ dV + (C_p - C_v)\ T\ dM - M\ C_v\ dT = 0. \tag{vi}$$

Assuming that the exhaust gas behaves like an ideal gas, we can write

$$\frac{dp}{p} + \frac{dV}{V} = \frac{dM}{M} + \frac{dT}{T} \tag{vii}$$

Eliminating dT between (vi) and (vii), we get

$$\frac{1}{k_p}\frac{dp}{p} + \frac{dV}{V} - \frac{dM}{M} = 0, \tag{9.1}$$

where $k_p = C_{pp}/C_{vp}$

Integration of eq.(9.1) yields

$$p\left(\frac{V}{M}\right)^{k_p} = pv^{k_p} = \text{constant}. \tag{9.2}$$

Equation (9.2) could have been written down without going through this analysis, merely by noting that the gas that remains inside the cylinder undergoes an adiabatic, reversible change of state; whether the change is caused by piston motion or by gas flow or by some combination of the two is immaterial. Since we wish to follow events as the piston moves, we write eq.(9.1) in the form

$$\frac{dp}{dt} = k_p p \left(\frac{1}{M}\frac{dM}{dt} - \frac{1}{V}\frac{dV}{dt} \right)_{\text{exhaust}} \tag{9.3}$$

Now let us consider the intake stroke; proceeding in the same fashion, the energy in the control volume at time t is

$$MC_vT + U_a dN_a.$$

The energy entering with mass dM (a positive quantity) is

$$C_p T_a dM,$$

where T_a is the temperature of the fresh air in the intake pipe.

The energy that enters the control volume as a result of the action of force F is

$$\begin{aligned} -F\,dy &= -(p - p_0)A_p\,dy \\ &= -(p - p_0)dV, \end{aligned}$$

dy being positive, as shown in Fig.9.1(b).

Air is pushed out of the control volume by piston movement and carries with it energy amounting to

$$h_a dN_a = (U_a + p_0 v_a)dN_a = U_a dN_a + p_0 dV.$$

The energy in the control volume at time $t + dt$ is

$$(M + dM)C_v(T + dT)$$

Combining these terms into an energy conservation statement, cancelling and dropping second-order terms, results in

$$\frac{C_v}{C_p}\frac{dp}{p} + \frac{C_v}{C_p}\left(\frac{R}{C_v} + 1\right)\frac{dV}{V} - \frac{T_a}{T}\frac{dM}{M} = 0. \tag{9.4}$$

Here C_v and R refer to gases in the cylinder, while C_p refers to the air in the intake pipe.

Now

$$\frac{C_p}{C_v} = k_r.$$

Therefore, the working form for the intake stroke is

$$\frac{dp}{dt} = k_r p \left(\frac{1}{M}\frac{T_a}{T}\frac{dM}{dt} - \frac{1}{V}\frac{dV}{dt} \right)$$

A more convenient form can be

$$\frac{dp}{dt} = k_r \left(\frac{R\,T_a}{V}\frac{dM}{dt} - \frac{p}{V}\frac{dV}{dt} \right)_{\text{intake}} \tag{9.5}$$

Both eqs.(9.3) and (9.5) require mass flows rates dM/dt, which are to be obtained from the equations of fluid mechanics.

When a gas at p, T with a heat capacity ratio k flows through an opening with an effective area A (i.e. A is the product of the actual area opening multiplied by a suitable discharge coefficient) into a region at pressure p_0, the flow must be considered in two regimes: subsonic and supersonic. The critical pressure ratio that defines the two regimes is called PR_{crit} and depends only on the value of k of the gas.

$$PR_{\text{crit}} = \left(\frac{k+1}{2} \right)^{k/(k-1)} \tag{9.6}$$

When p/p_0 is less than PR_{crit}, the flow is subsonic and the mass flow rate is given by

$$\frac{dM}{dt} = Ap_0 \sqrt{\frac{2k}{RT(k-1)} \left(\frac{p}{p_0} \right)^{(k-1)/k} \left[\left(\frac{p}{p_0} \right)^{(k-1)/k} - 1 \right]}. \tag{9.7}$$

The flow will be supersonic when p/p_0 exceeds PR_{crit} and dM/dt is given by

$$\frac{dM}{dt} = AP \sqrt{\frac{k}{RT} \left(\frac{2}{k+1} \right)^{(k+1)/(k-1)}} \tag{9.8}$$

Note that eq.(9.8) does not contain p_0, which is characteristic of supersonic flow; *what matters is where the gas is coming from, and not where it is going.*

On the exhaust stroke, p is the cylinder pressure and p_0 is the exhaust manifold pressure. On the intake stroke, p is the intake manifold pressure, and p_0 is the cylinder pressure.

Two observations concerning the treatment of eqs.(9.3) and (9.5) may be useful. The first is concerned with the events at the end of the exhaust stroke. With the piston at TDC, the mass of exhaust in the working volume is M_{tdc} and represents the residual gases that will remain in the engine during the next cycle calculation. The cylinder pressure at TDC is greater than the intake manifold pressure, p_m, or at the very least equal to p_m. If there is no overlapping of the valves, then the exhaust valve would have just closed at TDC, and as the piston moves, the intake valve will begin to open. This volume increase will cause a reduction in the pressure in the working space, and at the same time, exhaust gas will flow back into the intake manifold, displacing the fresh air. This is identified in Fig.9.2 as Region I. The outward flow of exhaust will continue until p is reduced to p_m. With further piston motion, p will fall below p_m and the flow direction will reverse. Exhaust gas which first flowed into the intake manifold will return to the cylinder, as evident in Region II.

Fresh air will not begin to enter the cylinder until all the exhaust has been returned to the working space. It is necessary to identify the instant when $M = M_{tdc}$ to get the correct result from simulation. That condition marks the start of fresh air flow into the cylinder. The purpose of a detailed treatment of the intake stroke is, for the accurate computation of the mass of fresh air in the engine at the start of the compression process; and this is achieved by summing up the small amounts of fresh air, dM, that flow in during each step in the numerical integration. If the summation is to be accurate, we must know when to commence the summing process.

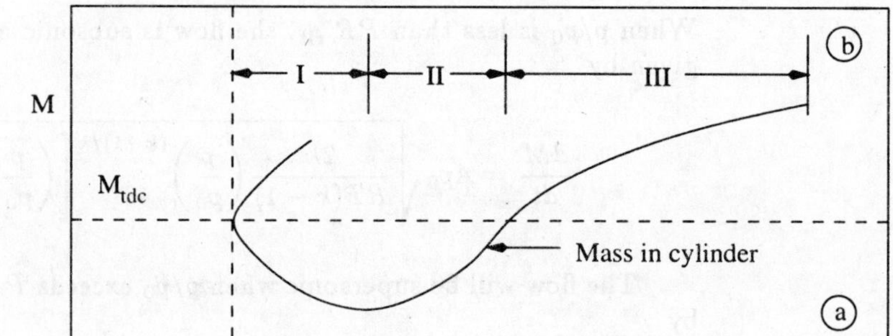

Fig.9.2 *Particulars of events in the early intake stroke*

The second comment is with regard to the technique for integrating eqs.(9.3) and (9.5). The following procedure is suggested. Let

$$Q_e = k_p p\left(\frac{1}{M}\frac{dM}{dt} - \frac{1}{V}\frac{dV}{dt}\right)_{\text{exhaust}} \tag{9.9}$$

$$Q_i = k_r\left(\frac{RT_a}{V}\frac{dM}{dt} - \frac{p}{V}\frac{dV}{dt}\right)_{\text{intake}} \tag{9.10}$$

Now eqs.(9.3) and (9.5) take the general form

$$\Delta p = Q\Delta t. \tag{9.11}$$

Let us define the maximum allowable pressure change for every step in the integration for the exhaust and the intake stroke. That is,

$$\Delta p_{\max}|_e = \frac{p - p_0}{m} \quad \text{(exhaust stroke)}, \tag{9.12}$$

$$\Delta p_{\max}|_i = \frac{p_m - p}{m} \quad \text{(intake stroke)}, \tag{9.13}$$

where m is a number say, between 3 and 10.

Let us define the maximum allowable time interval for each step in the integration. That is,

$$\Delta t_{\max} = \frac{n}{360}\frac{60}{\text{rpm}} \text{ [s]}, \tag{9.14}$$

i.e. $\Delta t_{\max}$ is the time for n degrees of crankshaft rotation. We could choose n also between, say, 3 and 10.

Now, either in the exhaust or in the intake stroke, first calculate $\Delta p_{\max}$, for the value of p (cylinder pressure) that prevails.

With this $\Delta p_{\max}$, calculate the maximum value of the flow rate dM/dt using eq.(9.7) or (9.8). Depending upon the value of PR_{crit}, dV/dt is calculated with respect to the engine speed.

The value of Q is calculated from eq.(9.9) or (9.10), depending upon whether it is the exhaust process or the intake process.

On examining eqs.(9.9) and (9.10), it is seen that Q can be either positive or negative depending upon whether dM/dt predominates over dV/dt or vice versa. In the limit (and very rarely) the first term $[(1/M)\cdot dM/dt$ or $R\cdot T_m$ $(dM/dt)]$ can become exactly equal to the second term in eqs.(9.9) and (9.10), respectively, so that Q can be zero.

With the values of Q and $\Delta p_{\max}$, Δt is calculated using eq.(9.11) and then compared with $\Delta t_{\max}$ obtained from eq.(9.14).

Use the smaller of the two as the determinant for that step in the integration process.

Figure 9.3 gives a flow-chart of the logic that controls each step in the integration. It may be more informative than a verbal description.

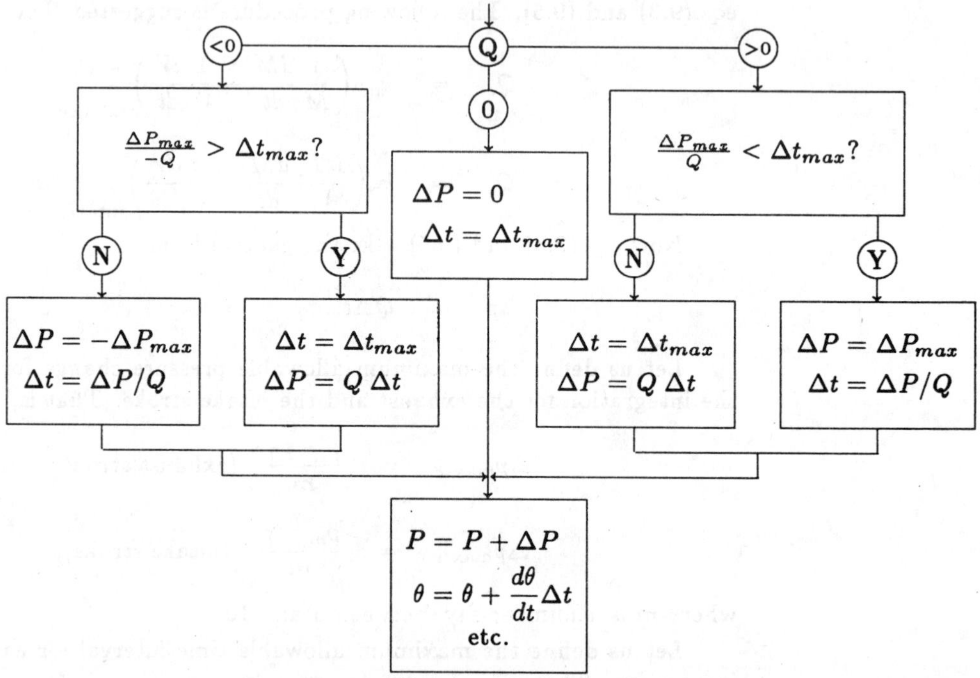

Fig.9.3 *Flow chart for integration of eqs.(9.3) and (9.5) [see eq.(9.11)]*

However, some form of control must oversee the integration. A uniform Δt at each step may lead to ΔP values that reduce cylinder pressure below p_0 during the exhaust process, or above p_m during the intake process.

On the other hand, with a fixed ΔP value, excessively large Δt values may result in overshooting the limits of piston travel.

The scheme described above will work satisfactorily for the entire exhaust stroke, and for that portion of the intake stroke identified as Region III in Fig.9.2. But it may not work during the early period of the intake stroke, because if we limit pressure changes to

$$\Delta p_{\max} = \frac{p - p_0}{m},$$

p cannot drop below p_0 or, in other words, we cannot use the relation

$$\Delta p_{\max} = \frac{p_m - p_0}{m}$$

for the intake stroke until p becomes less than p_m. Once TDC is reached on the exhaust stroke, the procedure is to decrease p repeatedly by small, prescribed amounts, using eq.(9.11) to compute the corresponding Δt, until p becomes less than p_m (Region I in Fig.9.2); after which intake of gas from the intake pipe will begin and Fig.9.2 can be applied. Note that the first portion of gas that flows in Region II (in Fig.9.2) will be returning exhaust that flowed out of the cylinder during Region I.

It is a common practice to have valve overlap, i.e. closing of the exhaust valve after TDC and opening of intake valve before TDC. This may result for the most part in improved scavenging and increased power. The elementary theory discussed here can be applied to valve overlap, although the calculation in Region I becomes more involved (Fig.9.2). With cylinder pressure p greater than exhaust manifold pressure, p_0, and inlet manifold pressure, p_m, when both the valves are open, exhaust gas will flow through both the valves. It is necessary to keep track of that portion of the exhaust which flows into the intake pipe, since it will return before fresh air can enter. If the exhaust valve remains open for a long period, exhaust gas may flow from the exhaust manifold through the cylinder and into the intake manifold. When this occurs, the engine performance will deteriorate.

A complete treatment of the gas exchange process would take into account the velocity distribution of gas in the cylinder, since its momentum affects the flow of gas out of the cylinder. Likewise, once the flow has begun to carry fresh air into the cylinder, its velocity along the intake manifold contributes to the flow rate. Simulation of these factors is considerably complicated and will not be examined beyond these qualitative remarks.

Now, let us define the term volumetric efficiency. It is the ratio of the volume occupied by the fresh air drawn into the engine on the intake stroke, measured at intake manifold conditions, to the displacement volume.

The mass of gas in the cylinder at TDC, M_{tdc} is known. By summing up the dM amounts of fresh air that enter during Region III, Fig.9.2, the mass in the cylinder at BDC, M_{bdc} is known:

$$M_{\text{bdc}} = M_{\text{tdc}} + \sum dM \tag{9.15}$$

Then the volumetric efficiency is given by

$$\eta_v = \frac{(M_{\text{bdc}} - M_{\text{tdc}})R\,T_{\text{a}}}{p_{\text{m}}V_{\text{disp}}}. \tag{9.16}$$

In order to carry out cycle calculations that incorporate details of the gas exchange process, it is necessary to specify the variation of the effective valve area A, that appears in eqs.(9.7) and (9.8) as a function of the crank angle. This valve area calculation depends upon the engine geometry and should be specified by the reader.

However, a simple scheme that can be used is given below:

$$\left.\begin{aligned} \text{Exhaust valve}: A &= A_{ex}(\sin\theta)^{1/3} \\ &\quad \text{opens at BDC, } \theta = 0 \\ &\quad \text{closes at TDC, } \theta = 180^\circ, \\ \text{Intake valve}: A &= A_{in}(|\sin\theta|)^{1/3} \\ &\quad \text{opens at TDC, } \theta = 180^\circ \\ &\quad \text{closes at BDC, } \theta = 360^\circ, \end{aligned}\right\} \tag{9.17}$$

where A_{ex} and A_{in} are the wide-open valve areas for A, and may be assumed to be identical for both valves. Generally, the exhaust valve area is larger than the intake valve area since the specific volume of the exhaust gas is much higher due to its high temperature. This can be very easily incorporated in the simulation.

Figure 9.4 shows A/A_{ex} or A/A_{in} against crank angle as per eq.(9.17). It may be noted that provisions must be made in the computer program to incorporate the relevant area variation of the valves of the engine concerned.

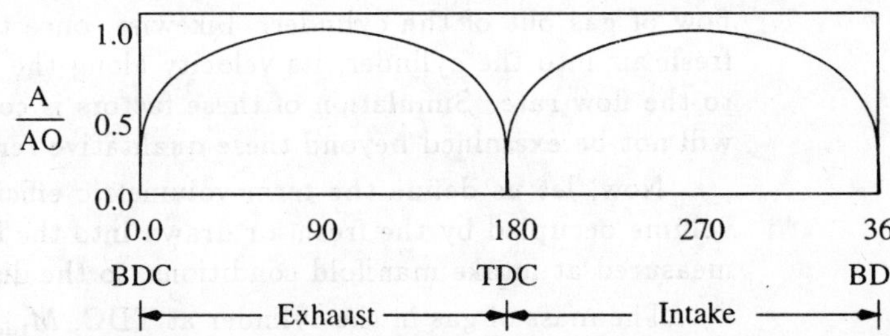

Fig.9.4 *Variation of valve area ratio A/A_{ex} or A/A_{in} with crank angle θ*

The final item required to complete the cycle calculation is W_{loop}, the work associated with the exhaust and intake strokes:

$$W_{loop} = -\sum\left(p + \frac{\Delta p}{2}\Delta V\right) \tag{9.18}$$

where Δp denotes the change in pressure accompanying the volume change ΔV. The summation extends from the point in the cycle at which the exhaust valve opens to the point at which the intake valve closes.

A number of tables have been included in this chapter to study the effect of various engine parameters on power output when the actual cycle simulation is carried out. The main idea is to provide the reader with sets of results, so that the program when compiled and executed should give the same identical results. By this, one can be sure that the program in the reader's computer is the same as that in the Appendix.

Unless otherwise specified, the tables and figures given in this chapter apply to an engine with the following specifications:

Bore	80.0 mm	
Stroke	110.0 mm	
V_{disp}	552.94 cc	
L	230.0 mm	
r	16.5	
Operation	Full load	
Intake manifold pressure	1 atm	
Intake manifold temperature	300 K	
Fuel	$C_{10}H_{22}$	
Air-fuel ratio	22.5	
Valve-timing	As per eq.(9.17)	(9.19)
Wide-open valve areas	3.0 cm^2	
Exhaust valve opens at	340°	
Exhaust valve closes at	554°	
Inlet valve opens at	527°	
Inlet valve closes at	750°	
Duration of combustion, $\Delta\theta_c$	50°	
Combustion model	Zero-dimensional	
Injection advance	27° bTDC	
Speed	1500 rpm	

Figures 9.5 and 9.6 illustrate the variation of cylinder pressure with volume, during the gas exchange process. Figure 9.5 clearly illustrates the effect of valve area at constant speed, whereas Fig.9.6 depicts the effect of speed at a particular valve area. It clearly shows that the work associated with the scavenging process may not be insignificant, and also reveals the profound effect the scavenging process exerts in the way of limiting power output.

Table 9.1 illustrates the effect of valve area on output power and volumetric efficiency. It may be noted that the increase in power for a larger valve area is obtained mainly due to the improvement in volumetric efficiency and comparatively reduced exhaust gas dilution. It may be noted that the volumetric efficiency improves from 85% to 99% in the CI engine and, if one compares the values for SI engine, one may find that the magnitude of volumetric efficiency is comparatively higher for CI engines (refer Table 9.1 of the book on *Computer Simulation of Spark-Ignition Engine Processes*, University Press, Hyderabad, 1996). It is mainly due to the fact that in a CI engine there is no throttle and the flow restriction is not as high as the SI engine. Further, higher compression ratio of the CI engine automatically reduces the exhaust gas dilution, which helps in the improvement of power output.

Table 9.1 Effect of valve area on power and volumetric efficiency [for the engine described by eq.(9.19)]

Speed	:	1500 rpm	r	:	16.5	RAF	:	1.5
Comdur	:	50°	Start of injection	:	153°			

A_{ex}/A_{in}	T_1 (K)	η_v	$\frac{N_m}{N_m + N_x}$	Power (kW)	η_{th}
2.0/2.0	344.530	85.116	0.980	3.918	28.882
2.5/2.5	312.099	90.771	0.952	4.586	31.458
3.0/2.5	311.440	90.883	0.950	4.635	31.744
3.0/3.0	299.173	94.008	0.950	4.912	32.413
3.5/3.5	289.797	96.612	0.949	5.145	32.938
4.0/4.0	279.816	99.145	0.943	5.347	33.220

Figure 9.5 shows that at 1500 rpm, with $A_{ex} = A_{in} = 4.0$ cm^2, pressure falls steadily after the exhaust valve opens at BDC; whereas with 2.5 cm^2 valve area, the pumping loss is larger as the result of competing effects of piston movement and flow going out of the cylinder. Another feature displayed in Fig.9.5 is the difference in throttling effects of valve area values on the intake stroke. With the smaller valve area, the pumping loop is larger. The pressure and temperature at the start of the compression stroke determine, in part, the quantity of fresh air in the cylinder, which in turn, controls the power developed.

In addition to changing the values of the inlet and exhaust valve areas the expression in eq.(9.17) itself may be altered, amounting to changing the valve cam profile itself. For best results the most desirable combination is quick opening and high lift valves, which will ensure best scavenging of the exhaust and the largest intake of fresh air. As for the thermodynamic analysis, any valve arrangement is permitted and may be examined for its effect on power. However, in practice there are limitations. Because of the inertia and design of the valve cam, there are limits to the rapidity with which a valve may be opened or closed. If either one is excessive, the cam follower will lose contact with the cam, resulting in valve burning and, very probably, failure of some piece in the valve.

Note in Table 9.2 how T_1 slightly decreases as the compression ratio, r, is increased. This slightly higher temperature at low compression ratio, viz. 12, is due to comparatively increased exhaust gas dilution which reduces the amount of fresh air in the cylinder, accounting for a part of the power decrease at lower compression ratios. The point to note is that the volumetric efficiency remains almost constant since variation of T_1 is very small with increased compression ratio, indicating compression ratio has negligible effect on volumetric efficiency. The trend of thermal efficiency variation is as expected due to the increase in compression ratio.

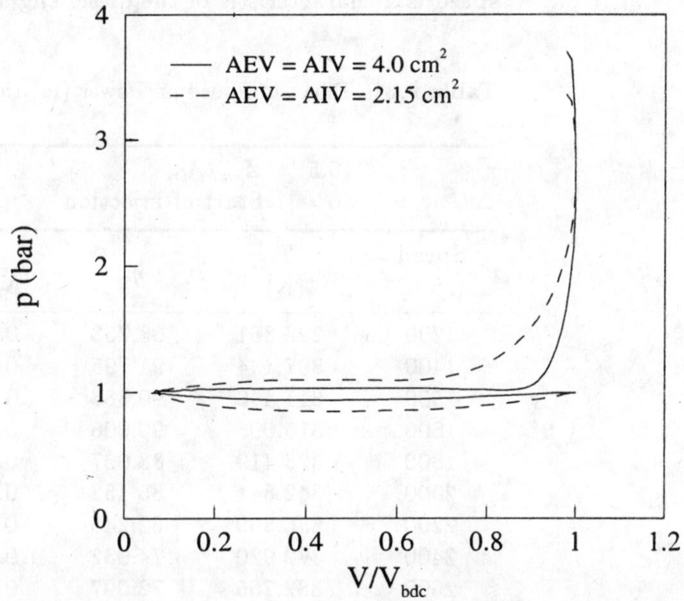

Fig.9.5 ***Effect of valve area on the gas exchange process***

Table 9.2 Effect of compression ratio on power and thermal efficiency [for the engine described by eq.(9.19)]

Speed : 1500 rpm		A_{ex}/A_{in} : 3.0/2.5 cm²		RAF : 1.5	
$\Delta\theta_c$: 50°		Start of injection : 153°			
r	T_1 (K)	η_v	$\frac{N_m}{N_m+N_x}$	Power (kW)	η_{th}
12.0	316.016	91.325	0.948	3.931	26.778
14.0	313.383	91.152	0.950	4.322	29.516
16.5	311.440	90.883	0.950	4.635	31.744
18.0	310.500	90.800	0.953	4.770	32.786
20.0	310.307	90.478	0.955	4.904	33.778
22.0	309.808	90.244	0.956	4.984	34.421

Table 9.3 illustrates the effect of engine speed on the power output. It can be observed that the power increases with speed, but the rate of increase drastically comes down and decreases after 2400 rpm. Power peak at a particular speed is a characteristic of the diesel engine.

Table 9.3 Effect of Speed on Power (for the engine described by eq.(9.19)

r : 16.5, A_{ex}/A_{in} : 3.0/2.5 cm^2, RAF : 1.5
$\Delta\theta_c$: 50°, Start of injection : 153°

Speed (rpm)	T_1 (K)	η_v	$\frac{N_m}{N_m + N_x}$	Power (kW)	η_{th}
1200	298.861	93.753	0.948	3.997	33.008
1400	307.434	91.795	0.954	4.450	32.284
1500	311.440	90.883	0.950	4.635	31.744
1600	315.095	90.006	0.953	4.825	31.369
1800	323.419	88.097	0.955	5.133	30.331
2000	342.844	85.132	0.975	5.184	28.682
2200	356.599	82.245	0.980	5.207	27.040
2400	372.920	74.932	0.987	5.049	24.985
2600	382.765	72.097	0.933	4.933	23.223

Figure 9.6 illustrates pressure volume traces for two speeds for the engine, specified by eq.(9.19). At 1500 rpm, pressure drops rapidly as soon as the exhaust valve opens at BDC and remains close to 1 atm during the remainder of the exhaust stroke and the subsequent intake stroke. At higher speeds, viz. 3000 rpm, pressure change is gradual from BDC to TDC, revealing how flow and piston movement compete. On the intake stroke, the pressure drops to 0.8 atm, reaching around 0.9 atm at the start of the compression stroke.

The arrow (↑) in the figure indicates the point in the intake stroke at 3000 rpm when fresh air begins to flow into the cylinder from the intake manifold. Between TDC and the arrow point, exhaust gas flows into the intake manifold and then returns to the cylinder. The arrow position is about 40° crank angle rotation after TDC.

As mentioned above, and as shown in Table 9.1, the wide-open valve area may be varied, and the shape of the valve area curve against the crank angle may be altered disregarding all the complexities of the mechanical motion of the valve train mechanism. In addition, the points in the cycle when the valves open and close may be altered. The effects of changes in valve-timing can be examined and are shown in Tables 9.4 to 9.7. A valve-timing diagram showing typical values for a CI engine is given in Fig.9.7.

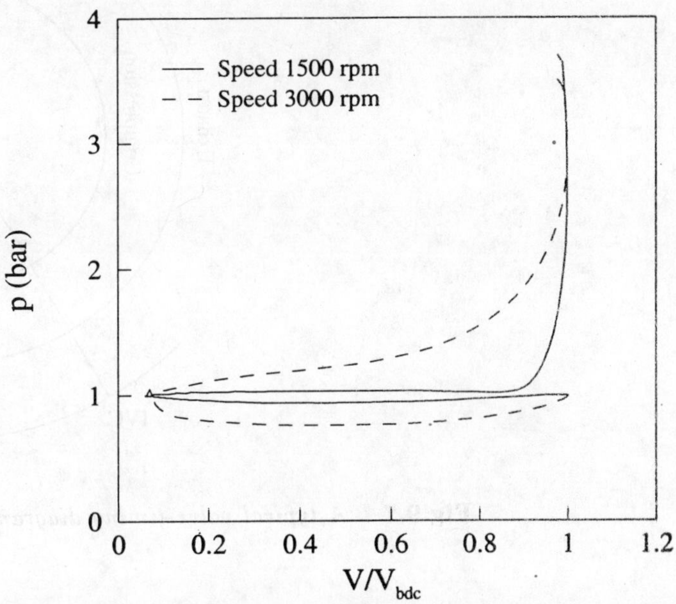

Fig.9.6 *Effect of speed on the gas exchange process*

Let us denote by θ_{ex} the crank angle at which the exhaust valve begins to open, and let θ_{in} denote the crank angle at which the intake valve closes. Let us express A_{ex} and A_{in} in terms of θ, as

$$\left.\begin{aligned} A_{ex} &= A_{exo}\sin\left\{\left|180\frac{\theta+\theta_{ex}}{180+\theta_{ex}}\right|\right\}^{1/3} \\ A_{in} &= A_{ino}\sin\left\{\left|180\frac{\theta-\theta_{in}}{180-\theta_{in}}\right|\right\}^{1/3} \end{aligned}\right\}. \tag{9.20}$$

These expressions are chosen for simplicity, since they reduce to eq.(9.17) for

$$\theta_{ex} = 0 \quad \text{and} \quad \theta_{in} = 360.$$

As shown in Table 9.4, valve-timing clearly has significant effect on power, especially at higher speeds. The reasons are made evident by Table 9.5.

The numbers in brackets in Table 9.5 refer to volumetric efficiency. The pressure p_1 is in atmospheres. Note that the engine is running at full load, with 1 atm pressure in the intake manifold, and that for some conditions of valve-timing and speed, the pressure in the cylinder at the start of compression

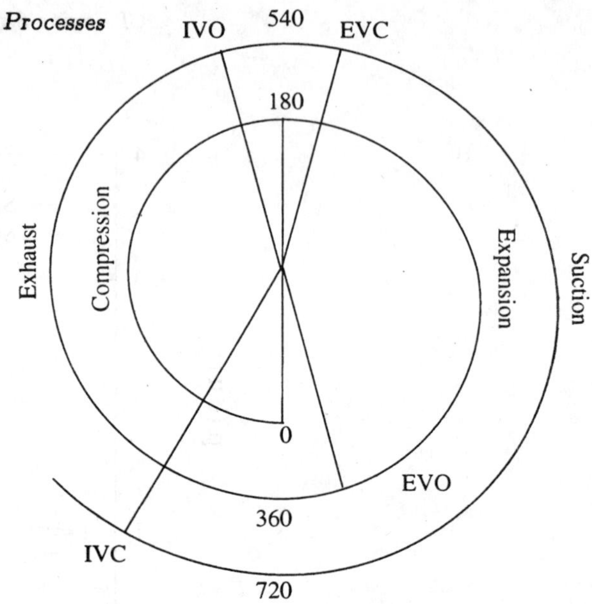

Fig.9.7 *A typical valve-timing diagram for a CI engine*

Table 9.4 Effect of valve-timing on power at various speeds

r : 16.5 A_{ex}/A_{in} : 3.0/2.5 cm^2 EVC : 554° RAF : 1.5
$\Delta\theta_c$: 50° Start of injection : 153° IVO : 527°

EVO/IVC (deg)	Speed (rpm)				
	1200	1500	1800	2100	2300
	Power (kW)				
360/720	3.326	3.926	4.120	4.149	3.963
340/735	3.632	4.288	4.622	4.727	4.778
340/750	3.997	4.635	5.133	5.229	5.167
320/750	3.822	4.504	5.124	5.276	5.327
290/765	–	4.098	4.547	4.845	4.984

is close to the manifold pressure. Once BDC has been passed on the intake stroke, the piston motion tends to increase the cylinder pressure opposed by flow out of the cylinder back to the intake manifold; which of the two prevails depends on the crank angle and speed, as well as on the valve cam profile given in eq.(9.17). It may be noted that instead of eq.(9.17), eq.(9.20) can also be used.

The analysis of valve-timing effects on power and other engine parameters may be carried a step further by altering exhaust valve opening and intake valve closing independently, as shown in Tables 9.6 and 9.7. Tables 9.6 and 9.7

Table 9.5 Effect of valve-timing on p_1 and volumetric efficiency at various speeds

r : 16.5 A_{ex}/A_{in} : 3.0/2.5 cm^2 EVC : 554° RAF : 1.5
$\Delta\theta_c$: 50° Start of injection : 153° IVO : 527°

P1 (atms) and Volumetric efficiency (%)

EVO/IVC (deg)	Speed (rpm)				
	1200	1500	1800	2100	2300
360/720	0.996 (89.479)	0.996 (86.949)	0.965 (81.687)	0.921 (77.311)	0.878 (73.961)
340/735	0.993 (91.849)	0.993 (88.775)	0.993 (85.292)	0.993 (80.097)	0.977 (76.181)
340/750	0.993 (92.531)	0.993 (89.853)	0.993 (87.336)	0.993 (81.379)	0.993 (77.920)
320/750	0.993 (92.721)	0.993 (89.821)	0.993 (87.406)	0.993 (81.724)	0.993 (76.816)
290/765	–	0.993 (90.810)	0.993 (88.107)	0.993 (83.551)	0.993 (77.818)

(* figures in brackets denote volumetric efficiency)

show, among other things, that the combination of valve events that produces maximum power for a given speed depends mainly on speed.

In Tables 9.4 to 9.7, the intake valve opens at TDC and the exhaust valve closes at TDC. In real engines, the intake valve is set to open before TDC while the exhaust valve closes after TDC. The period when both valves are open is referred to as valve overlap. The overlap period may be modelled using the principles of thermodynamics and fluid mechanics already described. Overlap requires a somewhat more complicated analysis. During the valve overlap period, one has to closely monitor the mass flow rate, not only through the exhaust manifold but also through the inlet manifold. When the cylinder pressure becomes less than the manifold pressure, whatever gases that have gone into the inlet manifold will first enter the cylinder. However, if the exhaust valve closing is delayed very much, there may even be some loss of fuel through the exhaust valve. All these details are to be taken into account.

With regard to computational schemes with arbitrary valve-timing, early exhaust valve opening does not present any problem. This is not so for the intake process. Early in the intake stroke, the cylinder pressure p drops below the intake manifold pressure, p_m, and remains below p_m until BDC. At that point,

$$p = p_m - \epsilon, \qquad \epsilon > 0$$

As the intake stroke continues, with intake valve or port open, p will increase owing to the combined effects of the inflow of gas and the piston or

Table 9.6 Effect of valve-timing on power and volumetric efficiency (speed = 1500 rpm)

r : 16.5 A_{ex}/A_{in} : 3.0/2.5 cm^2 EVC : 554° RAF : 1.5
$\Delta\theta_c$: 50° Start of injection : 153° IVO : 527° Speed : 1500 rpm

Brake power (kW) and Volumetric efficiency (%)

IVC (deg)	EVO (deg) 270	300	330	360
720	–	3.419 (86.586)*	4.042 (86.920)	3.926 (86.949)
735	–	3.613 (88.771)	4.252 (89.036)	4.152 (88.791)
750	–	4.009 (89.834)	4.654 (89.861)	4.539 (90.097)
765	–	4.458 (90.834)	5.058 (90.833)	4.937 (90.819)
780	–	4.452 (91.922)	5.056 (91.961)	4.957 (92.054)

(* figures in brackets denote volumetric efficiency)

rotor movement. As time passes, ϵ will decrease. If the point of the intake valve closing is delayed for a sufficiently long span of crankshaft rotation, p will eventually exceed p_m. To achieve this, however, "brute force" is required. That is, when ϵ becomes sufficiently small, say less than 1% of p_m, the calculation should be interrupted and p must be set as:

$$p = p_m + \epsilon.$$

This will reverse the direction of flow. The flow of fresh air and residual exhaust out of the cylinder will reduce p, while the piston motion will increase p, since BDC has been passed. These competing effects determine the cylinder pressure at the instant the intake valve closes, or the intake port is covered.

The engine size exerts a strong influence on power, as is to be expected. While comparing engines of different sizes, power output to unit volume displacement is a convenient measure. Table 9.8 compares geometrically similar engines. In each case, the stroke to bore ratio (S/B) and connecting rod to bore ratio (CRL/B) are as given in Table 9.1. Wide-open valve area is proportional to bore-square. Since combustion time $\Delta\theta_c$ can be assumed to be fixed, it has been taken to be proportional to the bore. In eq.(9.19), a bore of 8.0 cm is assumed with a combustion duration of 50°. Injection advance is, in all cases, set at one-half combustion duration. Other features of the engine that are independent of size are as listed in eq.(9.19). Large engines (in a geometrically similar series) have the disadvantage of poor volumetric efficiency

Table 9.7 Effect of valve-timing on power and volumetric efficiency (speed = 2000 rpm)

r : 16.5	A_{ex}/A_{in} : 3.0/2.5 cm^2	EVC : 554°	RAF : 1.5		
$\Delta\theta_c$: 50°	Start of injection : 153°	IVO : 527°	Speed : 2000 rpm		

Brake power (kW) and Volumetric efficiency (%)

IVC (deg)	EVO (deg) 270	300	330	360
720	–	3.908 (78.687)*	4.473 (79.275)	4.137 (79.053)
735	–	4.207 (81.963)	4.743 (81.209)	4.481 (80.903)
750	–	4.630 (82.698)	5.194 (83.227)	4.939 (83.489)
765	–	5.209 (85.034)	5.703 (84.420)	5.396 (84.136)
780	–	5.347 (86.456)	5.916 (86.462)	5.667 (87.014)

(* figures in brackets denote volumetric efficiency)

and long-duration combustion. They, therefore, require valve area values more closely proportional to the bore-cube, rather than the bore-square, since the volume of the exhaust to be sent out is proportional to the bore-cube. In addition, multiple injectors may reduce the combustion time. In theory, large engines can produce the same power per unit displacement volume as small engines can.

The final performance figures for the engine described by eq.(9.19) is given in Table 9.9, showing how the fuel–air ratio affects the operation. Here Y denotes the moles of oxygen/mole of fuel. Intake manifold temperature, T_m, is assumed to be constant at 300 K, by design. The duration of combustion varies according to the empirical expression given below. However, this expression is by no means a complete statement. It should be noted that diesel engines operate on lean mixtures and, therefore, the calculation shown is for $Y > Y_{cc}$. It is seen that with $Y > 17.5$, the power as well as the efficiency drops.

$$\Delta\theta_c \quad = \quad 40 + 5\left(\frac{N}{600} - 1\right) + 166\left(\frac{Y_{cc}}{Y} - 1.1\right)^2.$$

Table 9.8 Variation of specific power with engine size (geometrically similar engines)

Compression ratio	:	16.5	*RAF*	:	1.5
CRL	:	2.875 bore	Speed	:	2200 rpm
Stroke	:	1.375 bore	*ibc*	:	$180 - \frac{\Delta\theta_c}{2}$
for exhaust valve	:	$d2/D2 = 3.5/64.0 = 0.055$			
for inlet valve	:	$d2/D2 = 2.5/64.0 = 0.039$			

Bore (mm)	A_{ex}/A_{in} (cm^2)	Brake Power (kW)	$\Delta\theta_c$ (CA)	η_{vol} (%)	$\frac{N_m}{N_m + N_x}$	T_1 (K)
40	1.00/0.75	0.862	25.00	95.559	0.948	288.650
60	2.00/1.50	2.645	37.50	89.724	0.953	312.377
80	3.50/2.50	5.241	50.00*	78.316	0.984	359.486
100	5.50/4.00	8.775	62.50	70.850	0.980	386.245
120	8.00/5.75	11.683	75.00	60.006	0.982	397.879
140	11.00/7.75	11.171	87.50	50.583	0.983	401.063

* Start of injection = ($ibc = 153°$)

Table 9.9 Effect of air–fuel ratio on power [for the engine described by eq.(9.19), @ 1500 rpm]

Compression ratio	:	16.5	Speed	:	1500 rpm
Start of injection	:	$\frac{\Delta\theta_c}{2.0}$			

RAF	*Y*	Brake Power (kW)	η_{th}	$\Delta\theta_c$
1.06	16.5	4.118	28.265	51.57
1.13	17.5	6.001	31.344	55.17
1.19	18.5	5.714	31.133	58.69
1.26	19.5	5.312	30.623	63.07
1.32	20.5	4.996	30.177	66.96
1.50	23.5	4.121	28.277	78.67

9.3 Heat transfer process

Heat transfer is a must in IC engines to maintain cylinder walls, cylinder heads and piston faces at safe operating temperatures. Heat is transferred from or to the working fluid during every part of each cycle, and the net work done by the working fluid in one complete cycle is given by

$$W_{net} = \oint \left(p + \frac{\Delta p}{2}\right) \Delta V \tag{9.21}$$

where Δp is the pressure change inside the cylinder as a result of piston motion, combustion, flow into or out of the cylinder and heat transfer.

The pressure change Δp due to heat transfer is given by

$$\frac{\Delta p}{p} = \frac{h_c A(T_w - T)}{M C_v T} \Delta T \tag{9.22}$$

where h_c = heat transfer coefficient,
A = interior surface area of engine volume,
T_w = interior surface temperature,
M = mass of working fluid,
C_v = working fluid specific heat,
T = working fluid temperature.

The main problem with eq.(9.22) is the choice of a proper value for the heat transfer coefficient. The heat transfer between the working fluid and the interior surface is by forced convection, and the value of h_c depends on the gas velocity at the surfaces. As little is known about the gas motion inside; it is common to use some empirical formulae for calculating h_c. The formulae of (i) Ashley–Campbell, (ii) Sitkei and Ramanaiah, (iii) Hohenberg, (iv) Pflaum and (v) Annand are widely used.

(i) Ashley–Campbell equation

$$h_c = \frac{0.13 B^{0.2} P^{0.8} Z^{0.8}}{T^{0.5}} \text{ kJ/s m}^2 \text{ K.} \tag{9.23}$$

where B = cylinder bore in m,
p = cylinder pressure in atm,
T = working fluid temperature in K,
Z = working fluid velocity in m/s.

(ii) Sitkei and Ramanaiah equation

$$h_c = 0.04\,(1+b)\frac{p^{0.7} C_m^{0.7}}{T_g^{0.2} d_e^{0.3}} \text{ Kcal/m}^2\text{h}^\circ\text{C.} \tag{9.24}$$

where b = 0 – 0.03 fpr Hesselman-type direction combustion chamber,
= 0.05 – 0.10 for piston chamber,
= 0.15 – 0.25 for swirl chamber,
= 0.25 – 0.35 for precombustion chamber,
p = gas pressure in atm,

C_m = mean piston speed,
T_g = gas temperature,
d_e = equivalent diameter of cylinder = $4V/A$.

(iii) Hohenberg's equation

$$h_c = \frac{130p^{0.8}(C_m + 1.4)^{0.8}}{V_c^{0.06}T^{0.4}} \text{ W/m}^2\text{K}. \tag{9.25}$$

where V_c = cylinder volume, (m^3)
p = pressure (bar),
T = mean gas temperature,
C_m = mean piston speed.

(iv) Pflaum equation

$$h_c = \sqrt{p_g}T_g f(C_m) \text{ Kcal/m}^2 \text{ h}^\circ\text{C}. \tag{9.26}$$

where

$$f(C_m) = 3 \pm 2.57\left[1 - e^{\pm(1.5-0.416C_m)}\right].$$

The positive sign is used, if

$$C_m \geq 3.6 \text{ m/s},$$

and the negative sign is used, if

$$C_m \leq 3.6 \text{ m/s}.$$

where p_g = pressure (atm),
T_g = mean gas temperature (K),
C_m = mean piston speed (m/s).

(v) Annand's equation

$$h_c = a\left(\frac{\lambda}{B}\right)Re^{0.7} + \frac{C}{T - T_w} \times \left[\left(\frac{T}{100}\right)^4 - \left(\frac{T_w}{100}\right)^4\right] \text{ kcal h}^{-1} \text{ m}^{-2} \text{ K}^{-1}. \tag{9.27}$$

where a = 0.35 to 0.8 increasing with increased speed,

C = 0 for compression stroke of CI engine,
= 0.37 for other strokes and 2.81 for CI engines,
λ = thermal conductivity of gas in kcal h^{-1} m $°C^{-1}$,
Re = Reynold's number $= \dfrac{\rho D C_m}{\mu}$.
C_m = Mean piston speed,

A lot of research is being carried out to find a single equation to suit all engines, taking into account the various factors. This is, indeed, a very difficult job and till such an equation is arrived at, one has to depend largely upon empirical formulae for the determination of h_c.

The importance of heat transfer in simulation is worth noting. Heat transfer reduces the power output, as it reduces the expansion work and increases the compression work. During the exhaust stroke, heat transfer from the working fluid will lead to an increase in the quantity of residual gases in the cylinder. The heat transfer to the working fluid during the intake stroke will decrease the quantity of fresh air inhaled.

9.4 Friction calculations

A part of the power developed in the cylinder of an IC engine is absorbed to overcome friction in the various components, inlet and throttling losses and pumping losses. The empirical relations proposed by I.N.Bishop (*SAE Transactions*, Vol.**73**, 1965) have been used to calculate the power absorbed in friction, and the various expressions are as given below.

(i) Mean effective pressure (MEP) lost to overcome friction due to the gas pressure behind rings.

$$F_{\text{mep1}} = 0.42 \times (p_a - p_{\text{imf}}) \times \frac{S}{B^2} \times \left(0.0888 C_r + 0.182 C_r^{\,1.33 - 0.394 C_m/100}\right) \times 10 \qquad (9.28)$$

where

p_a = atmospheric pressure (bar),
p_{imf} = manifold vacuum (bar),
S = stroke (mm),
B = bore (mm),
r = compression ratio,
C_m = mean piston speed (m/min),
F_{mep} = friction mean effective pressure (bar).

(ii) Mean effective pressure absorbed in friction due to wall tension of rings

$$F_{\text{mep2}} = 10 \times \frac{0.377 S n_{\text{pr}}}{b^2}, \qquad (9.29)$$

where n_{pr} = number of rings.

(iii) MEP absorbed in friction due to piston and rings

$$F_{mep3} = 12.85 \times \frac{P_{sl}}{BS} \times \frac{100 \times C_m}{1000}, \tag{9.30}$$

where P_{sl} = piston skirt-length (mm).

(iv) Blow-by loss

$$F_{mep4} = \sqrt{p_a - p_{imf}} \times \left[0.121 r^{0.4} - (0.0345 + 0.001055 r) \times \left(\frac{N}{1000}\right)^{1.185}\right] \tag{9.31}$$

where N = speed in rpm.

(v) MEP lost in overcoming inlet and throttling losses

$$F_{mep5} = \frac{p_e}{2.75} + p_{imf} \tag{9.32}$$

where p_e = exhaust back pressure (bar).

(vi) MEP absorbed to overcome friction due to the valve gear

$$F_{mep6} = 0.226 \times \left(30 - \frac{4N}{1000}\right) \times \frac{GH^{1.75}}{B^2 S} \tag{9.33}$$

where G = number of intake valves/cylinder,
H = intake valve diameter (mm).

(vii) MEP lost in pumping

$$F_{mep7} = 0.0275 \times \left(\frac{N}{1000}\right)^{1.5} \tag{9.34}$$

(viii) MEP absorbed in bearing friction

$$F_{mep8} = 0.0564 \times \left(\frac{B}{S}\right) \times \left(\frac{N}{1000}\right) \tag{9.35}$$

(ix) MEP absorbed in overcoming the combustion chamber and wall pumping losses

$$F_{mep9} = \sqrt{\frac{p_{imep}}{11.45}} \times 0.0915 \times \left(\frac{N}{1000}\right)^{1.7} \tag{9.36}$$

Total MEP lost in friction, $F_{mep} = F_{mep1} + \ldots + F_{mep9}$

Net brake MEP = Indicated MEP − Friction MEP

Mechanical efficiency = $\dfrac{bmep}{imep}$

However, when gas exchange process is included, some of the frictional losses can be neglected in friction calculations . The above nine losses are only indicative, and should be applied with caution. The expressions are given in order to make the reader familiar with friction calculations. A separate subroutine in the computer program should take care of friction calculations.

9.5 Comparison of simulated results

Table 9.10 gives a comparison of simulated results, using the methods and equations described in Chapters 6 to 9, when the software given in the Appendix is just run. It is evident, taking almost all the processes into account (Chapter 9), how one can approach actual engine simulation. However, it may be cautioned here that the values predicted are only indicative. More refinements of various models should be attempted which, in the author's opinion, will be well rewarding and these are left to the reader. However, the demonstration of the capability of the code validation with experimental data has been done and the details are discussed in the following sections.

9.6 Validation of the computer code

In order to validate the computer code (given in Appendix) developed, experiments were conducted on a single-cylinder CI engine with a compression ratio of 16.5. Measurements of important parameters were made using standard instruments and power output by a swinging field dynamometer. The details of the measurements can be found in Ram Reddy, (1993 b).

The validation of the code has been attempted using the two-zone model. Progressive combustion and the zero-dimensional model cannot predict the details accurately since they are empirical in nature. Therefore, for better predictions the two-zone combustion model has been used. Readers may incorporate still better combustion models for better predictions.

9.7 Engine performance simulation

The engine performance data obtained from the dynamometer trails have been compared with the predicted results using the developed code. Experiments were conducted at full-load conditions. It may be noted that even at full-load operations in an actual engine, the manifold pressure need not be atmospheric due to restrictions in the flow passage.

9.8 Pressure–crank angle diagrams

Pressure histories for the experimental and zero-dimensional as well as two-zone model are plotted in Figs.9.8(a) and (b), for the rated operating conditions. In the single zone model, the cylinder temperature and equivalence ratio of the mixture are assumed to be uniform throughout the cylinder and the single Weibe's heat correlation (Miyamoto *et al.*, 1985) is used. The deficiency

Table 9.10 Comparison of various simulation method for the engine described in eq.(9.19) at relative air-fuel ratio, $RAF = 1.00$ and cut-off ratio, $V_r = 3.75$.

Variables	ICS	FCS	PCS	ACS
p_1 [bar]	1.000	1.000	1.000	0.993
V_1 [cc]	588.592	588.592	588.592	588.593
T_1 [K]	300.000	314.834	314.353	314.669
p_2 [bar]	50.638	50.314	50.340	18.845
V_2 [cc]	35.672	35.672	35.672	72.638
T_2 [K]	920.693	960.032	959.139	728.056
p_3 [bar]	50.638	50.314	50.342	77.765
V_3 [cc]	133.771	122.941	112.363	114.091
T_3 [K]	3452.598	2897.667	2572.085	2324.910
p_4 [bar]	6.363	7.186	6.365	4.061
V_4 [cc]	588.592	588.592	588.592	588.593
T_4 [K]	1908.820	1981.390	1752.610	1153.188
p_5 [bar]	–	1.000	1.000	0.989
V_5 [cc]	–	35.672	35.672	45.820
T_5 [K]	–	1347.986	1216.472	512.465
W_{exp} [J]	771.344	800.218	705.191	500.813
W_{comp} [J]	310.127	307.306	307.485	267.651
T_{wcomb} [J]	503.335	444.901	439.869	463.190
W_{loop} [J]	0.000	0.000	0.000	23.301
W_{net} [J]	964.552	937.813	837.575	673.050
ip [kW]	12.057	11.723	10.470	8.413
η_{ith}	54.613	46.220	43.943	38.562
η_{vol}	–	–	–	89.663
$\dfrac{N_{\mathrm{m}}}{N_{\mathrm{m}} + N_{\mathrm{x}}}$	1.000	0.986	0.984	0.959
$imep$ [bar]	17.217	16.739	14.950	12.013
$bmep$ [bar]	17.217	16.739	12.577	9.661
bp [kW]	12.057	11.723	8.807	6.766
η_{bth}	54.613	46.220	36.966	31.012
η_{m}	100.000	100.000	84.123	80.422

of this correlation is that it cannot handle the premixed and diffusive modes of combustion. So the model based on these assumptions, using single Weibe's heat release model, under-predicts the pressures pertaining to the premixed mode and overpredicts, in the later part corresponding to the diffusive mode. This trend is clearly observed in this figure. Heat transfer by radiation is not considered in this model as the burning zone temperature is not computed in this model. From Fig.9.8(b), for a compression ratio of 15.5, a similar trend of under prediction for the premixed and overprediction in the diffusive mode are revealed. So it may be concluded that the use of this type of model is limited and useful only for initial calculations.

In Fig.9.8(a), the computed pressure histories for the two-zone model is also presented for comparison with the experimental pressure histories. In this analysis double Weibe's heat release correlation is used, which adequately handles premixed and diffusive combustions. Heat transfer calculations are better in this model, because the burning zone and the non-burning zone temperatures are separately determined. It is observed that the computed pressures tally well with the experimental values. It is also observed that the computed peak pressure and its occurrence agree well with the experimental values. The pressure plots as shown in Fig. 9.8(b) for the two zone models at 15.5 compression ratio, also show that there is a reasonable level of agreement between the computed and experimental values.

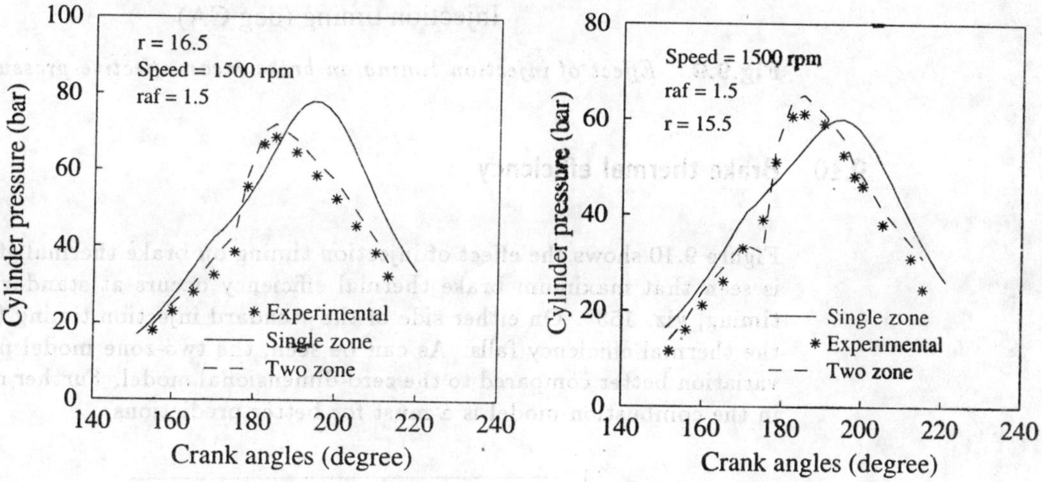

Fig.9.8 *Variation of cylinder pressure with crank angle for various models*

9.9 Brake mean effective pressure

Brake mean effective pressure is one of the important parameters in determining the performance of the engine. Figure 9.9 shows the predicted and experimental results of *bmep* with respect to injection timing. The standard injection timing of the experimental engine is 153°, i.e. 27° bTDC. Injection timings are varied ±20° to study the effect on *bmep*. It is seen that injection retard (moving closer towards TDC) reduces the *bmep*. As expected, it can be also seen that a two-zone model predicts details better than the zero-dimensional model. It is to be emphasized that further refinement in the combustion model is necessary for obtaining better predictions.

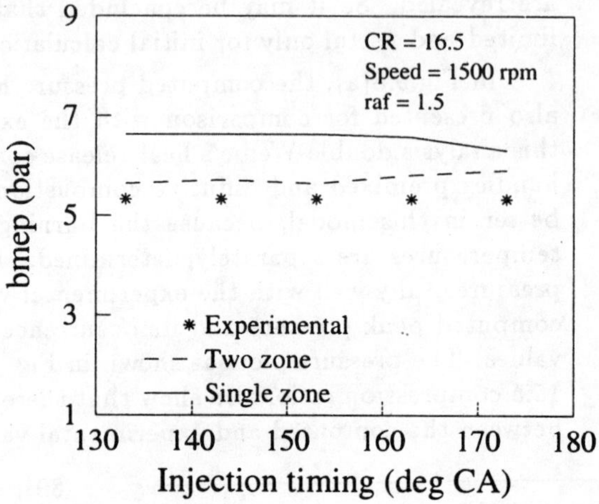

Fig.9.9 *Effect of injection timing on brake mean effective pressure*

9.10 Brake thermal efficiency

Figure 9.10 shows the effect of injection timing on brake thermal efficiency. It is seen that maximum brake thermal efficiency occurs at standard injection timing, viz. 153°. On either side of the standard injection timing (i.e., ±20°) the thermal efficiency falls. As can be seen, the two-zone model predicts the variation better compared to the zero-dimensional model. Further refinements in the combustion model is a must for better predictions.

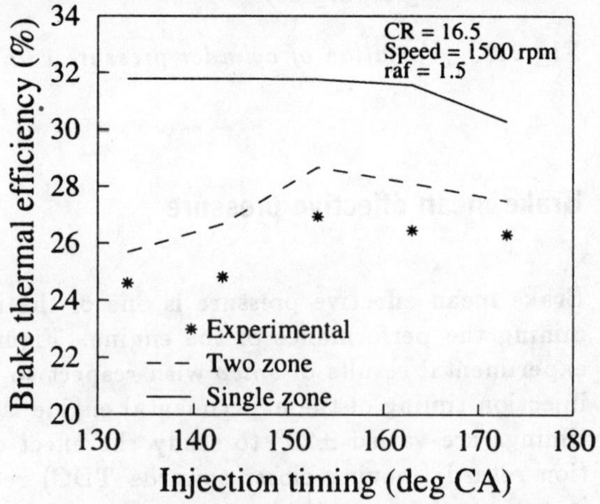

Fig.9.10 *Effect of injection timing on brake thermal efficiency*

9.11 Mechanical efficiency

Figure 9.11 shows the variation of mechanical efficiency with respect to injection timing. Experiments show that mechanical efficiency is at its maximum when the engine operates at standard injection timing. However, on either side of the standard injection timing the mechanical efficiency falls. it may be seen that neither of the models predict the details well. This is due to the empirical equations used in friction model calculations. Hence, proper friction model appropriate to the engine should be incorporated for better predictions.

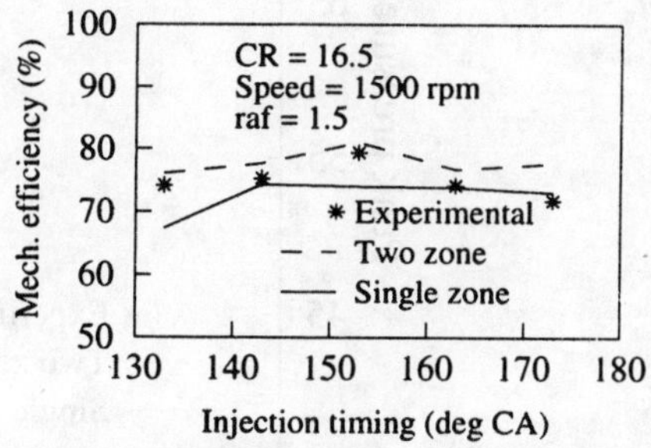

Fig.9.11 *Effect of injection timing on mechanical efficiency*

9.12 Volumetric efficiency

Figure 9.12 shows the variation of volumetric efficiency with respect to injection timing. It may be seen that injection timing has little effect on volumetric efficiency. As shown in the figure, volumetric efficiency is almost constant. Both the models predict the details well. However, it may be noted that combustion models have very little effect on the prediction of volumetric efficiency.

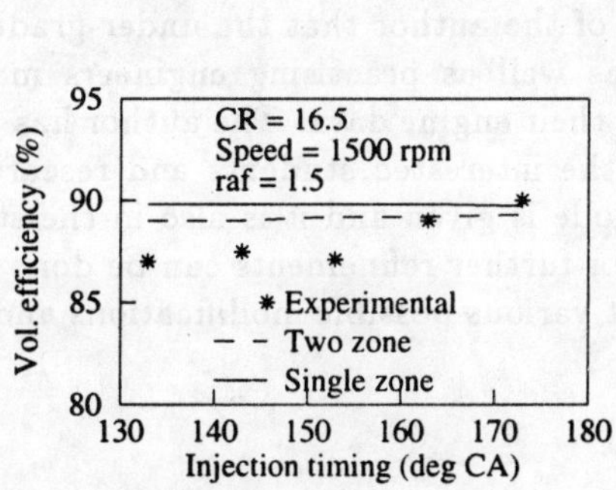

Fig.9.12 *Effect of injection timing on volumetric efficiency*

9.13 Effect of speed on performance

Figure 9.13 shows the variation of peak pressure with respect to injection timing. It is seen that the two-zone model predicts the details better than the zero-dimensional model.

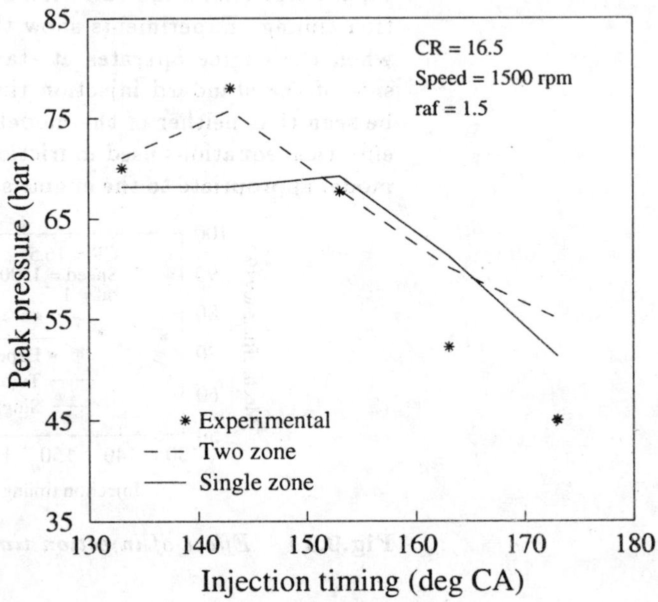

Fig.9.13 *Effect of injection timing on peak pressure*

From the performance predictions and the experimental comparison, it is seen that the developed code with the two-zone combustion model predicts the various parameters reasonably well. However, more refinements are required for still better agreement and this task is left to the reader.

Note that with this code a number of parametric studies can be made. It is the desire of the author that the under-graduate, post-graduate and doctoral students as well as practising engineers may use this code extensively for validating their engine data. The author has provided only a broad theoretical setup for the interested students and researchers to work on further. Since, a source code is given and it is also in the structured form, any modification required for further refinements can be done with ease. It is left to the reader to attempt various possible modifications and in this, only the sky is the limit!

Appendix A

Units and thermodynamic properties

In the SI unit system (Systeme International d'Unites), the base units are arbitrarily chosen. They are: length, metre (m); time, second (s); temperature, Kelvin (K); amount of substance, mole (mol).

The derived units are as follows:

The **Newton (N)** is the force that accelerates a mass of one kilogram at the rate of one metre per second.

The **Joule (J)** is the work done when the point of application of one newton is displaced by a distance of one metre in the direction of the force. (The joule is a relatively small quantity of energy. In terms of day-to-day experience, one kilojoule is the energy released by burning one 'strike-anywhere' kitchen match.)

The **Watt (W)** is the power that gives rise to the production of energy at the rate of one joule per second.

The **Pascal (Pa)** is the pressure exerted by one Newton distributed over one square metre.

In the SI unit system, Newton's second law does not require a dimensional conversion factor.

In the ideal equation, $pv = RT$, where

$$R = 8.314 \text{ kJ kmol}^{-1} \text{ K}^{-1}.$$

The following are more convenient R values when dealing with engines:

$$R = 82.06 \frac{\text{cm}^3 \text{ atm}}{\text{mol K}}$$

$$= 0.08206 \frac{\text{litre atm}}{\text{mol K}}.$$

The **mole** is the amount of a substance of a system that contains as many elementary entities as there are carbon atoms in 0.012 kg or 12 g of carbon 12. The elementary entities must be specified and they may be atoms, molecules, ions, electrons, other particles, or specified groups of such particles.

In the SI unit system, the mole replaces the gram mole (gmol).

The number of entities in a mole is 6.022×10^{23}, which is also known as Avogadro's constant.

1 mol of O_2 has a mass of 32 g,

1 mol of H_2 has a mass of 2 g,

1 mol of N_2 has a mass of 28 g,

1 mol of O has a mass of 16g, etc.

The first three are known as molecular weights and the last is known as atomic weight.

The internal energy, u, and enthalpy, h, are related by

$$h = u + pV. \tag{A.1}$$

For ideal gases, we can also write

$$h = u + RT. \tag{A.2}$$

Internal energy and enthalpy are defined by

$$du = C_v dT,$$

$$dh = C_p dT \tag{A.3}$$

$$C_p - C_v = R. \tag{A.4}$$

The ratio of the specific heats is designated by k, given by

$$k = \frac{C_p}{C_v}. \tag{A.5}$$

The heat capacities C_p and C_v are weak functions of pressure but strong functions of temperature. The values of C_p are tabulated in Table C.2. The superscript ° means that the values are for 1 atm pressure. Table C.3 gives coefficients to calculate C_p, for gases normally encountered in internal combustion engine calculations. The expression is of the form

$$C_p = a + bT \text{ (kJ/kmol K)}$$

and is valid for the temperature range $298 < T < 900$ K.

Internal energy and enthalpy are strong functions of temperature:

$$u(T) = \int_{T_0}^{T} C_v dT + u(T_0), \tag{A.6}$$

$$h(T) = \int_{T_0}^{T} C_p dT + u(T_0) + RT_0. \tag{A.7}$$

The temperature T_0 and $u(T_0)$ or $h(T_0)$ may be assigned arbitrarily. Entropy is a more complicated function and is derived from the first law,

$$ds = \frac{(du + pdv)}{T},$$

which can take any one of the following three forms (for $pV = RT$):

$$\left.\begin{aligned} ds &= C_v \frac{dT}{T} + R\frac{dv}{v}, \\ ds &= C_p \frac{dT}{T} - R\frac{dp}{p}, \\ ds &= C_p \frac{dv}{v} + C_v \frac{dp}{p}. \end{aligned}\right\} \tag{A.8}$$

Introducing a function $\phi(T)$ defined by

$$\phi(T) = \int_{T_0}^{T} C_p \frac{dT}{T} + \phi(T_0), \tag{A.9}$$

the entropy difference between two states 1 and 2 can be written as

$$s_2 - s_1 = \phi(T_2) - \phi(T_1) - R\ln\frac{p_2}{p_1} \tag{A.10}$$

The tabulated values of $\phi(T)$ are listed in Table C.5 (see Appendix C). Since k [eq.(A.5)] is not a strong function of temperature, eq.(A.8) may be integrated treating k as a constant:

$$\begin{aligned} pV^k &= \text{constant}, \\ Tp^{(k-1)/k} &= \text{constant } (s = \text{constant}), \\ Tv^{k-1} &= \text{constant}. \end{aligned} \tag{A.11}$$

Equation (A.11) will give quite accurate values for large temperature ranges. Equation (A.10) is, of course, more precise since the function $\phi(T)$ takes into account the temperature variation of C_p.

In a mixture of gases, with n_i denoting the mole number of gas i, the total mole number N is given by

$$N = \sum n_i.$$

The internal energy U, enthalpy H, and entropy S of a mixture are obtained by adding the contributions from each constituent gas:

$$\left.\begin{aligned} U(T) &= \sum n_i u_i(T), \\ H(T) &= \sum n_i h_i(T), \\ S(p,T) &= \sum n_i s_i(p_i, T), \end{aligned}\right\} \tag{A.12}$$

where the partial pressure p_i is

$$\left.\begin{aligned} p_i &= \frac{n_i}{N} p, \\ p &= \sum p_i. \end{aligned}\right\} \tag{A.13}$$

The internal energy, enthalpy and entropy of a mixture per mole of mixture can be expressed by introducing the mole fraction x_i, given by

$$x_i = \frac{n_i}{N}; \sum x_i = 1, \tag{A.14}$$

and then

$$\left.\begin{aligned} u(T) &= \sum x_i u_i(T), \\ h(T) &= \sum x_i h_i(T), \\ s(p,T) &= \sum x_i s_i(p_i, T). \end{aligned}\right\} \tag{A.15}$$

When the heat capacity of a mixture of gases is written with capital C,

$$C_p = \sum n_i c_{pi}; \quad C_v = \sum n_i c_{vi}, \tag{A.16}$$

the proper units are J K^{-1} or kJ K^{-1} . When written with lowercase c,

$$C_p = \sum x_i c_{pi}; \quad C_v = \sum x_i c_{vi}, \tag{A.17}$$

the proper units are J mol^{-1} of mixture K^{-1} or KJ mol^{-1} of mixture K^{-1}. Equations (A.16) and (A.17) apply only to mixtures with fixed compositions. If the composition changes as a result of chemical reaction, then the heat capacities are identified by C_p^* and C_v^* and are formulated from their basic definitions:

$$\begin{aligned} C_p^* &= \frac{d}{dT}H(T) \\ &= \frac{d}{dT}\sum n_i h_i \\ &= \sum n_i \frac{dh_i}{dT} + \sum h_i \frac{dn_i}{dT} \\ &= C_p + \sum h_i \frac{dn_i}{dT}, \quad p \text{ constant} \end{aligned} \tag{A.18}$$

and

$$C_v^* = C_v + \sum u_i \frac{dn_i}{dT}, \quad V \text{ constant.} \tag{A.19}$$

Under certain circumstances, the second terms in eqs.(A.18) and (A.19) may be substantially larger than C_p and C_v.

The molecular weight of a mixture, M_w, is simply related to the molecular weights of the constituent gases,

$$M_w = \sum x_i \cdot M_{wi}. \tag{A.20}$$

As a general rule, when the composition of a mixture of ideal gases is constant, any property of the mixture, per mole of mixture (when appropriate), is derived by weighing the corresponding property of each constituent according to each mole fraction.

In the region of small specific volume, the ideal gas equation is modified and appears as

$$p(v - b) = RT, \tag{A.21}$$

where R is still the universal constant and b is the *co-volume* which takes into account the volume occupied by the gas particles themselves. Values of b are shown to be one-third the critical specific volume and hence vary among gases, as the following values show:

Gas	Air	CO	H_2	N_2	O_2	CO_2	H_2O
b (cm^3/mol)	30.8	31.0	21.7	30.0	24.7	31.3	18.7

For a mixture of gases, the value of b can be approximated by

$$b_{\text{mixture}} = \sum x_i b_i. \tag{A.22}$$

The approximate character of eq.(A.22) can be observed by noting that air has a larger b value than both O_2 and N_2.

Air consists of nitrogen, oxygen and small amounts of several other gases. For engineering calculations, the latter may be ignored; the mole fractions assigned to nitrogen and oxygen are as follows:

$$x_{N_2} = 0.79; \quad x_{O_2} = 0.21.$$

The ratio is $x_{N_2}/x_{O_2} = 3.76$; thus, each oxygen molecule is accompanied by 3.76 nitrogen molecules.

While dealing with the flow of gases, it is useful to introduce the concept of *stagnation temperature* and to distinguish it from *stream temperature.* The former is measured with a thermometer that is stationary with respect to the moving gas, while the latter is measured with an infinitesimally small thermometer that moves with the gas. Stagnation temperatures are indicated as T^o, while T denotes the stream temperature. For a gas moving with velocity C, the relationship between the two temperatures is given by the energy equation

$$h(T) + \frac{1}{2}C^2 = h(T^o), \tag{A.23}$$

since the kinetic energy is converted into thermal energy as the fluid decelerates to zero velocity when it impacts against the stationary thermometer. Equation (A.23) contains enthalpy terms per unit mass. Writing them as C_pT products, we get

$$T^o = T + \left(\frac{C^2}{2C_p}\right).$$

As an example, for air $C_p = 29.2$ J mol^{-1} K^{-1} at room temperature, or about 1 J g^{-1} K^{-1}, since the molecular weight is 28.96. Thus,

$$T^o = T + \left(\frac{C^2}{2000}\right) \text{K}.$$

with C in (m/s).

Consequently, at a velocity of 45 m/s, the difference between T and T^o amounts to 1°C. When C becomes large, the variation of C_p with T must be taken into account to reach an accurate value for the temperature difference.

Appendix B

Solutions for $\mathbf{F(T) = 0}$

Solutions for $F(T) = 0$ can be obtained in a variety of ways. Two simple and well-known methods are described here.

In order to produce a successful algorithm, something must be known about the form of $F(T)$. The more we know, the easier it will be to write the algorithm and the better the chance that it will be successful in all situations. When $F(T) = 0$ arises in thermodynamic analysis, with T representing the absolute temperature, we know at once that we are concerned only with positive T values and that $F(T)$ must be single-valued. The forms for $F(T)$ encountered frequently, and prominently, are energy equations such as

$$\left.\begin{array}{rcl} F(T) & = & H_p(T) - H_r(T_r) \\ & \text{or} & \\ F(T) & = & U_p(T) - U_r(T_r) \end{array}\right\} \qquad (B.1)$$

or isentropic changes of state from 1 to 2, for which

$$\left.\begin{array}{rcl} F(T) & = & S(p_2, T) - S(p_1, T_1) \\ & \text{or} & \\ F(T) & = & S(V_2, T) - S(V_1, T_1) \end{array}\right\} \qquad (B.2)$$

In both cases, T is unambiguous; there is only one solution, so that in the range of interest, T positive, $F(T)$ is a single-valued function. We know more than that. In the case of eq.(B.1), we know that T is greater than T_r, where T_r represents the initial temperature of the reactants. When eq.(B.2) describes an expansion, then we know that T must be less than T_1. Information of this sort simplifies the construction of the program.

Newton–Raphson iteration technique

The strategy of this iteration technique is illustrated in Fig.B.1. Construct the tangent to the curve at T_1. The tangent intersects the T-axis at T_2, and by definition the slope at T_1 is

$$F'(T_1) = \frac{F(T_1)}{(T_1 - T_2)}, \qquad (B.3)$$

which can be solved for T_2 to give

$$T_2 = T_1 - \frac{F(T_1)}{F'(T_1)}, \qquad (B.4)$$

which is known as the recursion equation for T_2; a better approximation to the solution than T_1 can be computed from T_1. By repeated application of eq.(B.1), the solution can be approached as closely as we desire.

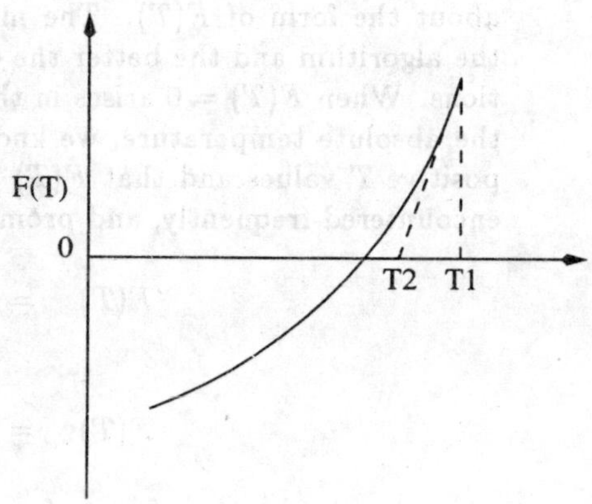

Fig.B.1 *Newton–Raphson iteration*

As a general rule, the Newton–Raphson iteration converges more rapidly than the other methods. But we need to know more about the character of $F(T)$ in order to use the Newton–Raphson iteration with assured success. For one thing, $F(T)$ must be differentiable. This is seldom a problem.

Figure B.2 illustrates the sort of problems which may arise; however, when, as in Fig.B.2(b), the curve is concave upwards, the solution can be found for any starting T value. Note that the solution is approached from above; successive approximations are each smaller than the preceding value. Trouble

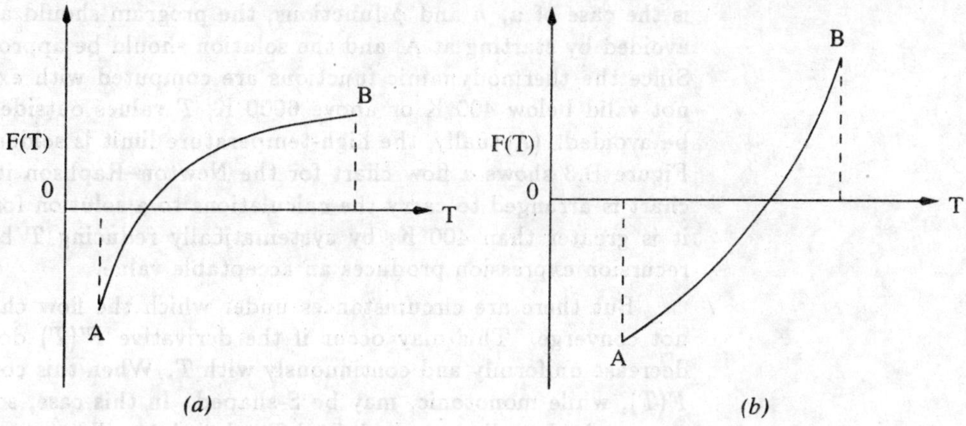

(a) ***for convex curves initial guess should be at A***

(b) ***for concave curves initial guess can be at A or B***

Fig.B.2 *Newton–Raphson iteration*

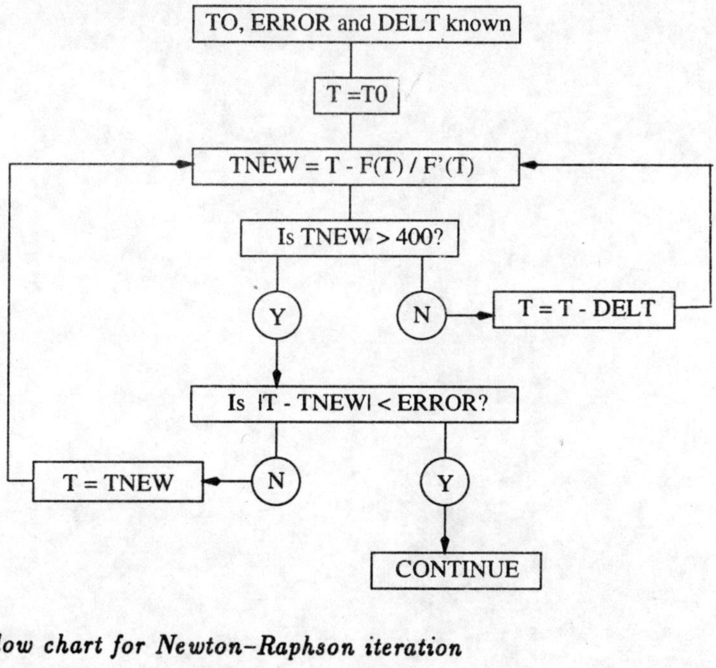

Fig.B.3 *Flow chart for Newton–Raphson iteration*

lurks in Fig.B.2(a), where the curvature is concave downwards. If we start at B, for example, the slope at that point may be such as to cause the tangent to intersect somewhere on the negative T-axis. If $F(T)$ contains $\log(T)$, as is the case of u, h and ϕ functions, the program should abort. This can be avoided by starting at A, and the solution should be approached from below. Since the thermodynamic functions are computed with expressions that are not valid below 400 K or above 6000 K, T values outside these limits must be avoided. (Actually, the high-temperature limit is seldom a real problem.) Figure B.3 shows a flow chart for the Newton–Raphson iteration. The flow chart is arranged to carry the calculations to a solution for any T_0, provided it is greater than 400 K, by systematically reducing T by DELT until the recursion expression produces an acceptable value.

But there are circumstances under which the flow chart in Fig.B.3 will not converge. This may occur if the derivative $F'(T)$ does not increase or decrease uniformly and continuously with T. When this condition is not met, $F(T)$, while monotonic, may be S-shaped. In this case, some manipulations are required to discover an initial T value that will guarantee convergence.

Appendix C

Algebraic expressions for thermodynamic functions

For hand calculations, the tabulated values of C_p, the constant-pressure heat capacity, h, the enthalpy, ϕ, the temperature portion of entropy and K_p, the reaction constant, are adequate. For computer programs, algebraic expressions are required. This can be accomplished in several ways.

The functions are related by

$$h(T) = \int_{T_0}^{T} C_p dT + h(T_0),$$

$$\phi(T) = \int_{T_0}^{T} \frac{C_p}{T} dT + \phi(T_0), \qquad (C.1)$$

and for the reaction

$$V_1 A_1 + V_2 A_2 \rightleftharpoons V_3 A_3 + V_4 A_4,$$

van't Hoff's equation provides the value of K:

$$\ln K_p(T) = \int_{T_0}^{T} \frac{\Delta H}{RT^2} dT + K(T_0)$$

$$= \int_{T_0}^{T} \frac{V_3 h_3 + V_4 h_4 - V_1 h_1 - V_2 h_2}{RT^2}. \qquad (C.2)$$

With experimentally determined values of C_p, formerly developed from calorimetric data and more recently from analysis of spectroscopic measurements, tabulated values of the enthalpy and entropy function can be prepared.

For the purpose of simulation, the following expression has been chosen to represent the enthalpy in this book.

$$h(T) = A + BT + C\ln(T) \qquad (\text{kJ mol}^{-1})$$

The remaining thermodynamic functions are then

$$
\begin{aligned}
C_p(T) &= B + \frac{C}{T} && \text{(kJ mol}^{-1}\text{ K}^{-1}\text{)},\\
C_v(T) &= B - 8.314 + \frac{C}{T} && \text{(kJ kmol}^{-1}\text{ K}^{-1}\text{)},\\
u(T) &= A + (B - 8.314)T + C\ln(T) && \text{(kJ kmol}^{-1}\text{ K}^{-1}\text{)},\\
\phi(T) &= B\ln(T) - \frac{C}{T} + D && \text{(kJ kmol}^{-1}\text{ K}^{-1}\text{)},\\
K_p(T) &= \exp\left[\frac{a}{T} + \left(b + \frac{c}{T}\right)\ln(T) + d\right] && \text{(P in atm).}
\end{aligned}
$$

Expressions with only three coefficients do not adequately fit the enthalpy and entropy functions over the temperature range 400 to 6000 K. Therefore, the range was sub-divided and the coefficients evaluated as follows:

1600 to 6000 K : A, B and C were evaluated at 2500, 4000 and 5500 K from the enthalpy tables, and D was evaluated at 3500 K from the entropy function, d was evaluated at 3500 K from the reaction constant tables.

400 to 1600 K : A, B and C were evaluated at 500, 1100 and 1600 K, and D was evaluated at 1600 K. (The reaction constants are not needed below 1600 K.)

Tables 3.1 and 3.2 in Chapter 3 list the values of A, B, C and D for 11 gases for the two temperature ranges. Table C.1 lists the values of a, b, c and d for nine reactions.

When the temperature range is sub-divided, it is important to have a precise *fit* at the point of sub-division. If this provision is not made, it is possible for an iterative routine to *stagger* about that point and not converge. The high-temperature range coefficients were first determined, and the low-temperature coefficients were adjusted to give enthalpy and entropy function values that coincide at 1600 K with the high-temperature coefficient values.

A single equation for each thermodynamic function could be developed by starting with an enthalpy expression containing, say, six or seven constants. As a general rule, the smaller the temperature span, the better is the agreement between the calculated and tabulated values. The important point to appreciate is that any algebraic expression, no matter how absurd, can be forced to pass through *any* n points of *any* curve, provided the expression contains n adjustable parameters. But if the chosen expression is indeed absurd, it will yield wildly inaccurate values in some or all of the intervals between the n points.

If the enthalpy expression is chosen at the starting point for the development of equations to compute thermodynamic functions, then

(i) the enthalpy expression must give satisfactory agreement with the tabulated values of $h(T)$ over the entire selected temperature range,

(ii) the expression for enthalpy must be differentiable to provide an equation for C_p,

(iii) $\left(\frac{C_p}{T}\right) dT$ must be integrable, in order to derive the expressions for $\phi(T)$ and

(iv) $\left(\frac{h}{T^2}\right) dT$ must be integrable in order to obtain the reaction constant equation.

Tables C.2 and C.3 give the values of C_p whereas Tables C.4 and C.5 give the values of h and ϕ at 100 K intervals in the range 300 to 1000 K, and at 500 K intervals in the range 1000 to 6000 K.

A more ambitious scheme for computing the thermodynamic properties of gases can found by Prothero, in Computing with Thermochemical Data, in *Combustion and Flame*, **Vol.13**, No.4, 1969. The expressions are derived starting with a seventh-order polynomial for C_p. Fourteen coefficients are listed for 47 gases, seven in the range 300 to 2000 K and seven in the range 2000 to 6000 K. The C_p values were drawn from the JANAF tables (Joint Army Navy Air Force Thermochemical Tables). With C_p calculable over the range 300 to 6000 K, the values of enthalpy and entropy are obtained by integration. Prothero lists the values of enthalpy and entropy at 300 K for each gas. These are the integration constants in eq.(C.1) and are chosen to incorporate the heats of formation. With a known value for the reaction constant $K_p(300)$, the reaction constants can then be found. However, the system developed by Prothero is more accurate than the equations listed in Appendix C.

Table C.1 Coefficients for calculations of the reaction constants K_p with the equation $K_p = \exp\left[\frac{a}{T} + \left(b + \frac{c}{T}\right)\ln(T) + d\right]$ valid for 1600 < T < 6000 K; pressures are in units of atmospheres

Reaction	*a*	*b*	*c*	*d*
$H_2 + \frac{1}{2}O_2 \rightleftharpoons H_2O$	42450.0	-1.0740	-2147.0	3.2515
$CO + \frac{1}{2}O_2 \rightleftharpoons CO_2$	33805.0	0.7422	165.8	-16.5739
$2H \rightleftharpoons H_2$	33587.0	0.5604	3327.0	-20.8683
$2O \rightleftharpoons O_2$	57126.0	-0.0100	599.0	-16.3201
$2H + O \rightleftharpoons H_2O$	104702.0	-0.5181	1480.0	-25.8073
$O + H \rightleftharpoons OH$	44216.0	-0.1319	1298.0	-13.1303
$CO + H_2O \rightleftharpoons CO_2 + H_2$	-8645.0	1.8162	2312.0	-19.8254
$O_2 + N_2 \rightleftharpoons 2NO$	-14096.0	-0.6893	-1375.3	9.6680
$2N \rightleftharpoons N_2$	108142.0	-1.7440	-3558.2	0.5950

Table C.2 c_p^o (kJ kmol^{-1} K^{-1}) for gases

$T(K)$	CO	CO_2	H	H_2	H_2O	N	NO	N_2	O	OH	O_2
300	29.14	37.21	20.79	28.85	33.58	20.79	29.85	29.12	21.90	29.87	29.38
400	29.34	41.30	20.79	29.18	34.25	20.79	29.97	29.25	21.48	29.60	30.11
500	29.79	44.61	20.79	29.26	35.21	20.79	30.50	29.58	21.26	29.49	31.09
600	30.44	47.33	20.79	29.32	36.30	20.79	31.25	30.11	21.12	29.51	32.09
700	31.17	49.58	20.79	29.43	37.48	20.79	32.04	30.76	21.04	29.65	32.98
800	31.90	51.46	20.79	29.61	38.72	20.79	32.77	31.43	20.98	29.92	33.74
900	32.58	53.04	20.79	29.87	39.99	20.79	33.43	32.10	20.94	30.27	34.36
1000	33.19	54.37	20.79	30.20	41.26	20.79	34.00	32.70	20.91	30.68	34.88
1100	33.71	55.50	20.79	30.58	42.45	20.79	34.49	33.25	20.89	31.13	35.31
1200	34.17	56.44	20.79	30.99	43.57	20.79	34.90	33.74	20.88	31.59	35.68
1300	34.58	57.24	20.79	31.42	44.63	20.79	35.25	34.16	20.86	32.06	36.00
1400	34.93	57.92	20.79	31.86	45.64	20.79	35.56	34.53	20.85	32.52	36.29
1500	35.23	58.53	20.79	32.30	46.58	20.79	35.82	34.85	20.84	32.95	36.56
2000	36.25	60.68	20.79	34.29	50.24	20.79	36.70	35.99	20.83	34.76	37.78
2500	36.84	61.99	20.79	35.83	52.53	20.82	37.22	36.65	20.85	36.04	38.92
3000	37.23	62.94	20.79	37.06	54.03	20.97	37.58	37.07	20.94	36.98	39.96
3500	37.50	63.66	20.79	38.13	55.01	21.28	37.86	37.38	21.09	37.72	40.84
4000	37.72	64.25	20.79	39.09	55.68	21.82	38.10	37.61	21.30	38.33	41.56
4500	37.90	64.75	20.79	39.97	56.17	22.56	38.32	37.80	21.55	38.87	42.09
5000	38.06	65.21	20.79	40.79	56.57	23.48	38.53	37.97	21.80	39.35	42.49
5500	38.20	65.67	20.79	41.55	56.96	24.50	38.73	38.13	22.05	39.79	42.79
6000	38.33	66.13	20.79	42.26	57.34	25.60	38.93	38.28	22.29	40.18	43.01

Table C.3 Expressions for the specific heat of gases and vapours: $c_p = a + bT$ (kJ kmol^{-1} K^{-1})$298 < T < 900$ K

Gas	a	b	Molecular weight
CO	27.40	0.0058	28.00
CO_2	28.80	0.0280	44.00
H_2	28.30	0.0019	2.00
H_20	30.50	0.0103	18.00
N_2	27.60	0.0051	28.00
O_2	27.00	0.0079	32.00
Air	27.50	0.0057	28.97
CH_4	20.10	0.0052	16.00
C_2H_6	52.30	0.1040	30.00
C_3H_8	25.30	0.1620	44.00
C_8H_{18}	38.40	0.4290	114.00
$C_{10}H_{22}$	38.10	0.6560	142.00
CH_3OH	8.37	0.1260	32.00
C_2H_5OH	18.80	0.1590	46.00
C_6H_6	27.20	0.2180	78.00

Table C.4 h° (kJ kmol^{-1}) for gases

$T(K)$	CO	CO_2	H	H_2	H_2O	N	N_2	NO	O	OH	O_2
298.16	283754	9364	363212	290540	57316	365894	15780	106855	256109	195948	17200
300.00	283807	9433	363250	290593	57376	365932	15834	106907	256149	190003	17254
400.00	286729	13367	365329	293499	60773	368011	18751	109895	257061	198975	20225
500.00	289684	17688	367408	296421	64252	370090	21691	112084	260452	201926	23284
600.00	292694	22269	369487	299346	67836	371974	24674	116005	262570	204880	26444
700.00	295775	27118	371566	302287	71557	374247	27717	120421	264678	207834	29699
800.00	298930	32172	373645	305241	75399	376326	30827	122400	266779	210811	33036
900.00	302155	37405	375724	308214	79353	378404	34004	125709	268876	213819	36442
1000.00	305443	42769	377803	311217	83425	380483	37245	129079	270968	216868	39904
1100.00	308788	48262	379879	314257	87610	382562	40543	132504	273058	219958	43414
1200.00	312182	53860	381958	317335	91911	384640	43892	135973	275147	223094	46963
1300.00	315620	59543	384036	320456	96321	386719	47287	139481	277234	226277	50547
1400.00	319096	65301	386115	323620	100835	388797	50721	143022	279320	229506	54161
1500.00	322604	71124	388194	326828	105446	390876	54190	146590	281405	232779	57804
2000.00	340499	100974	398587	343493	129722	401270	71929	164740	291821	249731	76394
2500.00	367154	131662	408980	361039	155455	411671	90101	183229	302238	267449	95569
3000.00	377309	162907	419373	379373	182117	422114	108539	201931	312682	285713	115294
3500.00	396000	194565	429766	398076	209392	432667	127156	220793	323186	304394	135501
4000.00	414806	226547	440159	417383	237073	443433	145906	239785	333783	323411	156108
4500.00	433713	258798	450552	437150	265039	454520	164760	258891	344494	342715	177025
5000.00	452704	291288	460945	457340	293225	466024	183705	278102	355331	362274	198176
5500.00	471769	324009	471338	477926	321609	478015	202732	297415	366293	382060	219501
6000.00	490903	356919	481731	498879	350186	490537	221837	316829	377379	402054	240954

Also, h° (sat. liquid H_2, 20 K) = 282 612 (kJ kmol^{-1}); h° (sat. liquid O_2, 90 K) = 4 315 (kJ kmol^{-1});
h° (solid C, 298.16 K) = 385 346 (kJ kmol^{-1}).

Table C.5 $\phi^\circ = \int_0^T c_p^\circ \frac{dT}{T}$ = absolute entropy at 1 atm (kJ kmol^{-1} K^{-1}) for gases

$T(K)$	CO	CO_2	H	H_2	H_2O	N	N_2	NO	O	O_2	OH
298.16	197.910	213.640	114.611	130.590	188.720	153.195	191.490	210.620	160.954	205.060	183.630
500.00	213.080	234.780	125.357	145.640	206.460	163.941	206.630	226.140	172.091	220.610	198.960
1000.00	234.789	269.161	139.764	166.122	232.706	178.348	228.066	248.404	186.683	243.505	219.622
1500.00	248.677	292.098	148.192	178.752	250.491	186.776	241.778	262.579	195.147	257.997	232.494
2000.00	258.967	309.258	154.172	188.327	264.433	192.756	251.976	273.016	201.140	268.685	242.235
2500.00	267.125	322.948	158.810	196.151	275.907	197.399	260.083	281.265	205.789	277.238	250.137
3000.00	273.879	334.339	162.600	202.797	285.625	201.206	266.805	288.084	209.597	284.427	256.794
3500.00	279.639	344.098	165.804	208.591	294.032	204.459	272.545	293.898	212.835	290.655	262.552
4000.00	284.661	352.638	168.580	213.746	301.424	207.334	277.551	298.970	215.665	296.158	267.630
4500.00	289.115	360.235	171.028	218.401	308.011	209.944	281.993	303.471	218.188	301.084	272.177
5000.00	293.116	367.081	173.218	222.655	313.950	212.368	285.985	307.519	220.471	305.541	276.298
5500.00	296.751	373.318	175.199	226.579	319.361	214.653	289.611	311.200	222.561	309.606	280.069
6000.00	300.080	379.052	177.008	230.225	324.333	216.831	292.936	314.578	224.490	313.339	283.548

Appendix D

```
*************************************************************
*                                                           *
*                                                           *
*               COMPUTER SIMULATION OF                      *
*                                                           *
*       COMPRESSION-IGNITION ENGINE PROCESSES               *
*                                                           *
*                  CODE DEVELOPED                           *
*                                                           *
*                        BY                                 *
*                                                           *
*                 PROF. V. GANESAN                          *
*                                                           *
*              I.C.ENGINES LABORATORY                       *
*                                                           *
*     DEPARTMENT OF MECHANICAL ENGINEERING                  *
*                                                           *
*           I.I.T. MADRAS 600 036, INDIA                    *
*                                                           *
*                      9.9.99                               *
*                                                           *
*************************************************************
```

```
C*********************************************************************
C         SIMULATION OF 4-STROKE COMPRESSION IGNITION ENGINE
C*********************************************************************
                            BLOCK DATA
C*********************************************************************
C     IN THIS SUBROUTINE VALUES WHICH ARE NOT LIKELY TO CHANGE ARE
C     GIVEN AS DATA
      REAL KA,KP,KR,MC,MEP,MH,MO,MOLWTP,NA,N,M,NM,NADNAX,NMO,
     #     NP,NPO,NX,KRR
      INTEGER EVO,EVC
      LOGICAL IPTTHR,IPRINT,ISUPCH,ISUPET,HT_INDEX
      CHARACTER*10 XV,YZ
      COMMON/GEOM/B,CR,CRL,S,VBDC,VDISP,VDVBDC(720),VOLUME(800),
     #          VTDC
      COMMON/THERM/HRP,MOLWTP(5),P1,P2,P3,P4,T1,T2,T3,T4,T5,T6,TA,
     #            V1,V2,V3,V4
      COMMON/CHEM/KA,KP,KR,N(5),NA,NADNAX,NMO,NP,NPO,NX,RMR,KRR,
     #           MC,MH,MO,R,RLITAT,RMIX,Y,YCC,YMIN,PMOLWT
      COMMON/CPCOEF/CV,ACPF,BCPF,ACPA,BCPA,AL(5),AH(5),
     #             BL(5),BH(5),CL(5),CH(5)
      COMMON/INDEX/IPTTHR,IPRINT,NCYCLE,HT_INDEX
      COMMON/GEN/CB(40,4),A(10,16),C(5),D(5),EETAH,RAF,F(5),
     #          FPM,FVM,G(5),MEP,PID4,POWER,RPM
      COMMON/INEXH/IVO,IVC,EVO,EVC,AEV,AIV
      COMMON/SUPECH/EFOCOM,EFOTUR,ISUPCH,ISUPET
      COMMON/COMBUN/WCOMB,BRMAX
      COMMON/IDIES/PA,VR,STROKE
      COMMON/HTMOD/MODFHT
      COMMON/VALARE/D1,BETA,MODFVA
      COMMON/OVERL/PID,OMEGA,DTMAX,CAINT,AM,BDCMAS
      COMMON/PSSA/CPR,DT,DTHDDT,IBC,IECPC,IEC,GASMAS,WCOMP,WEXP,NCEXG,
     #           WNET,WLOOP,PSPS,ML
      COMMON/ABC/WT,COMEFF,CPA,NM
      COMMON/FRICT/PIMF,PEMF,PSL,NPR,FMEP
      COMMON/FRPMOD/MODFRP
      COMMON/ABCD/DN,ITETA,ITETA3,L
      COMMON/TFCOM/COMDUR,M
      COMMON/MAX/PRMAX,ICAMAX,JCAMAX
      COMMON/COMOD/MODCOM
      COMMON/HRMOD/MODHR
      COMMON/PRINTS/XV(16),YZ(32)
      DATA   XV/'T1(K)','T2(K)','T3(K)','T4(K)','T5(K)','P2(ATM)',
     #          'P3(ATM)','P4(ATM)',' VR ',' KR ',' KP ','NADNAX',
     #          'POWER','EETAH','MEP(ATM)',' ITRNS '/
      DATA   YZ/'P1(KSC)','V1(CC)','T1(K)','P2(KSC)','V2(CC)','T2(K)',
     #          'PMAX(KSC)',
```

```
     #            'V3(CC)','TMAX(K)','P4(BAR)','V4(CC)','T4(K)',
     #            'P5(BAR)','V5(CC)','T5(K)', 'P6(BAR)', 'V6(CC)',
     #            'T6(K)','WEXP(J)','WCOMP(J)', 'WCOMB(J)', 'WLOOP(J)',
     #            'WNET(J)', 'POWER(KW)', 'EETATH', 'VOL. EFF.',
     #            'NADNAX', 'IMEP(BAR)', 'BMEP(BAR)', 'BPOWER(KW)',
     #            'BRTHEFF', 'MECHEFF' /
C    GIVE MOLE NUMBERS OF CARBON, HYDROGEN, & OXYGEN
C    IN THE FUEL. VALUES GIVEN HERE ARE FOR DIESEL.
C    (C10H22)
      DATA       MC    ,      MH    ,     MO   /
     #          10.0   ,     22.0   ,     0.0  /
C    HEATING VALUE(HRP) OF THE FUEL IS GIVEN HERE.
C    HRPF IS IN KJ/KMOL. C10H22
      DATA HRP/-0.62613E07/
C    COEFFICIENTS FOR THE CALCULATION OF THERMODYNAMIC
C    PROPERTIES OF THE EXHAUST GAS CONSTITUENTS.
C    THE VARIOUS EXHAUST GAS CONSTITUENTS ARE
C    CO    ,  CO2,     H2O    ,    N2,      O2
C    COEFFICIENTS  FOR LOW TEMPERATURES  (400<T<1600)
      DATA AL/299180.00, 56835.00, 88923.00, 31317.00, 43388.00/
      DATA  BL/    37.85,    66.27,    49.36,    37.46,    42.27/
      DATA  CL/ -4571.90,-11634.00, -7940.80, -4559.30, -6635.40/
C    COEFFICIENTS FOR HIGH TEMPERATURES (1600<T<6000)
      DATA AH/309070.00, 93048.00,154670.00, 44639.00,127010.00/
      DATA  BH/    39.29,    68.58,    60.43,    39.32,    46.25/
      DATA  CH/ -6201.90,-16979.00,-19212.00, -6753.40,-18798.00/
C    ACPA,BCPA ARE THE CONSTANTS TO EVALUATE SPECIFIC HEAT OF AIR
      DATA ACPA,BCPA/27.5,0.0057/
C    MOLWP IS THE MOLECULAR WEIGT OF PRODUCTS
C                    CO         CO2        H2O        N2         O2
      DATA MOLWTP/ 28.00,      44.00,     18.00,     28.00,     32.00/
C    R      :  UNIVERSAL GAS CONSTANT.
C    RLITAT :  UNIVERSAL GAS CONSTANT IN LITRE-ATMOSPHERE.
C    PID4:  PI DIVIDED BY 4  (I.E.  3.14/4.)
      DATA       R ,     RLITAT ,     PID4 /
     #         8.314,  0.082060,   .7853980/
C    FPM AND FVM ARE MULTIPLICATION FACTORS FOR PRESSURE & VOLUME
      DATA FPM,FVM/101325.0,0.001/
      DATA STROKE/4.0/
C    ENGINE DETAILS.  CHANGE THE DATA FOR YOUR ENGINE HERE.
C    NOTE: BORE(B),STROKE(S),CONNECTING ROD LENGTH(CRL) ARE IN MM.
C          VR IS THE FUEL CUT-OFF RATIO
      DATA B,S,CRL,VR/80.0,110.0,230.0,3.75/
C    GIVE THE COMPRESSION RATIO OF YOUR ENGINE HERE.
      DATA CR/16.5/
C    GIVE INITIAL PRESSURE AND TEMPERATURE VALUES HERE.
```

```
C     NOTE: PRESSURE IS IN ATMOSPHERES & TEMPERATURE IN KELVIN
       DATA        P1     ,      T1     ,   PA    ,      TA     /
      1           1.00    ,     300.00  ,  1.00   ,    300.00   /
       DATA RAF/1.5/
C     NCEXG :  NUMBER CONSTITUENTS IN THE EXHAUST GAS.
       DATA CPA,NX,NCEXG/29.0,0.,5/
C     BRMAX IS MAXIMUM ALLOWABLE BURNING RATE (LITRES/S)
C     THIS IS SPECIFIED FOR PROGRESSIVE COMBUSTION MODEL.
       DATA BRMAX/300.0/
C     IBC IS THE CRANK ANGLE AT WHICH FUEL IS INJECTED
C     IF PROGRESSIVE COMBUSTION MODEL(MODEL 1)IS USED THEN IBC=180
C      DATA IBC/153/
C     DN IS A CONSTANT CHOSEN BETWEEN 30 & 60 IN PROGRESSIVE COMBUS-
C     TION MODEL TO DETERMINE SMALL INCREMRNTS OF CRANK ANGLE.
       DATA DN/55.0/
C     IPTTHR IS TRUE ONLY FOR IDEAL CYCLE WITH SUPERCHARGER
       DATA IPTTHR,IPRINT/.FALSE.,.TRUE./
C     ISUPET IS .TRUE. FOR EXHAUST DRIVEN SUPERCHARGER.
C     ISUPCH IS .TRUE.FOR COMPRESSOR DRIVEN SUPERCHARGER OR GEAR DRIVEN
C     IF ANY ONE OF THE ABOVE IS TRUE, THEN IPTTHR SHOULD BE .TRUE.
C      DATA ISUPET,ISUPCH/.FALSE.,.TRUE./
C      DATA ISUPET,ISUPCH/.TRUE.,.FALSE./
       DATA ISUPET,ISUPCH/.FALSE.,.FALSE./
C     EFOCOM AND EFOTUR ARE EFFICIENCIES OF COMPRESSOR & TURBINE.
       DATA EFOCOM,EFOTUR/0.9,0.9/
C     AEV & AIV ARE MAX. AREA OF OPENING OF EXHAUST & INTAKE
C     VALVES IN SQUARE CM.
       DATA AEV,AIV/3.0,2.5/
C     VALVE TIMINGS ;
       DATA EVO,EVC,IVO,IVC/340,554,527,750/
C     CP & CV ARE  THE SPECIFIC HEAT AT CONSTANT VOLUME
C     AND CONSTANT PRESSURE RESPECTIVELY (KJ/KMOL)
       DATA KA,CV/1.4,20.896/
C     PIMF & PEMF ARE INLET & EXHAUST MANIFOLD PRESSURES.
C     PSL IS THE PISTON SKIRT LENGTH & NPR IS THE NUMBER OF
C     PISTON RINGS.
       DATA PIMF,PEMF,PSL,NPR/1.0,1.0,9.0,3/
C     MODFHT IS THE HEAT TRANSFER MODEL USED IN THE SUBROUTINE
C     HEAT TRANSFER (HTRANS)
       DATA MODFHT/4/
C     MODFVA IS MODEL FOR VALVE AREA USED IN THE SUBROUTINE
C     VALVAE.   SPECIFY HERE D1 & BETA IF MODFVA 2 IS USED.
       DATA MODFVA/1/
C     CAINT IS THE CRANK ANGLE INTERVAL  &  AM IS ANOTHER
C     FACTOR.     THESE ARE USED IN SUBROUTINE GASEX  AND
C     THEIR VALUES SHOULD BE BETWEEN 3 & 10.
```

```
      DATA CAINT,AM/6.,4./
C     'M' IS THE CONSTANT USED IN WIEBE'S HEAT RELEASE EQUATION;
C     IT IS GENERALLY DETERMINED FROM P-THETA DIAGRAM OBTAINED
C     FROM THE ACTUAL ENGINE
      DATA M/2.00/
C     COMDUR IS DURATION OF COMBUSTION IN DEGREES CARANK ANGLE
C     IT MAY BE ASSUMED BETWEEN 40 TO 80 DEGREES.
      DATA COMDUR/50.0/
C     WT IS THE MOLECULAR WEIGHT OF THE FUEL AND COMEFF IS COM-
C     BUSTION EFFICIENCY( NORMALLY BETWEEN 0.8 & 0.9)
      DATA WT,COMEFF/142.0,0.85/
C     PRMAX IS MAXIMUM ALLOWABLE PRESSURE RISE RATE IN ATM/DEG.CA
      DATA PRMAX/10.0/
C     MODCOM IS THE COMBUSTION MODEL USED.
C     FOR ZERO DIMENSIONAL COMBUSTION MODEL MODCOM =2 &
C     FOR PROGRESSIVE COMBUSTION MODEL MODCOM =1
C     DATA MODCOM/2/
C     MODHR IS THE HEAT RELEASE MODEL USED
      DATA MODHR/1/
C     MODFRP IS THE MODEL FOR ENGINE FRICTION
      DATA MODFRP/1/
C     SPEED OF THE ENGINE
      DATA RPM/1500.0/
      END
C*********************************************************************
C                                MAIN PROGRAM
C*********************************************************************
      COMMON/GEOM/B,CR,CRL,S,VBDC,VDISP,VDVBDC(720),VOLUME(800),
     #     VTDC
      COMMON/GEN/CB(40,4),A(10,16),C(5),D(5),EETAH,RAF,F(5),
     #       FPM,FVM,G(5),MEP,PID4,POWER,RPM
      COMMON/THERM/HRP,MOLWTP(5),P1,P2,P3,P4,T1,T2,T3,T4,T5,T6,TA,
     #        V1,V2,V3,V4
      OPEN(UNIT = 11, FILE = 'CIMJMM.OUT')
C     WRITE(*,*) 'ENTER COMPRESSION RATIO :'
C     READ(*,*) CR
C     WRITE(*,*) 'ENTER RAF :'
C     READ(*,*) RAF
C     WRITE(*,*) 'ENTER P1(ATM) :'
C     READ(*,*) P1
C     WRITE(*,*) 'ENTER SPEED (RPM) :'
C     READ(*,*) RPM
C     ================================================================
                                 CALL ICS
C     IN THIS SUBROUTINE AIR STANDARD DIESEL CYCLE (ASDEL) IS
C     SIMULATED.
```

```
C       IT CALCULATES P,V,T VALUES AT STATE POINTS 1 TO 4 IN
C       THE CYCLE.
C       WORKING MEDIUM IS ASSUMED TO BE AIR WITH CONSTANT CP
C       AND CV VALUES.
C       THERE IS NO PRESSURE RISE DURING COMBUSTION AND ONLY
C       CUT OFF RATIO IS TO BE GIVEN.
C       COMBUSTION IS ASSUMED TO BE ADIABATIC AND AT CONSTANT
C       PRESSURE.
C       ==================================================================
                                CALL FCS
C       IN THIS SUBROUTINE FUEL-AIR CYCLE (FCS) IS SIMULATED.
C       IT CALCULATES P,V,T VALUES AT STATE POINTS O TO 4 IN THE
C       THE CYCLE
C       THE WORKING MEDIUM IS ASSUMED TO BE FUEL AND AIR WITH
C       VARIABLE CP AND CV VALUES.
C       PRESSURE CHANGE DUE TO COMBUSTION IS CALCULATED USING
C       THE ADIABATIC FLAME TEMPERATURE CALCULATIONS.
C       THE COMBUSTION IS ASSUMED TO BE INSTANTANEOUS AND AT
C       CONSTANT PRESSURE.
C       ==================================================================
                                CALL PCS
C       THIS SUBROUTINE SIMULATES IDEAL DIESEL CYCLE WITH PROGRESSIVE
C       COMBUSTION (PCS)
C       IT CALCULATES P,V,T VALUES AT VARIOUS POINTS OF INTEREST
C       AND ALSO VALUES OF PRESSURE & VOLUME FOR EVERY DEGREE
C       CRANK ANGLE.
C       THE WORKING MEDIUM IS ASSUMED TO BE FUEL AND AIR WITH
C       VARIABLE CP AND CV VALUES
C       COMBUSTION IS ASSUMED TO TAKE PLACE OVER PERIOD OF CRANK
C       ANGLE ROTATION AND THE PRESSURE RISE DUE TO COMBUSTION
C       IS CALCULATED USING PREGRESSIVE COMBUSTION.
C       HEAT TRANSFER EFFECT IS INCLUDED.
C       ==================================================================
                                CALL ACS
C       THIS SUBROUTINE SIMULATES AN ACTUAL DIESEL CYCLE (ACS).
C       IT CALCULATES P,V,T VALUES AT THE VARIOUS POINT OF INTEREST
C       AND ALSO VALUES OF PRESSURE & VOLUME AT VARIOUS CRANK ANGLES.
C       THE WORKING MEDIUM IS ASSUMED TO BE FUEL AND AIR WITH
C       VARIABLE CP AND CV VALUES.
C       PROGRESSIVE COMBUSTION IS ASSUMED AND HEAT TRANSFER
C       EFFECT IS INCLUDED.
C       PROVISIONS ARE MADE TO INCORPORATE VARIOUS MODELS FOR
C       COMBUSTION, HEAT TRANSFER AND VALVE AREA CALCULATIONS.
C       GAS EXCHANGE PROCESSS IS INCLUDED AND THE EFFECT OF
C       VALVE OVERLAP CAN BE STUDIED.
C       ==================================================================
```

```
                    CALL PRINT2
C       THIS SUBROUTINE PRINTS OUT RESULTS
C       ALTERATIONS MAY BE MADE  TO GET THE PRINT OUT IN
C       THE REQUIRED STYLE
C       ================================================================
        CLOSE(UNIT = 11)
        STOP
        END
C*********************************************************************
                    SUBROUTINE ICS
C*********************************************************************
      REAL KA,KP,KR,MC,MEP, MH, MO, MOLWTP,NA, N,NADNAX,NMO,
     1     NP,NPO,NX
      CHARACTER*10 XV,YZ
      LOGICAL IPTTHR,IPRINT,ISUPCH,ISUPET,PVPRNT
       COMMON/GEOM/B,CR,CRL,S,VBDC,VDISP,VDVBDC(720),VOLUME(800),
     #           VTDC
       COMMON/THERM/HRP,MOLWTP(5),P1,P2,P3,P4,T1,T2,T3,T4,T5,T6,TA,
     #           V1,V2,V3,V4
       COMMON/CHEM/KA,KP,KR,N(5),NA,NADNAX,NMO,NP,NPO,NX,RMR,KRR,
     #           MC,MH,MO,R,RLITAT,RMIX,Y,YCC,YMIN,PMOLWT
       COMMON/CPCOEF/CV,ACPF,BCPF,ACPA,BCPA,AL(5),AH(5),
     #           BL(5),BH(5),CL(5),CH(5)
       COMMON/ARRAY/DELV(750),DV(750),P(800),DELN(800),DELP(800),
     #           THETA(800),V(800)
       COMMON/GEN/CB(40,4),A(10,16),C(5),D(5),EETAH,RAF,F(5),
     #           FPM,FVM,G(5),MEP,PID4,POWER,RPM
       COMMON/IDIES/PA,VR,STROKE
       COMMON/PSSA/CPR,DT,DTHDDT,IBC,IECPC,IEC,GASMAS,WCOMP,WEXP,NCEXG,
     #           WNET,WLOOP,PSPS,ML
       COMMON/PRINTS/XV(16),YZ(32)
       COMMON/ABC/WT,COMEFF,CPA,NM
C   ******    STATEMENT FUNCTION DEFINITION FOR THE CALCULATION OF
C   ******    VOLUME AT VARIOUS CRANK ANGLES.
       VOL(THETAR)=VDISP*(CR/(CR-1.)-(1.-COS(THETAR))/2. +
     1            (CRL/S)-.5*SQRT((2.*CRL/S)**2-(ABS(SIN(THETAR)))**2))
       WRITE(11,555)
 555   FORMAT(20X,'SIMULATION OF AIR STANDARD DIESEL CYCLE',//20X,
     1 38(1H-))
         IPRI=0
         PVPRNT=.TRUE.
         PSPS=RPM/120.
C        IF(STROKE.EQ.2.)PSPS=RPM/60.
         VDISP = PID4*B*B*S*1.0E-09
         VBDC = CR/(CR-1.)*VDISP
         VTDC = VBDC-VDISP
```

```
      V2 = VTDC
      V4 = VBDC
      V3 = V2*VR
      T2 = T1*CR**(KA-1.)
      P2 = P1*CR**KA
      T3 = VR*T2
      P3 = P2
      T4 = T3*(V3/VBDC)**(KA-1.)
      P4 = P3/((V4/V3)**KA)
      NA = (P1*FPM)*(VBDC*FVM)*1000.0/(R*T1)
C  ******      NM IS THE NUMBER OF KMOLS IN THE CYCLE.
      WCOMP = CV*(T2-T1)*NA
      WCOMB = R*(T3-T2)*NA
      WEXP = CV*(T3-T4)*NA
      WNET = WEXP + WCOMB - WCOMP
      EETAH = (1.0- (T4-T1)/(KA*(T3-T2)))*100.0
      POWER = WNET*PSPS*.001
      MEP = WNET/(VDISP*FPM)
      IF(IPRI.EQ.0) WRITE(11,25)
 25   FORMAT(//5X,72(1H-)/7X,'CR',5X,'T1(K)',5X,'T2(K)',6X,'T3(K)',7X,
     1        'T4(K)',3X,'WNET(KJ/KMOL)',4X,'EETAH',/5X,72(1H-))
      WRITE(11,30) CR,T1,T2,T3,T4,WNET,EETAH
 30   FORMAT(/5X,F5.2,4X,F4.0,3F11.2,F12.3,F14.3//5X,72(1H-))
      WRITE(11,40)EETAH
 40   FORMAT(//5X,'AIR STANDARD EFFFICIENCY OF DIESEL CYCLE =',F7.3,
     # ' %'//)
 132  FORMAT(3X,7F10.3)
      CB(1,1) = P1
      CB(2,1) = VBDC*1.0E06
      CB(3,1) = T1
      CB(4,1) = P2
      CB(5,1) = VTDC*1.0E06
      CB(6,1) = T2
      CB(7,1) = P3
      CB(8,1) = V3*1.0E+06
      CB(9,1) = T3
      CB(10,1) = P4
      CB(11,1) = VBDC*1.0E06
      CB(12,1) = T4
      CB(13,1) = 10000000
      CB(14,1) = 10000000
      CB(15,1) = 100000000
      CB(16,1) = 100000000
      CB(17,1) = 100000000
      CB(18,1) = 100000000
      CB(19,1) = WEXP
```

```
      CB(20,1) = WCOMP
      CB(21,1) = WCOMB
      CB(22,1) = 0.0
      CB(23,1) = WNET
      CB(24,1) = POWER
      CB(25,1) = EETAH
      CB(26,1) = 10000000
      CB(27,1) = 1.0
      CB(28,1) = MEP
      CB(29,1) = MEP
      CB(30,1) = POWER
      CB(31,1) = EETAH
      CB(32,1) = 100.0
C     TO GET P-V VALUES SET PVPRNT =.TRUE. IN THIS SUBROUTINE
      IF(.NOT.PVPRNT) GO TO 108
      WRITE(11,600)
  600 FORMAT(5X,'ANGLE',9X,'PRESSURE',6X,'VOLUME'/,
     #       5X,' DEG.',9X,'  (ATM) ',6X,' (M3) '/)
      PID=3.1415926/180.
      INCR=10
      V(1)=VOL(PID)
      P(1)=P1
      DO 700 I=1,179
      THETAR=(I+1)*PID
      V(I+1)=VOL(THETAR)
      P(I+1)=P(I)*(V(I)/V(I+1))**KA
  700 CONTINUE
      DO 800 J=1,180,INCR
      K=J-1
      WRITE(11,750) K,P(J),V(J)
  800 CONTINUE
      WRITE(11,750) I,P(180),V(180)
      P(180)=P3
      V(180)=VOL(180*PID)
      DO 900 I=180,359
      THETAR=(I+1)*PID
      V(I+1)=VOL(THETAR)
      P(I+1)=P(I)/((V(I+1)/V(I))**KA)
  900 CONTINUE
      DO 1000 J=180,360,INCR
      WRITE(11,750) J,P(J),V(J)
 1000 CONTINUE
  750 FORMAT(5X,I5,5X,F10.3,5X,F10.8/)
      WRITE(*,*) 'AIR STD. DIESEL CYCLE OVER'
  108 RETURN
      END
```

```
C*************************************************************************
                            SUBROUTINE FCS
C*************************************************************************
      REAL KA,KP,KR,MC,MEP, MH, MO, MOLWTP,NA, N,NM,NADNAX,NMO,
     1     NP,NPO,NX
      LOGICAL IPTTHR, ISUPCH, ISUPET, IPRINT, HT_INDEX
      CHARACTER*10 XV,YZ
      COMMON/GEOM/B,CR,CRL,S,VBDC,VDISP,VDVBDC(720),VOLUME(800),
     #          VTDC
      COMMON/THERM/HRP,MOLWTP(5),P1,P2,P3,P4,T1,T2,T3,T4,T5,T6,TA,
     #           V1,V2,V3,V4
      COMMON/CHEM/KA,KP,KR,N(5),NA,NADNAX,NMO,NP,NPO,NX,RMR,KRR,
     #          MC,MH,MO,R,RLITAT,RMIX,Y,YCC,YMIN,PMOLWT
      COMMON/CPCOEF/CV,ACPF,BCPF,ACPA,BCPA,AL(5),AH(5),
     #            BL(5),BH(5),CL(5),CH(5)
      COMMON/INDEX/IPTTHR,IPRINT,NCYCLE,HT_INDEX
      COMMON/GEN/CB(40,4),A(10,16),C(5),D(5),EETAH,RAF,F(5),
     #        FPM,FVM,G(5),MEP,PID4,POWER,RPM
      COMMON/SUPECH/EFOCOM,EFOTUR,ISUPCH,ISUPET
      COMMON/IDIES/PA,VR,STROKE
      COMMON/PSSA/CPR,DT,DTHDDT,IBC,IECPC,IEC,GASMAS,WCOMP,WEXP,NCEXG,
     #          WNET,WLOOP,PSPS,ML
      COMMON/PRINTS/XV(16),YZ(32)
      COMMON/III/IFPCO
      COMMON/ARRAY/DELV(750),DV(750),P(800),DELN(800),DELP(800),
     #          THETA(800),V(800)
C    ******     STATEMENT FUNCTION DEFINITION FOR THE CALCULATION OF
C    ******     VOLUME AT VARIOUS CRANK ANGLES.
      VOL(THETAR)=VDISP*(CR/(CR-1.)-(1.-COS(THETAR))/2. +
     1          (CRL/S)-.5*SQRT((2.*CRL/S)**2-(ABS(SIN(THETAR)))**2))
      IFPCO = 2
C    *****      CONVERSION OF BORE AND STROKE IN METERS.
      SR = 1.2
      BM = 0.001*B
      SM = 0.001*S
      RCR = CR/(CR-1.)
      AREA = PID4*BM*BM
      SAREA = PID4*4.*BM*SM*RCR
C    ******     CALCULATION OF VARIOUS VOLUMES
      VDISP = PID4*B*B*S*1.E-06
      VBDC = CR/(CR-1.)*VDISP
      IF(STROKE.EQ.2.) VBDC = (CR*SR/(SR*CR-1.))*VDISP
      VTDC = VBDC - VDISP
      IF(STROKE.EQ.2.) V1 = CR*VTDC
C   ******     INITIALLY KR IS ASSUMED TO BE 1.40
      KR = 1.4
```

```
      IF(ISUPET.OR.ISUPCH) TA = 300.
      IF(ISUPET.OR.ISUPCH) T1 = TA*(((P1/PA)**((KR-1.)/KR)-1.)
     #                       /EFOCOM+1.)
      IF(STROKE.NE.2) V1 = VBDC
C  ******INITIALISE NX=0.
      NX = 0.
C   ******    CALCULATION OF AIR-FUEL RATIO.
C   ******    YCC REPRESENTS CHEMICALLY CORRECT O2/FUEL RATIO.
C   ******    Y   REPRESENTS ACTUAL O2/FUEL RATIO.
C   ******    Y < YCC  MEANS RICH MIXTURE.
C   ******    Y > YCC  MEANS LEAN MIXTURE.
C   ******    YMIN REPRESENTS MINIMUM O2 REQUIRED.
      YCC = MC+0.25*MH-0.5*MO
      YMIN = YCC-.5*MC
      Y = YCC*RAF
      AFR = 4.76*Y
C   ******    CALCULATION OF TEMPERATURE DROP DUE TO THE
C   ******    VAPORISATION OF FUEL.
C     DELTAT(INDF)=HFGF(INDF)/(AFR*CPA+(ACPF(INDF)+BCPF(INDF)*TA))
C     IF(.NOT.NODROP)  TM=TA-DELTAT(INDF)
C     IF(.NOT.NODROP)  T1=TM
C     TM=300.
C     YMIN=YCC-MC/2.
      IF(STROKE.NE.2.)GO TO 8
      V12S = V1
      VO = 2.*VDISP
      T1 = TA
      EE = 1./CR-1.
      M1 = PA*(V1-VTDC)/(RLITAT*TA)
      X1 = PA*V1/RLITAT
    8 CONTINUE
      IF(Y.GE.YCC)GO TO 101
C   ******    N(1) TO N(5) REPRESENT THE EXHAUST GAS CONSTITUENTS.
C   ******    N(1):CO;  N(2):CO2;  N(3):H2O;   N(4):N2;  N(5):O2.
      N(1) = 2.*(YCC-Y)
      N(2) = 2.*(Y-YMIN)
      N(3) = MH/2.
      N(4) = 3.76*Y
      N(5) = 0.
      NPO = N(1)+N(2)+N(3)+N(4)+N(5)
      GO TO 102
  101 N(1) = 0.
      N(2) = MC
      N(3) = MH/2.
      N(4) = 3.76*Y
      N(5) = Y-YCC
```

```
      NPO = N(1)+N(2)+N(3)+N(4)+N(5)
 102  CONTINUE
C  ****** CALCULATION OF AVERAGE MOL. WT. AND GAS CONSTANT.
      NMO = 1.0+4.76*Y
      NA = P1*VBDC/(RLITAT*T1)
      NM = NA + NA/AFR
      IF(STROKE.EQ.2.) NA = P1*V1/(RLITAT*T1)
      J= 0
      L= 0
      SN = 0.0
      SUM = 0.0
      DO 65 I = 1,NCEXG
      SN = SN + N(I)
      SUM = SUM + N(I)*MOLWTP(I)
  65  CONTINUE
      AMOLWT = SUM/SN
      RMIX= R/AMOLWT
      K = 0
      NCYCLE = 0
 108  NCYCLE = NCYCLE+1
      K = K+1
      TREF = T1
      CPR = ACPA+BCPA*T1
      CPR = (CPR*NA+NX*CP(T1))/(NA+NX)
      KR = CPR/(CPR-R)
C     NMDNMX = NM/(NM+NX)
C  ******    CALCULATION OF INDEX FOR COMPRESSION(KR)
C  ******    FOR THE RELATION P*V**KR=C.
C     T = T1
C     IF(ITMT1.EQ.1) T = TM
C     CPF = ACPF(INDF)+BCPF(INDF)*T
C     CPO2 = ACPO2+BCPO2*T
C     CPN2 = ACPN2+BCPN2*T
C     CPR = (CPF+Y*CPO2+3.76*Y*CPN2)/NMO
C     CPR = (CPR*NM+NX*(CP(T)+R))/(NM+NX)
C     KR  = CPR/(CPR-R)
C   *****     P, V, T VALUES AT STATE POINT 2.
      P2 = P1*CR**KR
      V2 = VTDC
      T2 = T1*CR**(KR-1.)
C  *****      CALCULATION OF QP
      CM = NM/NMO+NX/NPO
      NP = NPO*CM
C     URPF = HRPF(INDF)-R*298.*(NPO-NMO)
C     IF(Y.LE.YCC) QV = -(URPF+2.*(YCC-Y)*281400.)*NM/NMO
C     IF(Y.GT.YCC) QV = -URPF*NM/NMO
```

```
      QP = -(HRP + N(1)*282800.0)*(NM/NMO)
C *****      CALCULATION OF T3 USINGING NEWTON-RAPHSON METHOD.
      NITRN = 0
      T = 3000.
151   TNEW = T-(CM*(HP(T)-HP(T2))-QP)/CP(T)
      NITRN = NITRN+1
      IF(ABS(T-TNEW).LT.0.1) GO TO 16
      IF(NITRN.GT.100) GO TO 16
      T = TNEW
      GO TO 151
16    CONTINUE
C  *****      P, V, T VALUES AT STATE POINT 3.
      T3 = TNEW
      P3 = P2
      V3 = NP*RLITAT*T3/P2
      VR = V3/V2
      V1 = VBDC
C  *****     CALCULATION OF INDEX FOR EXPANSION (KP)
C  *****     FOR THE RELATION P*V**KP = C.
      CPP = CP(T3)
      KP = CPP/(CPP-R)
C  *****     P, V, T VALUES AT STATE POINT 4.
      P4 = P3/((VBDC/V3)**KP)
      V4 = VBDC
      IF(STROKE.EQ.2.) V4 = V1
      T4 = T3*(V3/VBDC)**(KP-1.)
      P5 = PA
      IF(IPTTHR) P5 = P1
      IF(ISUPCH) P5 = PA
C  ******     CALCULATION OF NET WORK OUTPUT,THERMAL EFFICIENCY
C  ******     AND MEAN EFFECTIVE PRESSURE.
      WLOOP = 0.
      WCOMP = (NA+NX)*(CPR-R)*(T2-T1)
      UPT3 = CM*HP(T3)-R*NP*T3
      UPT4 = CM*HP(T4)-R*NP*T4
      WCOMB = (P2*FPM)*(V3-V2)*FVM
      WEXP = UPT3-UPT4
C  ******     CALCULATIONS FOR SUPERCHARGED ENGINES.
C  ******     BOTH GEAR DRIVEN COMPRESSOR & EXHAUST
C  ******     DRIVEN SUPERCHARGERS ARE CONSIDERED.
      IF(.NOT. ISUPET) GO TO 200
      RHS = (1.+NA*CPR*(T1-TA)*(P4/PA)**((KP-1.)/KP)/
     #      (NP*CPP*T4*EFOTUR))
C  ******    P5 REPRESENT THE EXHAUST GAS PRESSURE ENTERING THE TURBINE.
      P5 = RHS**(KP/(KP-1.))*PA
      WLOOP = 101.325*(P1-P5)*VDISP
```

```
      WNET = WEXP + WCOMB - WCOMP + WLOOP
      GO TO 300
  200 CONTINUE
      WNET = WCOMB + WEXP - WCOMP - WLOOP
      IF(.NOT.ISUPCH) GO TO 300
      WSPCH = NA*CPR*(T1-TA)
      WLOOP = 101.325*(P1-PA)*VDISP
      WNET = WCOMB + WEXP - WCOMP - WSPCH + WLOOP
  300 CONTINUE
      EETATH = (WNET*NMO)/(-HRP*NM)*100.
      T5 = T4*(P5/P4)**((KP-1.)/KP)
      IF(STROKE.NE.2.) GO TO 18
      TX = T4*(PA/P4)**((KP-1.)/KP)
      T5 = TA/(1.-(TX-TA)/TX*EXP(EE))
      V5 = V4
      V6 = VBDC
      VO = 2.*VDISP
      VR = VO/(V1-V2)
      X2 = X1*EXP(EE)
      T52S = TA/(1.-((TX-TA)/TX)*EXP(EE))
      NX5 = PA*V1*EXP(EE)/(RLITAT*T5)
      NA5 = PA*V1/(RLITAT*T5)-NX5
      NA1 = (NA5+PA*(VBDC-V1)/(RLITAT*TA))/SR
      T62S = ((NA5+NX5)*T52S+PA*(VBDC-V12S)/(RLITAT*TA)*TA)/
     1       ((NA5+NX5)+PA*(VBDC-V12S)/(RLITAT*TA))
      NX1 = NX5/SR
      T6 = T62S
      T12S = T62S
      WEXP2S = (HP(T3)-HP(T4))*CM
      WCOMP2 = (NA1+NX1)*CP(T2)*(T2-T1)
      WCC2S = PA*V2*(CR-1.)*((VR/(KR-1.))*(((VR/(VR-1.))**(KR-1.))
     1       -1.)-1.)
      WCC2S = 101.325*WCC2S
      WNET = WEXP2S-WCOMP2-WCC2S
   18 CONTINUE
      MEP = WNET/(VDISP*101.325)
C     ******    PSPS IS THE NUMBER OF POWER STROKES PER SEC.
      PSPS = RPM/120.
      IF(STROKE.EQ.2.) PSPS = RPM/60.
C     *******   NOTE:  WNET IS IN JOULES.
      POWER  =  WNET*PSPS*0.001
      IF(IPTTHR) T6 = T5*(P1/P5)**((KP-1.)/KP)
      NX = P1*VTDC/(RLITAT*T5)
      IF(IPTTHR) NX = PA*VTDC/(RLITAT*T5)
      NA = P1*VBDC/(RLITAT*T1)-NX
      NADNAX = NA/(NA+NX)
```

```
      IF(STROKE.EQ.2.) NA = NA1
      IF(STROKE.EQ.2.) NX = NX1
      IF(IPTTHR) GO TO 888
      TEMP = TA/T5-T6/T5
      T1 = CR*TA/(CR+P5/P1*TEMP)
      WLOOP = (P5-P1)*VDISP*101.325
      WNET = WCOMB+WEXP-WCOMP-WLOOP
      EETATH = (WNET*NMO)/(-HRP*NM)*100.
888   IF(NCYCLE.EQ.1) CALL WRITE1
 78   IF(STROKE.EQ.2) T1 = T62S
      A(K,1) = TREF
      A(K,2) = T2
      A(K,3) = T3
      A(K,4) = T4
      A(K,5) = T5
      A(K,6) = P2
      A(K,7) = P3
      A(K,8) = P4
      A(K,9) = VR
      A(K,10) = KR
      A(K,11) = KP
      A(K,12) = NADNAX
      A(K,13) = POWER
      A(K,14) = EETATH
      A(K,15) = MEP
      A(K,16) = NITRN
      IF(.NOT.IPTTHR) T1 = CR*TA/(CR-1.+(TA/T5))
      IF(ISUPET .OR. ISUPCH) GOTO 109
      IF(ABS(T1-TREF).GT.0.01) GO TO 108
109   IF(IPRINT) CALL WRITE2
      CB(1,2) = P1
      CB(2,2) = VBDC/FVM
      CB(3,2) = T1
      CB(4,2)  = P2
      CB(5,2)  = VTDC/FVM
      CB(6,2)  = T2
      CB(7,2)  = P3
      CB(8,2)  = V3/FVM
      CB(9,2)  = T3
      CB(10,2) = P4
      CB(11,2) = VBDC/FVM
      CB(12,2) = T4
      CB(13,2) = P5
      CB(14,2) = VTDC/FVM
      CB(15,2) = T5
      CB(16,2) = P1
```

```
      CB(17,2) = VTDC/FVM
      CB(18,2) = T6
      CB(19,2) = WEXP
      CB(20,2) = WCOMP
      CB(21,2) = WCOMB
      CB(22,2) = WLOOP
      CB(23,2) = WNET
      CB(24,2) = POWER
      CB(25,2) = EETATH
      CB(26,2) = 1000000
      CB(27,2) = NADNAX
      CB(28,2) = MEP
      CB(29,2) = MEP
      CB(30,2) = POWER
      CB(31,2) = EETATH
      CB(32,2) = 100.0
      PID = 3.1415926/180.
      DO 121 TH = 180.0,360.0,0.5
         DIFF = ABS(VOL(TH*PID)-V3)
 IF(DIFF.LE.0.001) THEN
    THETA3 = TH
    GOTO 122
         ENDIF
121   CONTINUE
122   WRITE(*,*) ' THETA3 = ', THETA3
      WRITE(11,600)
600   FORMAT(///5X,'ANGLE',9X,'PRESSURE',6X,'VOLUME',9X,'VOLUME',/
   #        5X,' DEG.',9X,' (ATM) ',6X,' (M3) ',9X, ' RATIO'/)
      INCR = 10
      V(1) = VOL(PID)
      P(1) = 0.8
      DO 700 I = 1,179
      THETAR = (I+1)*PID
      V(I+1) = VOL(THETAR)
      P(I+1) = P(I)*(VOL(I*PID)/VOL(THETAR))**KA
      VDVBDC(I+1) = V(I+1)/VBDC
700   CONTINUE
      DO 800 J = 1,180
      WRITE(11,750) J,P(J),V(J),VDVBDC(J)
800   CONTINUE
      V3RATIO = VOL(THETA3*PID)/VBDC
      ITHETA3 = IFIX(THETA3)
      DO 801 J = 181,ITHETA3
      P(J) = P2
      V(J) = VOL(J*PID)
      VDVBDC(J) = V(J)/VBDC
```

```
      WRITE(11,750) J,P(J),V(J),VDVBDC(J)
 801  CONTINUE
      DO 900 I = ITHETA3,359
      THETAR = (I+1)*PID
      V(I+1) = VOL(THETAR)
      P(I+1) = P(I)/(VOL(THETAR)/VOL(I*PID))**KA
      VDVBDC(I+1) = V(I)/VBDC
      WRITE(11,750) I+1,P(I+1),V(I+1),VDVBDC(I+1)
 900  CONTINUE
 750 FORMAT(5X,I5,5X,F10.3,5X,F10.8,5X,F10.8/)
      WRITE(*,*) 'IDEAL DIESEL CYCLE OVER'
      RETURN
      END
C*********************************************************************
                         SUBROUTINE PCS
C*********************************************************************
      REAL KP,KR,MC,MEP, MH, MO, MOLWTP,N,NA,NM,NADNAX,NMO,
     &    NP,NPO,NX,MECHEF
      INTEGER EVO,EVC
      LOGICAL IPTTHR,IPRINT, HT_INDEX
      CHARACTER*10 XV,YZ
      COMMON/GEOM/B,CR,CRL,S,VBDC,VDISP,VDVBDC(720),VOLUME(800),
     #           VTDC
      COMMON/THERM/HRP,MOLWTP(5),P1,P2,P3,P4,T1,T2,T3,T4,T5,T6,TA,
     #            V1,V2,V3,V4
      COMMON/CHEM/KA,KP,KR,N(5),NA,NADNAX,NMO,NP,NPO,NX,RMR,KRR,
     #           MC,MH,MO,R,RLITAT,RMIX,Y,YCC,YMIN,PMOLWT
      COMMON/CPCOEF/CV,ACPF,BCPF,ACPA,BCPA,AL(5),AH(5),
     #            BL(5),BH(5),CL(5),CH(5)
      COMMON/INDEX/IPTTHR,IPRINT,NCYCLE,HT_INDEX
      COMMON/GEN/CB(40,4),A(10,16),C(5),D(5),EETAH,RAF,F(5),
     #          FPM,FVM,G(5),MEP,PID4,POWER,RPM
      COMMON/INEXH/IVO,IVC,EVO,EVC,AEV,AIV
      COMMON/COMBUN/WCOMB,BRMAX
      COMMON/IDIES/PA,VR,STROKE
      COMMON/HTMOD/MODFHT
      COMMON/VALARE/D1,BETA,MODFVA
      COMMON/OVERL/PID,OMEGA,DTMAX,CAINT,AM,BDCMAS
      COMMON/PSSA/CPR,DT,DTHDDT,IBC,IECPC,IEC,GASMAS,WCOMP,WEXP,NCEXG,
     #           WNET,WLOOP,PSPS,ML
       COMMON/ARRAY/DELV(750),DV(750),P(800),DELN(800),DELP(800),
     #           THETA(800),V(800)
      COMMON/PROG/CM,BR,P3D
      COMMON/ABC/WT,COMEFF,CPA,NM
      COMMON/HEATRA/AREA,BM,RCR,SAREA,SM,TW,VP
      COMMON/FRICT/PIMF,PEMF,PSL,NPR,FMEP
```

```
      COMMON/FRPMOD/MODFRP
      COMMON/ABCD/DN,ITETA,ITETA3,L
      COMMON/PRINTS/XV(16),YZ(32)
      COMMON/III/IFPCO
      COMMON/STORE/PRR(800),TEMP(800),HRR(800)
      COMMON/ANGLE/ICB,ICE,IMX,ID
      COMMON/TFCOM/COMDUR,M
      COMMON/MAX/PRMAX,ICAMAX,JCAMAX
      COMMON/COMOD/MODCOM
      COMMON/HRMOD/MODHR
      COMMON/MATRX/CRANG(800),PRESS(800),VOLRAT(800),TMPR(800)
      COMMON/COMB/PMAX,TPMAX
      VOL(THETAR)=VDISP*(CR/(CR-1.)-(1.-COS(THETAR))/2. +
     1             (CRL/S)-.5*SQRT((2.*CRL/S)**2-(ABS(SIN(THETAR)))**2))
      WRITE(*,*)
      WRITE(*,*)
      WRITE(*,*) 'ENTER IBC VALUE FOR PROGRESSIVE COMBUSTION'
      WRITE(*,*) 'FOR P.C IBC IS 170 TO 190 DEG C.A'
      READ(*,*) IBC
      URP = -6274940.0
      IFPCO = 0
      MODCOM = 1
      HT_INDEX = .FALSE.
      CALL WRITE1
      ML = 0
      NX = 0.0
      T1 = 300.0
      ICYC = 1
  111 CONTINUE
      CALL PRECAL
      CALL COMPRN
      CALL COMBN
      CALL EXPN
C     IF(ICYC .EQ. 1) CALL WRITE1
      ICYC = ICYC+1
      TREF = T1
      P4 = P(EVO)
      P5 = PA
      T5 = T4*(P5/P4)**((KP-1.0)/KP)
      NX = P1*VTDC/(RLITAT*T5)
      NA = P1*VBDC/(RLITAT*T1) - NX
      NM = NA+NA/(4.76*Y)
      T1 = CR*TA/(CR-1.0 + (TA/T5))
      IF(ABS(TREF-T1).GT.0.05) GO TO 111
      IF(IPRINT) CALL PRINT1
      PSPS = RPM/120.0
```

```
      POWER = WNET*PSPS*0.001
      EETAH = (WNET*NMO)/(-HRP*NM)*100.0
      MEP = WNET/(VDISP*101.325)
      CALL FMEPC
      BMEP = MEP-FMEP
      BPOWER = BMEP*101.325*VDISP*PSPS/1000.0
      MECHEF = BMEP/MEP*100.0
      BRTHEF = MECHEF*EETAH/100.0
      IF(MODCOM.EQ.2) IBC = ICB
      CB(1,3) = P1
      CB(2,3) = VBDC/FVM
      CB(3,3) = T1
      CB(4,3) = P(IBC)
      AIBC = FLOAT(IBC)*PID
      CB(5,3) = VOL(AIBC)/FVM
      CB(6,3) = TEMP(IBC)
      CB(7,3) = PMAX
      CB(8,3) = VOL(ICE*PID)/FVM
      IF(MODCOM .EQ. 1) CB(8,3) = V3/FVM
      CB(9,3)   = TPMAX
      CB(10,3) = P4
      CB(11,3) = VBDC/FVM
      CB(12,3) = T4
      CB(13,3) = P5
      CB(14,3) = VTDC/FVM
      CB(15,3) = T5
      CB(16,3) = 1000000
      CB(17,3) = 1000000
      CB(18,3) = 1000000
      CB(19,3) = WEXP
      CB(20,3) = WCOMP
      CB(21,3) = WCOMB
      CB(22,3) = 0.0
      CB(23,3) = WNET
      CB(24,3) = POWER
      CB(25,3) = EETAH
      CB(26,3) = 10000000
      CB(27,3) = NADNAX
      CB(28,3) = MEP
      CB(29,3) = BMEP
      CB(30,3) = BPOWER
      CB(31,3) = BRTHEF
      CB(32,3) = MECHEF
      WRITE(*,*) 'IDEAL DIESEL CYCLE WITH P.C OVER'
      RETURN
      END
```

```
C       ******************************************************************
                            SUBROUTINE ACS
C       ******************************************************************
        REAL KA,KP,KR,MC,MEP, MH, MO, MOLWTP,NA, N,NM,NADNAX,NMO,
     #       NP,NPO,NX,MECHEF,KRR
        INTEGER EVO,EVC
        LOGICAL IPTTHR,IPRINT,HT_INDEX
        COMMON/GEOM/B,CR,CRL,S,VBDC,VDISP,VDVBDC(720),VOLUME(800),
     #          VTDC
        COMMON/THERM/HRP,MOLWTP(5),P1,P2,P3,P4,T1,T2,T3,T4,T5,T6,TA,
     #            V1,V2,V3,V4
        COMMON/CHEM/KA,KP,KR,N(5),NA,NADNAX,NMO,NP,NPO,NX,RMR,KRR,
     #           MC,MH,MO,R,RLITAT,RMIX,Y,YCC,YMIN,PMOLWT
        COMMON/CPCOEF/CV,ACPF,BCPF,ACPA,BCPA,AL(5),AH(5),
     #            BL(5),BH(5),CL(5),CH(5)
        COMMON/INDEX/IPTTHR,IPRINT,NCYCLE,HT_INDEX
        COMMON/GEN/CB(40,4),A(10,16),C(5),D(5),EETAH,RAF,F(5),
     #           FPM,FVM,G(5),MEP,PID4,POWER,RPM
        COMMON/INEXH/IVO,IVC,EVO,EVC,AEV,AIV
        COMMON/COMBUN/WCOMB,BRMAX
        COMMON/IDIES/PA,VR,STROKE
        COMMON/PSSA/CPR,DT,DTHDDT,IBC,IECPC,IEC,GASMAS,WCOMP,WEXP,NCEXG,
     #           WNET,WLOOP,PSPS,ML
        COMMON/ARRAY/DELV(750),DV(750),P(800),DELN(800),DELP(800),
     #           THETA(800),V(800)
        COMMON/FRICT/PIMF,PEMF,PSL,NPR,FMEP
        COMMON/ABCD/DN,ITETA,ITETA3,L
        COMMON/III/IFPCO
        COMMON/STORE/PRR(800),TEMP(800),HRR(800)
        COMMON/ANGLE/ICB,ICE,IMX,ID
        COMMON/TFCOM/COMDUR,M
        COMMON/MAX/PRMAX,ICAMAX,JCAMAX
        COMMON/COMOD/MODCOM
        COMMON/HRMOD/MODHR
        COMMON/MATRX/CRANG(800),PRESS(800),VOLRAT(800),TMPR(800)
        COMMON/COMB/PMAX,TPMAX
        COMMON/GAS/PR(800),VOLD(800),TE(800),NV,T,PEVC,VOLEFF
        WRITE(*,*)
        WRITE(*,*)
        WRITE(*,*) 'ENTER IBC VALUE FOR ZERO-DIMENSIONAL MODEL'
        WRITE(*,*) 'FOR Z.D.M IBC IS 153 DEG C.A (FOR THIS ENGINE)'
        READ(*,*) IBC
        URP = -6274940.0
        PSPS = RPM/120.0
        IFPCO = 1
        MODCOM = 2
```

```
      HT_INDEX = .TRUE.
      ML = 0
      NX = 0.0
      T1 = TA
      P1 = PA
      IPRIN = 1
      KOUNT = 0
 222  CONTINUE
      TREF = T1
      CALL PRECAL
      CALL COMPRN
      CALL COMBN
      CALL EXPN
      CALL GASEX
      NA = P1*VOLUME(IVC-719)/(RLITAT*T1)-NX
      NM = NA+NA/(4.76*Y)
      KOUNT = KOUNT+1
      IF(KOUNT.GT.20) GOTO 223
      IF((ABS(TREF-T1).GT.0.5).OR.(KOUNT.EQ.1)) GO TO 222
      CALL WRITE1
      IF(IPRINT) CALL PRINT1
      IF(IPRINT) CALL PRINT3
223   WNET = WNET-WLOOP
      POWER = WNET*PSPS*.001
      EETAH = WNET/(-HRP*NM/NMO)*100.0
      MEP = WNET/(VDISP*101.325)
      CALL FMEPC
      BMEP = MEP-FMEP
      MECHEF = BMEP/MEP
      BPOWER = BMEP*101.325*VDISP*PSPS/1000.0
      BRTHEF = MECHEF*EETAH
      CB(1,4)  = P1
      CB(2,4)  = VOLUME(EVO)/FVM
      CB(3,4)  = T1
      CB(4,4)  = P(IBC)
      CB(5,4)  = VOLUME(IBC)/FVM
      CB(6,4)  = TEMP(IBC)
      CB(7,4)  = PMAX
      CB(8,4)  = VOLUME(IEC)/FVM
      CB(9,4)  = TPMAX
      CB(10,4) = P(EVO)
      CB(11,4) = VOLUME(EVO)/FVM
      CB(12,4) = T4
      CB(13,4) = PEVC
      CB(14,4) = VOLUME(EVC)/FVM
      CB(15,4) = T5
```

```
      CB(16,4) = 1000000
      CB(17,4) = 1000000
      CB(18,4) = 1000000
      CB(19,4) = WEXP
      CB(20,4) = WCOMP
      CB(21,4) = WCOMB
      CB(22,4) = WLOOP
      CB(23,4) = WNET
      CB(24,4) = POWER
      CB(25,4) = EETAH
      CB(26,4) = VOLEFF
      CB(27,4) = NADNAX
      CB(28,4) = MEP
      CB(29,4) = BMEP
      CB(30,4) = BPOWER
      CB(31,4) = BRTHEF
      CB(32,4) = MECHEF*100.0
      IF(.NOT.IPRINT) GO TO 1091
 1091 CONTINUE
      RETURN
      END
C***********************************************************************
                              SUBROUTINE PRECAL
C***********************************************************************
      REAL KA,KP,KR,MC,MEP,MH,MO,MOLWTP,NA,N,NM,NADNAX,NMO,
     #     NP,NPO,NX,KRR
      LOGICAL IPTTHR,IPRINT,ISUPCH,ISUPET
      COMMON/GEOM/B,CR,CRL,S,VBDC,VDISP,VDVBDC(720),VOLUME(800),
     #           VTDC
      COMMON/THERM/HRP,MOLWTP(5),P1,P2,P3,P4,T1,T2,T3,T4,T5,T6,TA,
     #            V1,V2,V3,V4
      COMMON/CHEM/KA,KP,KR,N(5),NA,NADNAX,NMO,NP,NPO,NX,RMR,KRR,
     #           MC,MH,MO,R,RLITAT,RMIX,Y,YCC,YMIN,PMOLWT
      COMMON/CPCOEF/CV,ACPF,BCPF,ACPA,BCPA,AL(5),AH(5),
     #             BL(5),BH(5),CL(5),CH(5)
      COMMON/INDEX/IPTTHR,IPRINT,NCYCLE,HT_INDEX
      COMMON/GEN/CB(40,4),A(10,16),C(5),D(5),EETAH,RAF,F(5),
     #          FPM,FVM,G(5),MEP,PID4,POWER,RPM
      COMMON/SUPECH/EFOCOM,EFOTUR,ISUPCH,ISUPET
      COMMON/IDIES/PA,VR,STROKE
      COMMON/PSSA/CPR,DT,DTHDDT,IBC,IECPC,IEC,GASMAS,WCOMP,WEXP,NCEXG,
     #           WNET,WLOOP,PSPS,ML
      COMMON/ARRAY/DELV(750),DV(750),P(800),DELN(800),DELP(800),
     #           THETA(800),V(800)
      COMMON/PROG/CM,BR,P3D
      COMMON/HEATRA/AREA,BM,RCR,SAREA,SM,TW,VP
```

```
      COMMON/III/IFPCO
      COMMON/COMOD/MODCOM
      COMMON/HRMOD/MODHR
      PID = 3.1415927/180.
      URP = -6274940.0
C     CONVERSION OF BORE AND STROKE IN METERS.
      IF(ML.NE.0) GO TO 999
      ML = ML+1
      ITN = 0
      SR = 1.2
      BM = 0.001*B
      SM = 0.001*S
      RCR = CR/(CR-1.0)
      AREA = PID4*BM*BM
      SAREA = PID4*4.0*BM*SM*RCR
C     CALCULATION OF VARIOUS VOLUMES
      VDISP = PID4*B*B*S*1.0E-06
      VBDC = CR/(CR-1.0)*VDISP
      VTDC = VBDC-VDISP
      CALL VOLCAL
C     INITIALLY KR IS ASSUMED TO BE 1.4
      KR = 1.4
      IF(ISUPET.OR.ISUPCH)TA=300.
      IF(ISUPET.OR.ISUPCH)T1=TA*(((P1/PA)**((KR-1.)/KR)-1.)/EFOCOM+1.)
      IF(STROKE.NE.2)V1=VBDC
C     CALCULATION OF AIR-FUEL RATIO.
C     YCC REPRESENTS CHEMICALLY CORRECT O2/FUEL RATIO.
C     Y   REPRESENTS ACTUAL O2/FUEL RATIO.
C     Y < YCC  MEANS RICH MIXTURE.
C     Y > YCC  MEANS LEAN MIXTURE.
C     YMIN REPRESENTS MINIMUM O2 REQUIRED.
      YCC = MC+0.25*MH-0.5*MO
      YMIN = YCC-0.5*MC
      Y = YCC*RAF
      AFR = 4.76*Y
      IF(STROKE.NE.2.0)GO TO 8
      V12S = V1
      VO = 2.0*VDISP
      T1 = TA
      EE = 1.0/CR-1.0
      M1 = PA*(V1-VTDC)/(RLITAT*TA)
      X1 = PA*V1/RLITAT
    8 CONTINUE
      IF(Y.GE.YCC) GO TO 101
C     N(1) TO N(5) REPRESENT THE EXHAUST GAS CONSTITUENTS.
C     N(1) = CO ; N(2) = CO2 ; N(3) = H2O ; N(4) = N2 ; N(5) = O2.
```

```
      N(1) = 2.0*(YCC-Y)
      N(2) = 2.0*(Y-YMIN)
      N(3) = MH/2.0
      N(4) = 3.76*Y
      N(5) = 0.0
      NPO = N(1)+N(2)+N(3)+N(4)+N(5)
      GO TO 102
  101 N(1) = 0.0
      N(2) = MC
      N(3) = MH/2.0
      N(4) = 3.76*Y
      N(5) = Y-YCC
      NPO = N(1)+N(2)+N(3)+N(4)+N(5)
 102  CONTINUE
C    CALCULATION OF AVERAGE MOL. WT. AND GAS CONSTANT.
      NMO = 1.0+4.76*Y
      NA = P1*VBDC/(RLITAT*T1)
      NM = NA+NA/AFR
      IF(STROKE.EQ.2.) NA = P1*V1/(RLITAT*T1)
      SN = 0.0
      SUM = 0.0
      DO 65 I=1,NCEXG
         SN = SN+N(I)
         SUM = SUM+N(I)*MOLWTP(I)
   65 CONTINUE
      PMOLWT = SUM/SN
      RMOLWT = (NA*28.96+NX*PMOLWT)/(NA+NX)
      RMIX = R/PMOLWT
      RMR = R/RMOLWT
 999  CONTINUE
      NADNAX = NA/(NA+NX)
      CPR = ACPA+BCPA*T1
      CPR = (CPR*NA+NX*CP(T1))/(NA+NX)
      KR = CPR/(CPR-R)
C    P, V, T VALUES AT STATE POINT 2.
      P2 = P1*CR**KR
      V2 = VTDC
      T2 = T1*CR**(KR-1.0)
C    CALCULATION OF QV
C    URP FOR C10H22 IS GIVEN HERE,  URP = -6274940.0
C    WHEN PROGRESSIVE COMBUSTION MODEL IS USED IN ORDER TO
C    CALCULATE 'P3D' CONSTANT VOLUME ADIABATIC COMBUSTION
C    PROCESS IS USED AND NOT CONSTANT PRESSURE ADIABATIC
C    COMBUSTION. HENCE QV IS TO BE CALCULATED INSTEAD OF QP.
      CM = NM/NMO+NX/NPO
      NP = NPO*CM
```

```
      QV = -(URP+N(1)*281400.0)*(NA/NMO)
C     CALCULATION OF T3 USING NEWTON-RAPHSON METHOD.
      NITRN = 0
      T = 3000.0
 151  TNEW = T-(CM*(UP(T)-UP(T2))-QV)/CVG(T)
      NITRN = NITRN+1
      IF(ABS(T-TNEW).LT.0.1) GO TO 16
      IF(NITRN.GT.100) GO TO 16
      T = TNEW
      GO TO 151
 16   CONTINUE
C     P, V, T VALUES AT STATE POINT 3.
      T3  = TNEW
      P3D = P2*(T3/T2)*NP/(NA+NX)
      P3  = P2
      CPP = CP(T2)
      KP  = CP(T2)/(CP(T2)-R)
      WRITE(*,*) ' PRECAL OVER'
      RETURN
      END
C*********************************************************************
                              SUBROUTINE COMPRN
C*********************************************************************
C     THIS SUBROUTINE CALCULATES THE VARIATION OF PRESSURE
C     AND VOLUME FOR EVERY DEGREE CRANK ANGLE TAKING HEAT
C     TRANSFER INTO ACCOUNT FROM THE START OF COMPRESSION
C     TO THE START OF COMBUSTION
C     NOTE : ONLY AN EMPIRICAL FORMULA HAS BEEN USED FOR
C     HEAT TRANSFER.
      REAL KA,KP,KR,MC,MEP,MH,MO,MOLWTP,NA,N,NADNAX,NMO,
     #   NP,NPO,NX,KRR
      INTEGER EVO, EVC
      LOGICAL IPTTHR,IPRINT,HT_INDEX
      COMMON/GEOM/B,CR,CRL,S,VBDC,VDISP,VDVBDC(720),VOLUME(800),
     #          VTDC
      COMMON/THERM/HRP,MOLWTP(5),P1,P2,P3,P4,T1,T2,T3,T4,T5,T6,TA,
     #          V1,V2,V3,V4
      COMMON/CHEM/KA,KP,KR,N(5),NA,NADNAX,NMO,NP,NPO,NX,RMR,KRR,
     #          MC,MH,MO,R,RLITAT,RMIX,Y,YCC,YMIN,PMOLWT
      COMMON/INDEX/IPTTHR,IPRINT,NCYCLE,HT_INDEX
      COMMON/GEN/CB(40,4),A(10,16),C(5),D(5),EETAH,RAF,F(5),
     #          FPM,FVM,G(5),MEP,PID4,POWER,RPM
      COMMON/INEXH/IVO,IVC,EVO,EVC,AEV,AIV
      COMMON/IDIES/PA,VR,STROKE
      COMMON/PSSA/CPR,DT,DTHDDT,IBC,IECPC,IEC,GASMAS,WCOMP,WEXP,NCEXG,
     #          WNET,WLOOP,PSPS,ML
```

```
      COMMON/PROG/CM,BR,P3D
      COMMON/ARRAY/DELV(750),DV(750),P(800),DELN(800),DELP(800),
     #            THETA(800),V(800)
      COMMON/ABCD/DN,ITETA,ITETA3,L
      COMMON/III/IFPCO
      COMMON/STORE/PRR(800),TEMP(800),HRR(800)
      GASMAS = (P1*FPM)*(VBDC*FVM)/(RMIX*1000.0*T1)
      WEXP = 0.0
      CVR = CPR - R
      TEMP(IBC) = T1*(VBDC/VOLUME(IBC))**(KR-1.)
      WCOMP = (NA+NX)*CVR*(TEMP(IBC)-T1)
      DT = 60.0/(RPM*360.0)
      JJJ = IVC-719
      IF(IFPCO.EQ.0)JJJ = 1
      P(JJJ) = P1
      TEMP(JJJ) = T1
      PRR(JJJ) = 0.
      HRR(JJJ) = 0.
      DO 1000 ITETA = JJJ,IBC
      DELV(ITETA) = VOLUME(ITETA+1)-VOLUME(ITETA)
      F(1) = P(ITETA)
      F(2) = DT
      F(3) = GASMAS
      F(4) = T1*(VBDC/VOLUME(ITETA))**(KR-1.)
      F(5) = DELV(ITETA)*FVM/F(2)
      IF(HT_INDEX) THEN
        CALL HTRANS(F,PH)
      ELSE
   PH = 0.0
      ENDIF
      P(ITETA+1) = P(ITETA)*(VOLUME(ITETA)/VOLUME(ITETA+1))**KR
      P(ITETA+1) = P(ITETA+1)+PH
      PRR(ITETA) = P(ITETA+1)-P(ITETA)
      TEMP(ITETA) = T1*(VBDC/VOLUME(ITETA))**(KR-1.0)
      HRR(ITETA) = 0.0
C     WRITE(*,*) ITETA, P(ITETA), TEMP(ITETA)
 1000 CONTINUE
      WRITE(*,*) 'COMPRESSION OVER'
      RETURN
      END
C***********************************************************************
                          SUBROUTINE COMBN
C***********************************************************************
      REAL KA,KP,KR,MC,MEP, MH, MO, MOLWTP,NA, N,NADNAX,NMO,
     #     NP,NPO,NX,NDEL,KRR
      LOGICAL IPTTHR,IPRINT,ISUPCH,ISUPET,HT_INDEX
```

```
      COMMON/GEOM/B,CR,CRL,S,VBDC,VDISP,VDVBDC(720),VOLUME(800),
     #          VTDC
      COMMON/THERM/HRP,MOLWTP(5),P1,P2,P3,P4,T1,T2,T3,T4,T5,T6,TA,
     #          V1,V2,V3,V4
      COMMON/CHEM/KA,KP,KR,N(5),NA,NADNAX,NMO,NP,NPO,NX,RMR,KRR,
     #        MC,MH,MO,R,RLITAT,RMIX,Y,YCC,YMIN,PMOLWT
      COMMON/CPCOEF/CV,ACPF,BCPF,ACPA,BCPA,AL(5),AH(5),
     #          BL(5),BH(5),CL(5),CH(5)
      COMMON/INDEX/IPTTHR,IPRINT,NCYCLE,HT_INDEX
      COMMON/GEN/CB(40,4),A(10,16),C(5),D(5),EETAH,RAF,F(5),
     #        FPM,FVM,G(5),MEP,PID4,POWER,RPM
      COMMON/INEXH/IVO,IVC,EVO,EVC,AEV,AIV
      COMMON/SUPECH/EFOCOM,EFOTUR,ISUPCH,ISUPET
      COMMON/COMBUN/WCOMB,BRMAX
      COMMON/IDIES/PA,VR,STROKE
      COMMON/HTMOD/MODFHT
      COMMON/VALARE/D1,BETA,MODFVA
      COMMON/OVERL/PID,OMEGA,DTMAX,CAINT,AM,BDCMAS
      COMMON/PSSA/CPR,DT,DTHDDT,IBC,IECPC,IEC,GASMAS,WCOMP,WEXP,NCEXG,
     #          WNET,WLOOP,PSPS,ML
      COMMON/ARRAY/DELV(750),DV(750),P(800),DELN(800),DELP(800),
     #          THETA(800),V(800)
      COMMON/PROG/CM,BR,P3D
      COMMON/HEATRA/AREA,BM,RCR,SAREA,SM,TW,VP
      COMMON/FRICT/PIMF,PEMF,PSL,NPR,FMEP
      COMMON/FRPMOD/MODFRP
      COMMON/ABCD/DN,ITETA,ITETA3,L
      COMMON/III/IFPCO
      COMMON/STORE/PRR(800),TEMP(800),HRR(800)
      COMMON/ANGLE/ICB,ICE,IMX,ID
      COMMON/TFCOM/COMDUR,M
      COMMON/MAX/PRMAX,ICAMAX,JCAMAX
      COMMON/COMOD/MODCOM
      COMMON/HRMOD/MODHR
      COMMON/MATRX/CRANG(800),PRESS(800),VOLRAT(800),TMPR(800)
      COMMON/COMB/PMAX,TPMAX
      COMMON/HEAT/HR
      DIMENSION FUN(500)
      VOL(TETAR) = VDISP*(CR/(CR-1.)-(1.-COS(TETAR))/2. +
     #         (CRL/S)-.5*SQRT((2.*CRL/S)**2-(ABS(SIN(TETAR)))**2))
      VD(TETAR) = 0.5*VDISP*(0.5*SIN(2.*TETAR)/(SQRT((2.*CRL/S)**2-
     #          (ABS(SIN(TETAR)))**2))-SIN(TETAR))
      PID = 3.1415927/180.
      GO TO (11,12),MODCOM
 11   CONTINUE
C     THIS MODEL IS BASED ON PROGRESIVE COMBUSTION
```

```
           V3 = VTDC*(1.+(P3D-P2)/(KP*P2))
           ITETA = 1
      2    IF(ABS(VOLUME(ITETA)-V3).LT.5.E-03) GO TO 1
      9    ITETA =  ITETA+1
           GO TO 2
      1    IF(ITETA .LT.IBC) GO TO 9
           TETA        = FLOAT(ITETA)
           TETA3       = TETA
           P(TETA3)    = P(IBC)
           TETAR       = TETA*PID
           DTH         = (RPM*360.0)/60.0
           DT          = 1.0/DTH
           DTHDDT      = 8.0*PID4*RPM/60.0
           BR = VD(TETA3*PID)*DTHDDT/(V3-VTDC)
           IF(IBC .LT. 181) GO TO 25
           DO 30 I = 181,IBC
           ITETA = I
           TETA_R = FLOAT(I)*PID
           TETA1_R = FLOAT(I+1)*PID
           PH = 0.0
           KOUNT = KOUNT+1
           P(KOUNT) = P(ITETA)*(VOL(TETA_R)/VOL(TETA1_R))**KP
           P(KOUNT) = P(ITETA+1)+PH
           TEMP(ITETA)   = T2/((VOL(TETA1_R)/
         &               VOL(TETA_R))**(KP-1.0))
           PP = P(KOUNT)
           TT = TEMP(ITETA)
           KP   = CP(TT)/(CP(TT)-R)
     30    CONTINUE
     25    CONTINUE
           IF(BR.GT.BRMAX)GO TO 20
           D(1) = P2
           D(2) = DT
           D(3) = GASMAS
           D(4) = TT
           D(5) = DELV(ITETA)*FVM/D(2)
           IF(HT_INDEX) THEN
             CALL HTRANS(D,PH)
           ELSE
             PH = 0.0
           ENDIF
           P2 = P2+PH
           T3 = (P2*V3)/(RLITAT*NP)
           T4 = T3*(V3/VBDC)**(KP-1.0)
           UPT3 = CM*HP(T3)-R*NP*T3
           UPT4 = CM*HP(T4)-R*NP*T4
```

```
      WEXP = UPT3-UPT4
      WCOMB = P2*FPM*(V3-V2)*FVM
      IEC = IFIX(TETA3)
      IECPC = IEC
      DO 144 ITETA = IBC,IEC
         P(ITETA) = P(IBC)
 144  CONTINUE
      WNET = WEXP + WCOMB - WCOMP
      GO TO 220
 20   CONTINUE
      DELTE = (TETA3-FLOAT(IBC))/DN
      SUMN = 0.0
      WCOMB = 0.0
      L = 0
      TETA = FLOAT(IBC)
      TETAR = TETA*PID
      PRS = P(IBC)
 4    VDEL = (VD(TETAR)-VD(IBC*PID))*DELTE*PID
      IF(IBC .LT. 180) DELTAN = VD(TETAR-FLOAT(IBC)*PID)*DELTE*PID/
     & (V3-VTDC)
      DELTAV = VOL((TETA+DELTE)*PID)-VOL(TETA*PID)
      BR = ((VD(TETAR)-VD(IBC*PID))*DTHDDT)/(V3-VTDC)
      IF(BR.GE.BRMAX) GO TO 5
      NDEL = ABS(VDEL/(V3-VTDC))
      GO TO 6
 5    NDEL = BRMAX*DELTE/DTH
      IF(IBC.LT.180) GO TO 98
 6    SUMN = SUMN+ABS(NDEL)
      GO TO 97
 98   SUMN = SUMN+ABS(DELTAN)
 97   CONTINUE
      TETAR = TETA*PID
      IF(IBC .LT. 180) GO TO 7
      PDEL = -PRS*KP*VDEL/VOL(TETAR)
     &      +(P3D-P2)*VTDC/VOL(TETAR)*ABS(NDEL)
      GO TO 99
 7    PTERM1 = -PRS*KP*DELTAV/VOL(TETAR)
      PTERM2 = (P3D-P2)*VTDC/VOL(TETAR)*ABS(DELTAN)
      PDEL = PTERM1+PTERM2
 99   CONTINUE
      D(1) = PRS
      D(2) = DT
      D(3) = GASMAS
      D(4) = PRS*FPM*VOL(TETAR)*FVM/(RMIX*GASMAS*1000.)
      D(5) = VDEL*FVM/D(2)
      IF(HT_INDEX) THEN
```

```
         CALL HTRANS(D,PH)
      ELSE
         PH = 0.0
      ENDIF
      PDEL = PDEL+PH
      PRS = PRS+PDEL
      WCOMB = WCOMB+(PRS+PDEL*0.5)*VDEL*FPM*FVM
      ITETA = IFIX(TETA+DELTE)
      P(ITETA) = PRS
      TEMPER = PRS*FPM*VOL(ITETA*PID)*FVM/(GASMAS*RMIX*1000.)
      L = L+1
      CRANG(L) = TETA
      PRESS(L) = PRS
      VOLRAT(L) = VOL(TETAR)/VBDC
      TMPR(L) = TEMPER
      IF(SUMN.GE.1) GO TO 8
      TETA = TETA+DELTE
C     NEW ADDITION
      TETAR = TETA*PID
      GO TO 4
  8   IEC = IFIX(TETA)
      PMAX = P(IBC)
 220  PMAX = P(IBC)
      TPMAX = TEMP(IBC)
      DO 222 I = IBC,IEC
      PMAX = AMAX1(PMAX,P(I))
      TPMAX = AMAX1(TPMAX,TEMP(I))
 222  CONTINUE
      DO 221 I = IBC,IEC
      IF(P(I)-P(I+1) .GE. 0.01) GO TO 224
 221  CONTINUE
 224  IECPC = I
      WRITE(*,*) 'COMBUSTION OVER (PROGRESSIVE COMBUSTION MODEL)'
 223  RETURN
C======================================================================
  12  CONTINUE
C   THIS IS ZERO DIMENSIONAL GLOBAL MODEL
C   DELAY PERIOD IS CALCULATED BY INTEGRATING WOLFER'S RELATION
C   USING TRAPEZOIDAL RULE.
      SUM = 0.
      ID = 0
      I = 1
      ITETA = IBC
 200  FUN(I) = 1./(.00044*P(ITETA)**(-1.19)*EXP(4650./TEMP(ITETA))*
     #          6.*RPM)
      DELV(ITETA) = VOLUME(ITETA+1)-VOLUME(ITETA)
```

```
      F(1) = P(ITETA)
      F(2) = DT
      F(3) = GASMAS
      F(4) = T1*(VBDC /VOLUME(ITETA))**(KR-1.)
      F(5) = DELV(ITETA)*FVM/F(2)
      IF(HT_INDEX) THEN
         CALL HTRANS(F,PH)
      ELSE
   PH = 0.0
      ENDIF
      P(ITETA+1) = P(ITETA)*(VOLUME(ITETA)/VOLUME(ITETA+1))**KR
      TEMP(ITETA+1) = T1*(VBDC/VOLUME(ITETA+1))**(KR-1.)
      FUN(I+1) = 1.0/(0.00044*P(ITETA+1)**(-1.19)*
     #        EXP(4650.0/TEMP(ITETA+1))*6.0*RPM)
      SUM = SUM+(FUN(I)+ FUN(I+1))/2.0
      IF(SUM.GE.1.0) GO TO 100
      I = I+1
      ITETA = ITETA+1
      GO TO 200
 100  CONTINUE
      ID = ITETA-IBC
      ICB = IBC+ID
      DO 121 ITETA = IBC,ICB
      DELV(ITETA) = VOLUME(ITETA+1)-VOLUME(ITETA)
      F(1) = P(ITETA)
      F(2) = DT
      F(3) = GASMAS
      F(4) = T1*(VBDC/VOLUME(ITETA))**(KR-1.)
      F(5) = DELV(ITETA)*FVM/F(2)
      IF(HT_INDEX) THEN
         CALL HTRANS(F,PH)
      ELSE
   PH = 0.0
      ENDIF
      P(ITETA+1) = P(ITETA)*(VOLUME(ITETA)/VOLUME(ITETA+1))**KR
      P(ITETA+1) = P(ITETA+1)+PH
      PRR(ITETA) = P(ITETA+1)-P(ITETA)
      HRR(ITETA) = 0.0
      TEMP(ITETA) = T1*(VBDC/VOLUME(ITETA))**(KR-1.)
C     WRITE(*,*) ITETA, P(ITETA), TEMP(ITETA)
 121  CONTINUE
      CVR = CPR-R
      T = TEMP(ITETA)
      WCOMP = (NA+NX)*CVR*(TEMP(ICB)-T1)
      ICE = ICB+COMDUR
      WCOMB = 0.
```

```
      ITETA = ICB
      TEMP(ITETA) = TEMP(ICB)
C    RUNGE-KUTTA METHOD IS USED TO FIND TEMPERATURES AT VARIOUS
C    CRANK ANGLES
   44 T = TEMP(ITETA)
      I2 = 2
      I1 = I2/2
   55 CONTINUE
      RK1 = I2*TRR(ITETA,T)
      RK2 = I2*TRR(ITETA+I1,T+0.5*RK1)
      RK3 = I2*TRR(ITETA+I1,T+0.5*RK2)
      RK4 = I2*TRR(ITETA+I2,T+RK3)
      ITETA = ITETA+2
      TEMP(ITETA) = T+(RK1+(RK2+RK3)*2.+RK4)/6.0
      P(ITETA) = TEMP(ITETA)*(RMIX*GASMAS*1000.)/(FPM*VOLUME(ITETA)*
     #            FVM)
      DELP(ITETA) = P(ITETA)-P(ITETA-2)
C     MAXIMUM ALLOWABLE PRESSEURE IS ASSUMED AS 0.6 TIMES THE
C     PRESSURE WHICH WOULD HAVE BEEN ATTAINED IF COMBUSTION
C     TAKES PLACE AT CONSTANT VOLUME.
      PMX = 0.6*P3D
      PRR(ITETA) = DELP(ITETA)/I2
      IF(PRR(ITETA).GT.PRMAX) GO TO 600
      IF(P(ITETA).GT.PMX) GO TO 600
      HRR(ITETA) = HR
      VDEL = VOLUME(ITETA+2)-VOLUME(ITETA)
      WCOMB = WCOMB+(P(ITETA)+0.5*DELP(ITETA))*VDEL*FPM*FVM
      IF(ITETA.GE.ICE) GO TO 500
      GO TO 44
  600 ITETA = ITETA-2
      IMX = ITETA
      MODHR = 2
      T = TEMP(ITETA)
      GO TO 55
  500 CONTINUE
      IF(ITETA.GT.ICE) ICE = ITETA-2
      ICE = ITETA
      PMAX = P(ICB)
C     TO FIND MAXIMUM PRESSURE
      DO 110 I = ICB,ICE,2
      IF(PMAX-P(I))120,120,110
  120 PMAX = P(I)
      ICAMAX = I
  110 CONTINUE
C     TO FIND MAXIMUM TEMPERATURE
      TPMAX = TEMP(ICB)
```

```
      DO 290 I = ICB,ICE,2
      IF(TPMAX-TEMP(I)) 300,300,290
 300  TPMAX = TEMP(I)
      JCAMAX = I
 290  CONTINUE
      WRITE(*,*) 'COMBUSTION OVER (ZERO-DIME COMB MODEL)'
      RETURN
      END
C*******************************************************************
                       SUBROUTINE EXPN
C*******************************************************************
      REAL KA,KP,KR,MC,MEP, MH, MO, MOLWTP,NA, N,NADNAX,NMO,
     #   NP,NPO,NX,KRR
      INTEGER EVO,EVC
      LOGICAL IPTTHR,IPRINT,HT_INDEX
      COMMON/GEOM/B,CR,CRL,S,VBDC,VDISP,VDVBDC(720),VOLUME(800),
     #            VTDC
      COMMON/THERM/HRP,MOLWTP(5),P1,P2,P3,P4,T1,T2,T3,T4,T5,T6,TA,
     #            V1,V2,V3,V4
      COMMON/CHEM/KA,KP,KR,N(5),NA,NADNAX,NMO,NP,NPO,NX,RMR,KRR,
     #            MC,MH,MO,R,RLITAT,RMIX,Y,YCC,YMIN,PMOLWT
      COMMON/CPCOEF/CV,ACPF,BCPF,ACPA,BCPA,AL(5),AH(5),
     #             BL(5),BH(5),CL(5),CH(5)
      COMMON/INDEX/IPTTHR,IPRINT,NCYCLE,HT_INDEX
      COMMON/GEN/CB(40,4),A(10,16),C(5),D(5),EETAH,RAF,F(5),
     #           FPM,FVM,G(5),MEP,PID4,POWER,RPM
      COMMON/INEXH/IVO,IVC,EVO,EVC,AEV,AIV
      COMMON/COMBUN/WCOMB,BRMAX
      COMMON/IDIES/PA,VR,STROKE
      COMMON/PSSA/CPR,DT,DTHDDT,IBC,IECPC,IEC,GASMAS,WCOMP,WEXP,NCEXG,
     #            WNET,WLOOP,PSPS,ML
      COMMON/ARRAY/DELV(750),DV(750),P(800),DELN(800),DELP(800),
     #            THETA(800),V(800)
      COMMON/PROG/CM,BR,P3D
      COMMON/ABCD/DN,ITETA,ITETA3,L
      COMMON/III/IFPCO
      COMMON/STORE/PRR(800),TEMP(800),HRR(800)
      COMMON/ANGLE/ICB,ICE,IMX,ID
      COMMON/COMOD/MODCOM
      COMMON/MATRX/CRANG(800),PRESS(800),VOLRAT(800),TMPR(800)
C     TEAC IS THE TEMPERATURE AT THE CRANK ANGLE WHEN COMBUSTION ENDS.
      GO TO (3,4),MODCOM
 3    IF(BR.LT.BRMAX) GO TO 1
      VOLUME(IEC) = VOLRAT(L)*VBDC
      IF(BR.GT.BRMAX)P(IEC) = PRESS(L)
      TEAC = P(IEC)*VOLUME(IEC)/(RLITAT*NP)
```

```
      GO TO 5
    4 IEC = ICE
      TEAC = P(ICE)*VOLUME(ICE)/(RLITAT*NP)
    5 KP = CP(TEAC)/(CP(TEAC)-R)
      T4 = TEAC*((VOLUME(IEC)/VOLUME(EVO))**(KP-1.))
      UPTEAC = CM*HP(TEAC)-R*NP*TEAC
      UPT4 = CM*HP(T4)-R*NP*T4
      WEXP = UPTEAC-UPT4
      WNET = WEXP+WCOMB-WCOMP
      GO TO 2
    1 P(IEC) = P(IBC)
      TEAC = P(IEC)*VOLUME(IEC)/(RLITAT*NP)
      T4 = TEAC*((VOLUME(IEC)/ VOLUME(EVO))**(KP-1.))
    2 IF(IFPCO.EQ.0) EVO = 360
      DO 145 ITETA = IEC,EVO
      G(1) = P(ITETA)
      G(2) = DT
      G(3) = GASMAS
      G(4) = TEAC*(VOLUME(IEC)/VOLUME(ITETA))**(KP-1.)
      G(5) = (VOLUME(ITETA)-VOLUME(ITETA-1))/G(2)*FVM
      IF(HT_INDEX) THEN
        CALL HTRANS(G,PH)
      ELSE
   PH = 0.0
      ENDIF
      P(ITETA+1) = P(ITETA)*(VOLUME(ITETA)/VOLUME(ITETA+1))**KP
      P(ITETA+1) = P(ITETA+1)+PH
      PRR(ITETA) = P(ITETA+1)-P(ITETA)
      TEMP(ITETA) = TEAC*(VOLUME(IEC)/VOLUME(ITETA))**(KP-1.)
      HRR(ITETA) = 0.0
      TT = TEMP(ITETA)
C     WRITE(*,*) 'EXPN : ', ITETA, P(ITETA), TEMP(ITETA)
  145 CONTINUE
      WRITE(*,*) 'EXPANSION OVER'
      RETURN
      END
C***********************************************************************
                          SUBROUTINE GASEX
C***********************************************************************
      REAL KA,KP,KR,MC,MEP, MH, MO, MOLWTP,NA, N,NADNAX,NMO,
     #     NP,NPO,NX,INMASS,KRR
      INTEGER EVO,EVC
      LOGICAL HT_INDEX
      COMMON/GEOM/B,CR,CRL,S,VBDC,VDISP,VDVBDC(720),VOLUME(800),
     #            VTDC
      COMMON/THERM/HRP,MOLWTP(5),P1,P2,P3,P4,T1,T2,T3,T4,T5,T6,TA,
```

```
#                V1,V2,V3,V4
      COMMON/CHEM/KA,KP,KR,N(5),NA,NADNAX,NMO,NP,NPO,NX,RMR,KRR,
#              MC,MH,MO,R,RLITAT,RMIX,Y,YCC,YMIN,PMOLWT
      COMMON/CPCOEF/CV,ACPF,BCPF,ACPA,BCPA,AL(5),AH(5),
#                BL(5),BH(5),CL(5),CH(5)
      COMMON/GEN/CB(40,4),A(10,16),C(5),D(5),EETAH,RAF,F(5),
#             FPM,FVM,G(5),MEP,PID4,POWER,RPM
      COMMON/INEXH/IVO,IVC,EVO,EVC,AEV,AIV
      COMMON/OVERL/PID,OMEGA,DTMAX,CAINT,AM,BDCMAS
      COMMON/PSSA/CPR,DT,DTHDDT,IBC,IECPC,IEC,GASMAS,WCOMP,WEXP,NCEXG,
#                WNET,WLOOP,PSPS,ML
      COMMON/ARRAY/DELV(750),DV(750),P(800),DELN(800),DELP(800),
#              THETA(800),V(800)
      COMMON/HEATRA/AREA,BM,RCR,SAREA,SM,TW,VP
      COMMON/GAS/PR(800),VOLD(800),TE(800),NV,T,PEVC,VOLEFF
      COMMON/GAS1/THETAS,THETAU
      COMMON/FRICT/PIMF,PEMF,PSL,NPR,FMEP
      COMMON/FRPMOD/MODFRP
      COMMON/ABCD/DN,ITETA,ITETA3,L
      COMMON/III/IFPCO
      COMMON/INDEX/IPTTHR,IPRINT,NCYCLE,HT_INDEX
      COMMON/SUCTION/THETA_SUC,PR_SUC,TE_SUC,VOLD_SUC
C     STATEMENT FUNCTION DEFINITION FOR THE CALCULATION OF
C     VOLUME AT VARIOUS CRANK ANGLES.
      VOL(THETAR) = VDISP*(CR/(CR-1.)-(1.-COS(THETAR))/2. +
#              (CRL/S)-.5*SQRT((2.*CRL/S)**2-(ABS(SIN(THETAR)))**2))
      DATA ISUBPR,ISUPPR/2*0/
      NV = 0
      TM = TA
      PIMF = PIMF*FPM
      PEMF = PEMF*FPM
      PRESS = P(EVO)*FPM
      IVAR = 0
      DTMAX = CAINT*60.0/(360.0*RPM)
      WLOOP = 0.0
      EPSLON = .01*PIMF
      PID = 3.1415926/180.0
      THETAC = EVO
      NV = NV+1
      THETA(NV) = THETAC
      THETAR = THETAC*PID
      OMEGA = 2.0*3.1416*RPM/60.0
      EXMASS = VOL(THETAR)*FVM*PRESS*0.001/(RMIX*T4)
   10 CONTINUE
C    ANALYSIS OF EXHAUST PROCESS
      PDPO = PRESS/PEMF
```

```
      IF(PRESS.LE.PEMF)PDPO = PEMF/PRESS
      THETAR = THETAC*PID
      CALL VALVAE(AEV,AREXV,THETAC)
      DPMAX = (PRESS-PEMF)/AM
      T = PRESS*VOL(THETAR)*FVM/(EXMASS*RMIX*1000.0)
      CPP = CP(T)+R
      KP = CPP/(CPP-R)
      GA = (KP-1.0)/KP
      GK = (KP+1.0)/(KP-1.0)
      GP = (2./(KP+1.0))**GK
      CRIT = (0.5*(KP+1.0))**(KP/(KP-1.0))
      TE(NV) = T
      UNDR = SQRT((2.0*CRL/S)**2-((ABS(SIN(THETAR)))**2))
      DVDDT = VDISP*0.5*FVM*(.5*SIN(2.*THETAR)/UNDR-SIN(THETAR))*OMEGA
      IF(PDPO-CRIT) 100,200,200
  100 VP = PDPO**GA
      DMDDT = AREXV*PEMF*SQRT(2./(GA*RMIX*T)*VP*(VP-1.)/1000.)*(-1.)
      IF(ISUBPR.EQ.0)THETAS = THETAC
      ISUBPR = 1
      GO TO 300
  200 DMDDT = AREXV*PRESS*SQRT(KP/(RMIX*T*1000.)*GP)*(-1.)
      IF(ISUPPR.EQ.0)THETAU = THETAC
      ISUPPR = 1
  300 CONTINUE
      QEX = KP*PRESS*((DMDDT/EXMASS)-(DVDDT/(VOL(THETAR)*FVM)))
      IF(QEX)260,270,280
  260  CONTINUE
       IF( (-DPMAX/QEX) - DTMAX) 20,30,30
   20  DELTAP = -DPMAX
       DELTT = ABS(DELTAP/QEX)
       GO TO 50
   30  DELTT = DTMAX
       DELTAP = QEX*DELTT
       GO TO 50
  270  DELTAP = 0.
       DELTT = DTMAX
       GO TO 50
  280  IF((DPMAX/QEX)-DTMAX)40,60,60
   40  DELTAP = DPMAX
       DELTT = ABS(DELTAP/QEX)
       GO TO 50
   60  DELTT = DTMAX
       DELTAP = QEX*DELTT
   50  CONTINUE
C     CALCULATION OF PRESSURE DORP DUE TO HEAT TRANSFER
       DELTV = DVDDT*DELTT
```

```
           C(1) = PRESS/FPM
           C(2) = DELTT
           C(3) = EXMASS
           C(4) = T
           C(5) = DVDDT
           IF(HT_INDEX) THEN
              CALL HTRANS(C,PDHT)
           ELSE
      PDHT = 0.0
           ENDIF
           PDHT = PDHT*FPM
C     TOTAL PRESSURE DROP CALCULATIONS
           DELTAP = DELTAP+PDHT
           VDVBC = VOL(THETAR)/VBDC
           PR(NV) = PRESS/FPM
           VOLD(NV) = VDVBC
           PRESS = PRESS+DELTAP
           EXMASS = EXMASS+DELTT*DMDDT
           THETAC = THETAC+360.0*RPM*DELTT/60.0
           NV = NV+1
           THETA(NV) = THETAC
C     WLOOP IS THE WORK DONE ON GASES DURING EXHAUST AND INTAKE STROKES.
           WLOOP = WLOOP+(PRESS+(DELTAP/2.0))*DELTV
C          WRITE(*,*)'EXHAST : ', THETAC, PRESS, T
           IF(THETAC.LE.IVO)GO TO 10
           THETA(NV) = THETAC
           BDCMAS = EXMASS
           WRITE(*,*)   ' EXHAST  OVER'
           IF((EVC-IVO).EQ.0) GO TO 3000
           CALL OVERLP(EXMASS,PRESS,THETAC)
 3000      CONTINUE
           EXMEVC = EXMASS
           PEVC = PRESS/FPM
           T5 = T
C   ******   ANALYSIS OF THE INTAKE STROKE.
           INMASS = EXMASS
           NV_REF = NV
  950      CONTINUE
           THETAR = THETAC*PID
           CALL VALVAI(AIV,ARINV,THETAC)
           T = PRESS*VOL(THETAR)*FVM/(INMASS*RMR*1000.0)
C   ******  CALCULATION OF KP & KR
           CPR = ACPA+BCPA*TA
           CPR = (CPR*NA+NX*CP(TA))/(NA+NX)
           CVT = CP(T)-R
           KRR = CPR/CVT
```

```
          CPR1 = ACPA+BCPA*T
          CPR1 = (CPR1*NA+NX*CP(T))/(NA+NX)
          CVT1 = CP(TA)-R
          KR = CPR1/CVT
          KP = CP(T)/CVT
          TE(NV) = T
C         WRITE(*,*) 'INTAKE 1', T, NV, TE(NV)
          UNDR = SQRT((2.*CRL/S)**2-((ABS(SIN(THETAR)))**2))
          IF(ABS(PRESS-PIMF).LE.EPSLON) PRESS = PIMF-EPSLON
          FACTOR = PRESS-PIMF
          IF(FACTOR) 17,17,18
   17     CONTINUE
          ITAG = 0
          IVAR = 1
          DPMAX = ABS(PIMF-PRESS)/AM
          PDPO = PIMF/PRESS
          GO TO 21
   18     DPMAX = ABS(PRESS-PIMF)/AM
          PDPO = PRESS/PIMF
   21     CONTINUE
          CRIT = (0.5*(KR+1.))**(KR/(KR-1.))
          DVDDT = VDISP*.5*FVM*(.5*SIN(2.*THETAR)/UNDR-SIN(THETAR))*OMEGA
          IF(PDPO - CRIT) 960,970,970
  960     GA = (KR-1.)/KR
          VP = PDPO**GA
          SQT = 2.0/(GA*RMR*T)*VP*(VP-1.)/1000.
          DMDDT = ARINV*PIMF*SQRT(SQT)*(-1.)
          IF(IVAR.EQ.1) DMDDT = ARINV*PRESS*SQRT(SQT)
          GO TO 980
  970     GK = (KR+1.)/(KR-1.)
          GP = (2./(KR+1.))**GK
          DMDDT = ARINV*PRESS*SQRT(KR/(RMR*T*1000.)*GP)*(-1.)
          IF(IVAR.EQ.1) DMDDT = ARINV*PIMF*SQRT(KR/(RMR*T*1000.)*GP)
  980     CONTINUE
          IF(IVAR.EQ.1) GO TO 199
          QEX = KRR*PRESS*(DMDDT/INMASS-DVDDT/(VOL(THETAR)*FVM))
          GO TO 299
  199     QEX = KRR*((RMR*TM*DMDDT*1000./(VOL(THETAR)*FVM))-
     #          (PRESS*DVDDT/(VOL(THETAR)*FVM)))
  299     CONTINUE
          IF(QEX)990,1000,1100
  990     IF((DPMAX/(-QEX))-DTMAX)130,140,140
  130     DELTAP = -DPMAX
          DELTT = ABS(DELTAP/QEX)
          GO TO 150
  140     DELTT = DTMAX
```

```
      DELTAP = QEX*DELTT
      GO TO 150
1000  DELTAP = 0.
      DELTT = DTMAX
      GO TO 150
1100  IF(DPMAX/QEX-DTMAX)160,170,170
 160  DELTAP = DPMAX
      DELTT = ABS(DELTAP/QEX)
      GO TO 150
 170  DELTT = DTMAX
      DELTAP = QEX*DELTT
 150  CONTINUE
C     CALCULATION OF PRESSURE DROP DUE TO HEAT TRANSFER.
      DELTV = DVDDT*DELTT
      C(1) = PRESS/FPM
      C(2) = DELTT
      C(3) = INMASS
      C(4) = T
      C(5) = DVDDT
      IF(HT_INDEX) THEN
         CALL HTRANS(C,PDHT)
      ELSE
         PDHT = 0.0
      ENDIF
      PDHT = PDHT*FPM
C     TOTAL PRESSYRE DROP CALCULATION DURING INTAKE PROCESS.
      VDVBC = VOL(THETAR)/VBDC
      DELTAP = DELTAP+PDHT
      PRESS = PRESS+DELTAP
      IF(ABS(PRESS-PREST).LE.0.001) GOTO 1410
      PR(NV) = PRESS/FPM
      VOLD(NV) = VDVBC
      THETAC = THETAC+360.0*RPM*DELTT/60.0
      IF(THETAC.GE.IVC) GOTO 1400
      IF(THETAC.GT.715.0.AND.THETAC.LT.722.0)TDCMAS = INMASS
C      WRITE(*,*) 'TDCMAS', THETAC, TDCMAS
      NV = NV+1
      THETA(NV) = THETAC
      INMASS = INMASS+DELTT*DMDDT
      WLOOP = WLOOP+(PRESS+(DELTAP/2.0))*DELTV
      IF(THETAC.GE.IVC)THETAC = IVC
      PREST = PRESS
      GO TO 950
1410  CONTINUE
      T1 = T
      PRES1 = ((INMASS*RMR*T1)/VOL(THETAC*PID))*FPM
```

```
      PRES2 = ((INMASS*RMR*T1)/VOL((THETAC+1.0)*PID))*FPM
      DP = PRES1-PRES2
      DELTV = (VOL((THETAC+1.0)*PID)-VOL(THETAC*PID))*FVM
      WLOOP = WLOOP+(PRES1+(DP/2.0))*DELTV
      IF(THETAC.GE.IVC) GOTO 1400
      THETAC = THETAC+1.0
      GOTO 1410
 1400 CONTINUE
      THETA(NV) = THETAC
      NX = EXMEVC*PMOLWT
      T1 = T
      PIVC = PRESS/FPM
      P1 = PIVC
      WLOOP = ABS(WLOOP)
      AINMAS = INMASS
      NMDNMX = (AINMAS-EXMEVC)/AINMAS
      PIMF = PIMF/FPM
      PEMF = PEMF/FPM
      VOLEFF = (TDCMAS-BDCMAS)*RMR*TM*1000.0/(PIMF*VDISP)
C     LOCATION OF THE CRANK ANGLE WHERE THE MASS FLOW IS ZERO
C     DURING GAS EXCHANGE PROSESS
      PREF = PR(NV_REF)
      DO 113 I = NV_REF, NV_REF+180
         IF( PR(I).GT.PREF) THEN
           LOC = I-1
     THETA_SUC = THETA(LOC)
     PR_SUC = PR(LOC)
     TE_SUC = TE(LOC)
     VOLD_SUC = VOLD(LOC)
             GO TO 114
         ELSE
             PREF = PR(I)
             GO TO 113
         ENDIF
  113 CONTINUE
  114 WRITE(*,*) 'LOCATION', THETA_SUC, PR_SUC, TE_SUC, VOLD_SUC
      WRITE(*,*) 'GAS EXCHANGE OVER'
      RETURN
      END
C***********************************************************************
                      SUBROUTINE OVERLP(EXMASS,PRESS,THETAC)
C***********************************************************************
      REAL KA,KP,KR,MC,MEP, MH, MO, MOLWTP,NA, N,NADNAX,NMO,
     #     NP,NPO,NX,KRR
      INTEGER EVO,EVC
      LOGICAL HT_INDEX
```

```
      COMMON/GEOM/B,CR,CRL,S,VBDC,VDISP,VDVBDC(720),VOLUME(800),
     #            VTDC
      COMMON/THERM/HRP,MOLWTP(5),P1,P2,P3,P4,T1,T2,T3,T4,T5,T6,TA,
     #            V1,V2,V3,V4
      COMMON/CHEM/KA,KP,KR,N(5),NA,NADNAX,NMO,NP,NPO,NX,RMR,KRR,
     #            MC,MH,MO,R,RLITAT,RMIX,Y,YCC,YMIN,PMOLWT
      COMMON/CPCOEF/CV,ACPF,BCPF,ACPA,BCPA,AL(5),AH(5),
     #            BL(5),BH(5),CL(5),CH(5)
      COMMON/GEN/CB(40,4),A(10,16),C(5),D(5),EETAH,RAF,F(5),
     #            FPM,FVM,G(5),MEP,PID4,POWER,RPM
      COMMON/INEXH/IVO,IVC,EVO,EVC,AEV,AIV
      COMMON/OVERL/PID,OMEGA,DTMAX,CAINT,AM,BDCMAS
      COMMON/PSSA/CPR,DT,DTHDDT,IBC,IECPC,IEC,GASMAS,WCOMP,WEXP,NCEXG,
     #            WNET,WLOOP,PSPS,ML
      COMMON/ARRAY/DELV(750),DV(750),P(800),DELN(800),DELP(800),
     #            THETA(800),V(800)
      COMMON/HEATRA/AREA,BM,RCR,SAREA,SM,TW,VP
      COMMON/GAS/PR(800),VOLD(800),TE(800),NV,T,PEVC,VOLEFF
      COMMON/GAS1/THETAS,THETAU
      COMMON/FRICT/PIMF,PEMF,PSL,NPR,FMEP
      COMMON/FRPMOD/MODFRP
      COMMON/ABCD/DN,ITETA,ITETA3,L
      COMMON/III/IFPCO
      COMMON/INDEX/IPTTHR,IPRINT,NCYCLE,HT_INDEX
C     STATEMENT FUNCTION DEFINITION FOR THE CALCULATION
C     THE VOLUME.
      VOL(THETAR) = VDISP*(CR/(CR-1.)-(1.-COS(THETAR))/2. +
     #            (CRL/S)-.5*SQRT((2.*CRL/S)**2-(ABS(SIN(THETAR)))**2))
      EPSLON = .01*PEMF
      TM = TA
      DPMAX = 0.0
 950  CONTINUE
      THETAR = THETAC*PID
      PDPO = PRESS/PEMF
      IF(ABS(PRESS-PEMF).LE.EPSLON)PRESS = PEMF-EPSLON
      IF(PRESS.LE.PEMF)PDPO = PEMF/PRESS
      DPMAX1 = ABS(PRESS-PEMF)/AM
      IF(DPMAX1.GT.DPMAX) DPMAX = DPMAX1
      CALL VALVAE(AEV,AREXV,THETAC)
      T = PRESS*VOL(THETAR)*FVM/(EXMASS*RMIX*1000.)
C     CALCILATION OF KP & KR
      CVT = CP(T) - R
      KP = CP(T)/CVT
      GA = (KP-1.)/KP
      GK = (KP+1.)/(KP-1.)
      GP = (2./(KP+1.))**GK
```

```
      CRIT = (.5*(KP+1.))**(KP/(KP-1.))
      TE(NV) = T
      UNDR = SQRT((2.*CRL/S)**2-((ABS(SIN(THETAR)))**2))
      DVDDT = VDISP*.5*FVM*(.5*SIN(2.*THETAR)/UNDR-SIN(THETAR))*OMEGA
     IF(PDPO-CRIT) 100,200,200
 100 VP = PDPO**GA
     DMDDT1 = AREXV*PEMF*SQRT(2./(GA*RMIX*T)*VP*(VP-1.)/1000.)*(-1.)
     IF(PRESS.LE.PEMF) DMDDT1  =  AREXV*PRESS*SQRT(2./(GA*RMIX*T)*VP*
    #                            (VP-1.0))/1000.0
     GO TO 300
 200 DMDDT1 = AREXV*PRESS*SQRT(KP/(RMIX*T*1000.)*GP)*(-1.)
     IF(PRESS.LE.PEMF) DMDDT1 = AREXV*PEMF*SQRT(KP/(RMIX*T*1000.)*GP)
 300 CONTINUE
C     ANALYSIS OF INTAKE PROTION WITH OVERLAP
      CALL VALVAI(AIV,ARINV,THETAC)
      IF(ABS(PRESS-PIMF).LE.EPSLON)PRESS = PIMF-EPSLON
      DPMAX2  =  ABS(PRESS-PIMF)/AM
      IF(DPMAX2.GT.DPMAX) DPMAX  =  DPMAX2
      IF(PRESS-PIMF) 17,17,18
 17   CONTINUE
      PDPO = PIMF/PRESS
      GO TO 21
 18   PDPO  =  PRESS/PIMF
 21   CONTINUE
      CRIT = (0.5*(KP + 1.0))**(KP/(KP-1.0))
      IF(PDPO-CRIT) 960,970,970
 960  GA = (KP-1.0)/KP
      VP = PDPO**GA
      SQT = 2.0/(GA*RMIX*T)*VP*(VP-1.0)/1000.0
      DMDDT2  =  ARINV*PIMF*SQRT(SQT)*(-1.)
      IF(PRESS.LE.PIMF) DMDDT2  =  ARINV*PRESS*SQRT(SQT)
      GO TO 980
 970  GK = (KP+1.)/(KP-1.)
      GP = (2./(KP+1.))**GK
      DMDDT2 = ARINV*PRESS*SQRT(KP/(RMIX*T*1000.)*GP)*(-1.)
      IF(PRESS.LE.PIMF)DMDDT2 = ARINV*PIMF*SQRT(KP/(RMIX*T*1000.)*GP)
 980  CONTINUE
      DMDDT = DMDDT1 + DMDDT2
      IF(DMDDT.LT.0.0) THEN
         Q = KRR*((RMIX*TM*DMDDT*1000./(VOL(THETAR)*FVM))-(PRESS*
    #    DVDDT/(VOL(THETAR)*FVM)))
      ELSE
         Q = KP*PRESS*(DMDDT/EXMASS-DVDDT/(VOL(THETAR)*FVM))
      ENDIF
      IF(Q) 990,1000,1100
 990  IF(ABS(-DPMAX/Q) - DTMAX) 130,140,140
```

```
  130  DELTP = -DPMAX
       DELTT = DELTP/Q
       GO TO 150
  140  DELTT = DTMAX
       DELTP = Q*DELTT
       GO TO 150
 1000  DELTP = 0.0
       DELTT = DTMAX
       GO TO 150
 1100  IF(DPMAX/Q - DTMAX)160,170,170
  160  DELTP = DPMAX
       DELTT = DELTP/Q
       GO TO 150
  170  DELTT = DTMAX
       DELTP = Q*DELTT
  150  CONTINUE
C      CALCULATION OF PRESSURE DROP DUE TO HEAT TRANSFER.
       DELTV = DVDDT*DELTT
       C(1) = PRESS/FPM
       C(2) = DELTT
       C(3) = EXMASS
       C(4) = T
       C(5) = DVDDT
       IF(HT_INDEX) THEN
         CALL HTRANS(C,PDHT)
       ELSE
         PDHT = 0.0
       ENDIF
       PDHT = PDHT*FPM
C      TOTAL PRESSURE DROP CALCULATION DURING INTAKE PROCESS.
        VDVBC =  VOL(THETAR)/VBDC
        PRESS =  PRESS+DELTP+PDHT
        PR(NV) =  PRESS/FPM
        VOLD(NV) =  VDVBC
        IF(THETAC.EQ.EVC)GO TO 1400
        THETAC = THETAC+360.0*RPM*DELTT/60.0
        IF(THETAC.GE.540.0.AND.THETAC.LT.548.0)BDCMAS = EXMASS
        NV = NV+1
        THETA(NV) = THETAC
        EXMASS = EXMASS+DMDDT*DELTT
        WLOOP = WLOOP+(PRESS+(DELTP/2.0))*DELTV
        IF(THETAC.GT.EVC)THETAC = EVC
C       WRITE(*,*) 'OVERLP :', THETAC, PRESS, T
        GO TO 950
 1400   CONTINUE
        THETA(NV) = THETAC
```

```
      WRITE(*,*) 'OVERLAP OVER'
      RETURN
      END
C***********************************************************************
                        FUNCTION HP(T)
C***********************************************************************
      REAL KA,KP,KR,MC, MH, MO, NA, N,NADNAX,NMO,NP,NPO,NX,KRR
      COMMON/CHEM/KA,KP,KR,N(5),NA,NADNAX,NMO,NP,NPO,NX,RMR,KRR,
     #          MC,MH,MO,R,RLITAT,RMIX,Y,YCC,YMIN,PMOLWT
      COMMON/CPCOEF/CV,ACPF,BCPF,ACPA,BCPA,AL(5),AH(5),
     #            BL(5),BH(5),CL(5),CH(5)
      HP = 0.
      IF(T.GT.1600.0) GO TO 20
      DO 1 I = 1,5
    1 HP = HP+N(I)*(AL(I)+BL(I)*T+CL(I)*ALOG(T))
      RETURN
   20 DO 3 I = 1,5
    3 HP = HP+N(I)*(AH(I)+BH(I)*T+CH(I)*ALOG(T))
      RETURN
      END
C***********************************************************************
    FUNCTION UP(T)
C***********************************************************************
      REAL KA,KP,KR,MC, MH, MO, NA, N,NADNAX,NMO,
     &    NP,NPO,NX
      COMMON/CHEM/KA,KP,KR,N(5),NA,NADNAX,NMO,NP,NPO,NX,RMR,KRR,
     #          MC,MH,MO,R,RLITAT,RMIX,Y,YCC,YMIN,PMOLWT
      COMMON/CPCOEF/CV,ACPF,BCPF,ACPA,BCPA,AL(5),AH(5),
     #            BL(5),BH(5),CL(5),CH(5)
      UP = 0.
      IF(T.GT.1600.0) GO TO 20
      DO 1 I = 1,5
    1 UP = UP+N(I)*(AL(I)+(BL(I)-R)*T+CL(I)*ALOG(T))
      RETURN
   20 DO 3 I = 1,5
    3 UP = UP+N(I)*(AH(I)+(BH(I)-R)*T+CH(I)*ALOG(T))
      RETURN
      END
C***********************************************************************
                        FUNCTION CVG(T)
C***********************************************************************
      REAL KA,KP,KR,MC, MH, MO, NA, N,NADNAX,NMO,
     &    NP,NPO,NX
      COMMON/CHEM/KA,KP,KR,N(5),NA,NADNAX,NMO,NP,NPO,NX,RMR,KRR,
     #          MC,MH,MO,R,RLITAT,RMIX,Y,YCC,YMIN,PMOLWT
      COMMON/CPCOEF/CV,ACPF,BCPF,ACPA,BCPA,AL(5),AH(5),
```

```
#                  BL(5),BH(5),CL(5),CH(5)
      CVG = 0.0
      IF(T.GT.1600.)GO TO 58
      DO 61 I = 1,5
   61 CVG = CVG+((BL(I)-R)+CL(I)/T)*N(I)
      CVG = CVG/NPO
      RETURN
   58 DO 59 I = 1,5
   59 CVG = CVG+((BH(I)-R)+CH(I)/T)*N(I)
      CVG = CVG/NPO
      RETURN
      END
C*********************************************************************
                         FUNCTION CP(T)
C*********************************************************************
      REAL KA,KP,KR,MC, MH, MO, NA, N,NADNAX,NMO,NP,NPO,NX,KRR
      COMMON/CHEM/KA,KP,KR,N(5),NA,NADNAX,NMO,NP,NPO,NX,RMR,KRR,
     #              MC,MH,MO,R,RLITAT,RMIX,Y,YCC,YMIN,PMOLWT
      COMMON/CPCOEF/CV,ACPF,BCPF,ACPA,BCPA,AL(5),AH(5),
     #              BL(5),BH(5),CL(5),CH(5)
      CP = 0.0
      IF(T.GT.1600.)GO TO 58
      DO 61 I = 1,5
   61 CP = CP+(BL(I)+CL(I)/T)*N(I)
      CP = CP/NPO
      RETURN
   58 DO 59 I = 1,5
   59 CP = CP+(BH(I)+CH(I)/T)*N(I)
      CP = CP/NPO
      RETURN
      END
C*********************************************************************
                         SUBROUTINE VOLCAL
C*********************************************************************
      COMMON/GEOM/B,CR,CRL,S,VBDC,VDISP,VDVBDC(720),VOLUME(800),
     #            VTDC
      COMMON/ARRAY/DELV(750),DV(750),P(800),DELN(800),DELP(800),
     #            THETA(800),V(800)
      RCLS = CRL/S
      SRCLS = (2.0*RCLS)**2
      RCR = CR/(CR-1.)
      PID = 3.1415926/180.
      DO 100 ITETA = 1,720
      VTETA = ITETA*PID
      SX = SIN(VTETA)*SIN(VTETA)
      UDRT = SQRT(SRCLS-SX)
```

```
      CX = 1.-COS(VTETA)
      TERM = (RCR-CX*0.5+RCLS-UDRT*0.5)
      S2X = 2.*SIN(VTETA)*COS(VTETA)
      VOLUME(ITETA) = VDISP*TERM
      VDVBDC(ITETA) = VOLUME(ITETA)/VBDC
 100  CONTINUE
      RETURN
      END
C*********************************************************************C
                             SUBROUTINE DURCOM
C*********************************************************************C
      LOGICAL IPTTHR,IPRINT
      COMMON/CHEM/KA,KP,KR,N(5),NA,NADNAX,NMO,NP,NPO,NX,RMR,KRR,
     #           MC,MH,MO,R,RLITAT,RMIX,Y,YCC,YMIN,PMOLWT
      COMMON/INDEX/IPTTHR,IPRINT,NCYCLE,HT_INDEX
      COMMON/GEN/CB(40,4),A(10,16),C(5),D(5),EETAH,RAF,F(5),
     #          FPM,FVM,G(5),MEP,PID4,POWER,RPM
      COMMON/NEWGEN/CHAR(15),E(5),EQR,NN(5),ICOMBM,INDF,ITMT1,NODRO
      COMMON/COBUS/DC,ISTA,IENDA,NDC
C     SUBROUTINE DURCOM IS PROVIDED TO CALCULATE THE DURATION
C     OF COMBUSTION IF SUITABLE EXPRESSIONS ARE AVAILABLE
C     AT PRESENT IT IS GIVEN IN THE BLOCK DATA AS INPUT
C     PROVISION IS MADE FOR DIFFERENT MODELS
C     PUT APPROPRIATE INDEX (1,2,3,4 OR 5)FOR ICOMBM IN
C     BLOCK DATA DEPENDING UPON THE MODEL TO BE USED.
      GO TO (1,2,3,4,5),ICOMBM
C     DC IS  THE DURATION OF COMBUSTION
    1 CONTINUE
      COMDUR = 40.0 + 5.0*(RPM/600.0 - 1.0) + 166.0*(YCC/Y-1.1)**2
      GO TO 5
    2 CONTINUE
      COMDUR = 60.0
    3 CONTINUE
      COMDUR = 35.0
    4 CONTINUE
    5 CONTINUE
      COMDUR = 65.0
      RETURN
      END
C*********************************************************************
                          SUBROUTINE HTRANS(CA,X)
C*********************************************************************
C     NOTE : CA(1) = PRESS ; CA(2) = DELTT ; CA(3) = EXMASS ;
C       CA(4) = TEMP ; CA(5) = DVDTH
      REAL KA,KP,KR,MC,MEP, MH, MO, MOLWTP,NA, N,NADNAX,NMO,
     #     NP,NPO,NX,KRR
```

```
      DIMENSION CA(5)
      COMMON/GEOM/B,CR,CRL,S,VBDC,VDISP,VDVBDC(720),VOLUME(800),
     #            VTDC
      COMMON/THERM/HRP,MOLWTP(5),P1,P2,P3,P4,T1,T2,T3,T4,T5,T6,TA,
     #             V1,V2,V3,V4
      COMMON/CHEM/KA,KP,KR,N(5),NA,NADNAX,NMO,NP,NPO,NX,RMR,KRR,
     #            MC,MH,MO,R,RLITAT,RMIX,Y,YCC,YMIN,PMOLWT
      COMMON/GEN/CB(40,4),A(10,16),C(5),D(5),EETAH,RAF,F(5),
     #           FPM,FVM,G(5),MEP,PID4,POWER,RPM
      COMMON/HTMOD/MODFHT
      COMMON/HEATRA/AREA,BM,RCR,SAREA,SM,TW,VP
      COMMON/ABCD/DN,ITETA,ITETA3,L
      COMMON/ADDN/PATM,VEL
C     MODFHT 1 IS DUE TO CAMPBELL ASHLEY
C     MODFHT 2 IS DUE TO SITKEI & RAMANAIAH
C     MODFHT 3 IS DUE TO HOHENBERG
C     MODFHT 4 IS DUE TO PFLAUM
      CV(T) = CP(T) - R
C     VP IS THE PISTON SPEED IN M/S.
      VP = SM*RPM/30.
      TW = T2
      PATM = CA(1)
      AREA = PID4*BM**2
      VEL = ABS(CA(5)/AREA)
C     ASSUMED WALL TEMPERATURE IS THE TEMPERATURE AT THE END
C     OF THE COMPRESSION STROKE.
      T = CA(4)
      GO TO(1,2,3,4),MODFHT
    1 HC = 0.13*(BM**(-0.2))*((PATM*VEL)**(0.8))*(T**(-0.5))
      GO TO 10
    2 HC=0.04*(1.0+.015)*(PATM*VP)**.7/((T**.2)*(B**.3))*(4.18/3600.)
      GO TO 10
    3 HC=0.13*((VOLUME(ITETA)*FVM)**(-.06))*((PATM*(VP+1.4))**(0.8))*
     #    (T**(-0.4))
      GO TO 10
    4 XXX = 1.5 - 0.416*VP
      YYY = EXP(XXX)
      IF(VP.GE.3.6) FVP = 3.0 + 2.57*(1.0 - YYY)
      IF(VP.LE.3.6) FVP = 3.0 - 2.57*(1.0 - (1.0/YYY))
      HC = (4.18/3600.)*SQRT(PATM*T*FVP)
   10 CONTINUE
      DELTPH = (CA(1)*HC*SAREA*(TW-T)*CA(2))*PMOLWT/(CA(3)*CV(T)*T)
      X = DELTPH
      RETURN
      END
C
```

```
C*********************************************************************
                    FUNCTION TRR(ITETA,T)
C*********************************************************************
      REAL KA,KP,KR,MC,MEP, MH, MO, MOLWTP,NA, N,M,NM,NADNAX,NMO,
     #     NP,NPO,NX,KRR
      COMMON/GEOM/B,CR,CRL,S,VBDC,VDISP,VDVBDC(720),VOLUME(800),
     #     VTDC
      COMMON/THERM/HRP,MOLWTP(5),P1,P2,P3,P4,T1,T2,T3,T4,T5,T6,TA,
     #          V1,V2,V3,V4
      COMMON/CHEM/KA,KP,KR,N(5),NA,NADNAX,NMO,NP,NPO,NX,RMR,KRR,
     #         MC,MH,MO,R,RLITAT,RMIX,Y,YCC,YMIN,PMOLWT
      COMMON/CPCOEF/CV,ACPF,BCPF,ACPA,BCPA,AL(5),AH(5),
     #          BL(5),BH(5),CL(5),CH(5)
      COMMON/INDEX/IPTTHR,IPRINT,NCYCLE,HT_INDEX
      COMMON/GEN/CB(40,4),A(10,16),C(5),D(5),EETAH,RAF,F(5),
     #        FPM,FVM,G(5),MEP,PID4,POWER,RPM
      COMMON/INEXH/IVO,IVC,EVO,EVC,AEV,AIV
      COMMON/SUPECH/EFOCOM,EFOTUR,ISUPCH,ISUPET
      COMMON/COMBUN/WCOMB,BRMAX
      COMMON/IDIES/PA,VR,STROKE
      COMMON/HTMOD/MODFHT
      COMMON/VALARE/D1,BETA,MODFVA
      COMMON/OVERL/PID,OMEGA,DTMAX,CAINT,AM,BDCMAS
      COMMON/PSSA/CPR,DT,DTHDDT,IBC,IECPC,IEC,GASMAS,WCOMP,WEXP,NCEXG,
     #     WNET,WLOOP,PSPS,ML
      COMMON/ARRAY/DELV(750),DV(750),P(800),DELN(800),DELP(800),
     #         THETA(800),V(800)
      COMMON/PROG/CM,BR,P3D
      COMMON/ABC/WT,COMEFF,CPA,NM
      COMMON/HEATRA/AREA,BM,RCR,SAREA,SM,TW,VP
      COMMON/FRICT/PIMF,PEMF,PSL,NPR,FMEP
      COMMON/FRPMOD/MODFRP
      COMMON/III/IFPCO
      COMMON/STORE/PRR(800),TEMP(800),HRR(800)
      COMMON/ANGLE/ICB,ICE,IMX,ID
      COMMON/TFCOM/COMDUR,M
      COMMON/MAX/PRMAX,ICAMAX,JCAMAX
      COMMON/COMOD/MODCOM
      COMMON/HRMOD/MODHR
      COMMON/MATRX/CRANG(800),PRESS(800),VOLRAT(800),TMPR(800)
      COMMON/COMB/PMAX,TPMAX
      COMMON/HEAT/HR
      COMMON /ADDN/PATM,VEL
C     CALCULATION OF HEAT RELEASE RATE USING WIEBE'S MODEL
      CVT =  CP(T)-R
      FKM = NA/(4.76*Y)*1.E-03
```

```
      FKG = COMEFF*FKM*WT
      HV = -HRP/142.
      C1 = FKG*HV/COMDUR
      YX = (ITETA-ICB)/COMDUR
      GO TO(50,60),MODHR
   50 HR = 6.908*C1*(M+1)*(YX**M)*EXP(-6.908*(YX**(M+1)))
      GO TO 25
   60 HRMAX = 6.908*C1*(M+1)*(YX**M)*EXP(-6.908*(YX**(M+1)))
      HR = (ICE-ITETA)/(ICE-IMX)*HRMAX
      GO TO 25
C     CALCULATION HEAT TRANSFER RATE
   25 PRS = (GASMAS*RMIX*T)/VOLUME(ITETA)*(1000000./101325.)
      GO TO(1,2,3,4),MODFHT
    1 HC = 0.13*(BM**(-0.2))*((PATM*VEL)**(0.8))*(T**(-0.5))
      GO TO 10
    2 HC=0.04*(1.0+.015)*(PRS*VP)**.7/((T**.2)*(B**.3))*(4.18/3600.)
      GO TO 10
    3 HC=0.13*((VOLUME(ITETA)*FVM)**(-.06))*((PRS*(VP+1.4))**(0.8))*
     1        (T**(-0.4))*0.001
      GO TO 10
    4 XXX = 1.5 - 0.416*VP
      YYY = EXP(XXX)
      IF(VP.GE.3.6) FVP = 3.0 + 2.57*(1.0 - YYY)
      IF(VP.LE.3.6) FVP = 3.0 - 2.57*(1.0 - (1.0/YYY))
      HC = (4.18/3600.)*SQRT(PRS*T*FVP)
   10 HTR = HC*SAREA*(TW-T)*DT*2.
C     CALCULATION OF RATE OF WORK TRANSFER
      VDEL = VOLUME(ITETA+2)-VOLUME(ITETA)
      WTR = (GASMAS*RMIX*T)*VDEL/(2.*VOLUME(ITETA))
C     TRR IS THE RATE OF TEMPERATURE RISE
      TRR = (HR+HTR-WTR)*PMOLWT/(GASMAS*CVT)
      RETURN
      END
C*****************************************************************C
                       SUBROUTINE FMEPC
C*****************************************************************C
      REAL MEP
      COMMON/GEOM/B,CR,CRL,S,VBDC,VDISP,VDVBDC(720),VOLUME(800),
     #        VTDC
      COMMON/GEN/CB(40,4),A(10,16),C(5),D(5),EETAH,RAF,F(5),
     #        FPM,FVM,G(5),MEP,PID4,POWER,RPM
      COMMON/IDIES/PA,VR,STROKE
      COMMON/INEXH/IVO,IVC,EVO,EVC,AEV,AIV
      COMMON/FRICT/PIMF,PEMF,PSL,NPR,FMEP
      COMMON/FRPMOD/MODFRP
C     EMPRICAL RELATIONS ARE USED TO ESTIMATE FRICTION.
```

```
C       RELATIONS ARE TAKEN FROM I.N.BISHOP 'AN ANALYSIS
C       IF EBGUBE FRICTION & ECONOMY'   SAE TRANSACTIONS
C       VOL.73, 1965.
C       FMEP  IS THE FRICTIONAL MEAN EFFECTIVE PRESSURE.
C       FMEP1 IS THE FRICTION DUE TO GAS PRESSURE BEHIND RINGS.
C       FMEP2 IS THE FRICTION DUE TO WALL TENSION OF RINGS.
C       FMEP3 IS FRICTION DUE TO PISTON & RING FRICTION
C       FMEP4 IS THE BLOWBY LOSS
C       FMEP5 IS THE INLET AND THROTTLE LOSS.
C       FMEP6 IS FRICTION DUE TO VALVE GEAR
C       FMEP7 IS THE PUMPING LOSS
C       FMEP8 IS THE BEARING FRICTION.
C       FMEP9 IS THE COMBUSTION CHAMBER & VALVE PUMPING LOSS.
C       PS IS THE PISTON SPEED IN M/MIN.
C       H  IS THE INLET VALVE DIAMETER.
C       GH IS THE NUMBER OF INLET VALVE/CYLINDER.
        GO TO (1,2),MODFRP
  1     CONTINUE
        PS = 3.14*B*RPM/1000.
        H = SQRT(4.*AIV/3.14)
        GH = 1.0
      FMEP1 = 0.42*(PA-PIMF)*S/(B*B)*(.0888*CR+.182*CR+.182*CR**(1.33-
     #        .394*PS/100.))*10.
      FMEP2 = 0.377*S*NPR/(B*B)*10.
      FMEP3 = (12.85*PSL/(B*S)*100.)*PS/1000.
      FMEP4 = SQRT(PA-PIMF)*(0.121*CR**.4-(.0345+.001055*CR)*(RPM/1000.)
     #         **1.185)
      FMEP5 = PEMF/2.75+PIMF
      FMEP6 = .226*(30.-(4.*RPM/1000.))*H**1.75/(B*B*S)*GH
      FMEP7 = 0.0275*(RPM/1000.)**1.5
      FMEP8 = 0.0564*(B/S)*RPM/1000.
      FMEP9 = SQRT(MEP/11.45)*.0915*(RPM/1000.)**1.7
      FMEP = FMEP1+FMEP2+FMEP3+FMEP4+FMEP5+FMEP6+FMEP7+FMEP8+FMEP9
        GO TO 3
C       THIS MODEL IS PROPOSED BY GISCH
  2     V = S/1000.*RPM/30.
        FMEP = 0.068*(CR-4.)+RPM/2000.+1.11E-06*(V**2)
  3     CONTINUE
        RETURN
        END
C**********************************************************************
                         SUBROUTINE VALVAE(X,Y,THETAC)
C**********************************************************************
C       AN EMPRICAL FORMULA IS USED FOR THE RELATIONSHIP
C       BETWEEN CRANK ANGLE AND VALVE AREA.
C       EXACT RELATION, IF AVAILABLE FOR YOUR ENGINE, YOU MAY
```

```
C       INCLUDE IT HERE.
C       MODFA=2 IS USED WHEN THE RELATION BETWEEN HEIGHT OF
C       VALVE OPENING & CRANKSHAFT ANGLE IS KNOWN.  THIS
C       DEPENDS ON CAM PROFILE & IT MUST BE INCLUDED HERE.
C       D1 IS THE DIAMETER AT THE POINT WHERE VALVE STEM
C       REACHES VALVE SEAT.(IN MM)
C       HEIGHT IS THE INSTANTANEOUS HEIGHT OF VALVE OPENING
C       DEPENDING ON THE RELATION INCLUDED.  (IN MM)
C       BETA IS THE VALVE SEAT ANGLE IN DEGREES.
        INTEGER EVO,EVC
        COMMON/INEXH/IVO,IVC,EVO,EVC,AEV,AIV
        COMMON/GAS1/THETAS,THETAU
        COMMON/VALARE/D1,BETA,MODFA
        HEIGHT = 0.0
        EXP = 0.3333
        PID = 3.1415926/180.
        GO TO (1,2,3), MODFA
    1   BBDCB = EVO-360.
        ATDCA = EVC-540.
        DWELAE = ABS(BBDCB+ATDCA)
        TETAME = EVO+90.
        TETADE = TETAME+DWELAE
        IF(THETAC.LE.TETAME)Y=.0001*X*(ABS(SIN((360.-THETAC+BBDCB)*PID)))
     #                   **EXP
        IF(THETAC.GE.TETAME.AND.THETAC.LE.TETADE)Y=.0001*X*(ABS(SIN((360.
     #          -TETAME+BBDCB)*PID)))**EXP
        IF(THETAC.GE.TETADE)Y=.0001*X*(ABS(SIN((360.-THETAC+ATDCA)
     #                   *PID)))**EXP
        GO TO 100
    2   Y=3.14/1000.*(D1+HEIGHT*SIN(BETA*PID)*COS(BETA*PID))*HEIGHT*
     #   COS(BETA*PID)*.0001
        GO TO 100
    3   CONTINUE
  100   CONTINUE
        RETURN
        END
C**********************************************************************
                        SUBROUTINE VALVAI(X,Y,THETAC)
C**********************************************************************
        INTEGER EVO,EVC
        COMMON/GAS1/THETAS,THETAU
        COMMON/INEXH/IVO,IVC,EVO,EVC,AEV,AIV
        EXP = .3333
        PID = 3.1415926/180.
        BTDCB = IVO-540.
        ATDCA = IVC-720.
```

```
      DWELAI = ABS(BTDCB+ATDCA)
      TETAMI = IVO+90.
      TETADI = TETAMI+DWELAI
      IF(THETAC.LE.TETAMI)Y=.0001*X*(ABS(SIN((540.-THETAC+BTDCB)*
     #                 PID)))**EXP
      IF(THETAC.GE.TETAMI.AND.THETAC.LE.TETADI) Y = .0001*X*
     #     (ABS(SIN((540. - TETAMI + BTDCB)*PID)))**EXP
      IF(THETAC.GE.TETADI) Y = .0001*X*(ABS(SIN((540.-THETAC+ATDCA)
     #                   *PID)))**EXP
      RETURN
      END
C*********************************************************************
                          SUBROUTINE OUTPUT
C*********************************************************************
      REAL KA,KP,KR,MC,MEP, MH, MO, MOLWTP,NA, N,NADNAX,NMO,
     #     NP,NPO,NX,KRR
      INTEGER EVO,EVC
      LOGICAL IPTTHR,IPRINT
      CHARACTER*10 XV,YZ
      CHARACTER*4 BLANKS,BLANK
      DIMENSION BLANK(10)
      COMMON/GEOM/B,CR,CRL,S,VBDC,VDISP,VDVBDC(720),VOLUME(800),
     #          VTDC
      COMMON/THERM/HRP,MOLWTP(5),P1,P2,P3,P4,T1,T2,T3,T4,T5,T6,TA,
     #          V1,V2,V3,V4
      COMMON/CHEM/KA,KP,KR,N(5),NA,NADNAX,NMO,NP,NPO,NX,RMR,KRR,
     #          MC,MH,MO,R,RLITAT,RMIX,Y,YCC,YMIN,PMOLWT
      COMMON/CPCOEF/CV,ACPF,BCPF,ACPA,BCPA,AL(5),AH(5),
     #           BL(5),BH(5),CL(5),CH(5)
      COMMON/INDEX/IPTTHR,IPRINT,NCYCLE,HT_INDEX
      COMMON/GEN/CB(40,4),A(10,16),C(5),D(5),EETAH,RAF,F(5),
     #         FPM,FVM,G(5),MEP,PID4,POWER,RPM
      COMMON/INEXH/IVO,IVC,EVO,EVC,AEV,AIV
      COMMON/IDIES/PA,VR,STROKE
      COMMON/HTMOD/MODFHT
      COMMON/PSSA/CPR,DT,DTHDDT,IBC,IECPC,IEC,GASMAS,WCOMP,WEXP,NCEXG,
     #          WNET,WLOOP,PSPS,ML
      COMMON/FRPMOD/MODFRP
      COMMON/STORE/PRR(800),TEMP(800),HRR(800)
      COMMON/COMOD/MODCOM
      COMMON/HRMOD/MODHR
      COMMON/III/IFPCO
      COMMON/PRINTS/XV(16),YZ(32)
      DATA BLANKS/'    '/
C
C
```

```
C=================================================================
                         ENTRY WRITE1
C=================================================================
      WRITE(11,999)
  999 FORMAT(///6X,55(1H*),3(/6X,1H*,53X,1H*))
      IF(IFPCO.EQ.O)WRITE(11,998)
  998 FORMAT(1H ,5X,1H*,11X,'SIMULATION OF IDEAL DIESEL CYCLE',
     #       10X,1H*/6X,1H*,11X,30(1H-),12X,1H*/6X,1H*,53X,1H*/
     #       1H ,5X,1H*,11X,'  WITH PROGRESSIVE COMBUSTION ',
     #       12X,1H*/6X,1H*,13X,27(1H-),13X,1H*,2(/6X,1H*,53X,1H*))
      IF(IFPCO.EQ.2)WRITE(11,990)
  990 FORMAT(1H ,5X,1H*,11X,'SIMULATION OF IDEAL DIESEL CYCLE',
     #       10X,1H*/6X,1H*,11X,30(1H-),12X,1H*,2(/6X,1H*,53X,1H*))
      IF(IFPCO.EQ.1)WRITE(11,989)
  989 FORMAT(1H ,5X,1H*,11X,'SIMULATION OF ACTUAL DIESEL CYCLE',
     #        9X,1H*/6X,1H*,11X,31(1H-),11X,1H*,2(/6X,1H*,53X,1H*))
      WRITE(11,997)
  997 FORMAT(1H ,5X,1H*,23X,'DETAILS',23X,1H*,2(/6X,1H*,53X,1H*))
      WRITE(11,996) B,S,CRL,CR,RAF,Y,VDISP,TA,RPM
  996 FORMAT(6X,1H*,4X,'FUEL                           =','    C10H22',11X,
     # 1H*/6X,1H*,53X,1H*/
     #  6X,1H*, 4X,'BORE                          =',F10.3,'  MM',7X,1H*/
     #  6X,1H*,53X,1H*/
     #  6X,1H*, 4X,'STROKE                        =',F10.3,'  MM',7X,1H*/
     #  6X,1H*,53X,1H*/
     #  6X,1H*, 4X,'CONNECTING ROD LENGTH         =',F10.3,'  MM',7X,1H*/
     #  6X,1H*,53X,1H*/
     #  6X,1H*, 4X,'COMPRESSION RATIO             =',F10.3,'    ',7X,1H*/
     #  6X,1H*,53X,1H*/
     #  6X,1H*, 4X,'RELATIVE A/F RATIO            =',F10.3,'    ',7X,1H*/
     #  6X,1H*,53X,1H*/
     #  6X,1H*, 4X,'OXYGEN-FUEL RATIO             =',F10.3,'    ',7X,1H*/
     #  6X,1H*,53X,1H*/
     #  6X,1H*, 4X,'DISPLACEMENT VOLUME           =',F10.3,'   L',7X,1H*/
     #  6X,1H*,53X,1H*/
     #  6X,1H*, 4X,'INLET MANIFOLD TEMPERATURE =',F10.3,'  K ',7X,1H*/
     #  6X,1H*,53X,1H*/
     #  6X,1H*, 4X,'OPERATING SPEED               =',F10.3,' RPM',7X,1H*/
     #  6X,1H*,53X,1H*)
      WRITE(11,992) MODCOM,MODFHT,MODFRP,IBC
  992 FORMAT(6X,1H*,4X,'COMBUSTION MODEL              =',I8,13X,1H*/
     #       6X,1H*,53X,1H*/
     #       6X,1H*,4X,'HEAT TRANSFER MODEL           =',I8,13X,1H*/
     #       6X,1H*,53X,1H*/
     #       6X,1H*,4X,'FRICTION MODEL                =',I8,13X,1H*/
     #       6X,1H*,53X,1H*/
```

```
     #        6X,1H*,4X,'INJECTION ANGLE (DEG)        =',I8,13X,1H*/)
          IF(IFPCO.EQ.O.OR.IFPCO.EQ.2) GO TO 1
          WRITE(11,993) EVO,IVO,EVC,IVC
    993   FORMAT(6X,1H*,4X,'EVO    =',I10,12X,'IVO    =',I10,3X,1H*/
     #        6X,1H*,53X,1H*/
     #        6X,1H*,4X,'EVC   =',I10,12X,'IVC    =',I10,3X,1H*/
     #        2(6X,1H*,53X,1H*/),6X,55(1H*),//)
      1   CONTINUE
          WRITE(11,991)
    991   FORMAT(1H ,5X,55(1H*),2(/6X,1H*,53X,1H*)/
     #           6X,1H*,4X,'CRANK ANGLE  1 TO 180  COMPRESSION STROKE',
     #           8X,1H*/
     #           6X,1H*,53X,1H*/
     #           6X,1H*,4X,'CRANK ANGLE 181 TO 360 EXPANSION   STROKE',
     #           8X,1H*/
     #           6X,1H*,53X,1H*/
     #           6X,1H*,4X,'CRANK ANGLE 361 TO 540 EXHAUST     STROKE',
     #           8X,1H*/
     #           6X,1H*,53X,1H*/
     #           6X,1H*,4X,'CRANK ANGLE 541 TO 720 SUCTION     STROKE',
     #           8X,1H*,2(/6X,1H*,53X,1H*)/6X,55(1H*)//)
          RETURN
C=====================================================================
                          ENTRY WRITE2
C=====================================================================
          DO 1000 I = 1,NCYCLE
   1000   BLANK(I) = BLANKS
          IF(NCYCLE.LT.3) WRITE(11,995)(BLANK(I),I=1,NCYCLE)
          IF((NCYCLE.EQ.3).OR.(NCYCLE.GT.3))WRITE(11,995)(BLANK(I),I=1,3)
    995   FORMAT(/8X,'VARIABLES',A4,7X,'CYCLE1',A4,4X,'CYCLE2',A4,6X,
      1          'CYCLE3',4X)
          DO 1020 I = 1,15
          IF(NCYCLE.LT.3)WRITE(11,994)XV(I),(A(L,I),L=1,NCYCLE)
          IF(NCYCLE.GE.3)WRITE(11,994)XV(I),(A(L,I),L=1,3)
   1020   CONTINUE
          IF(NCYCLE.LE.3) RETURN
          WRITE(11,1030)(BLANK(I),I = 4,NCYCLE)
   1030   FORMAT(1H1/8X,'VARIABLES',A4,4X,'CYCLE4',A4,4X,'CYCLE5',A4,4X,
      1          'CYCLE6')
          DO 1040 I = 1,15
   1040   WRITE(11,994)(XV(I),A(L,I),L = 4,NCYCLE)
    994   FORMAT(///5X,A12,2X,3F15.4)
          RETURN
          END
C
C
```

```
C***********************************************************************
                     SUBROUTINE PRINT1
C***********************************************************************
      INTEGER EVO,EVC
      COMMON/GEOM/B,CR,CRL,S,VBDC,VDISP,VDVBDC(720),VOLUME(800),
     #          VTDC
      COMMON/INEXH/IVO,IVC,EVO,EVC,AEV,AIV
      COMMON/IDIES/PA,VR,STROKE
      COMMON/PSSA/CPR,DT,DTHDDT,IBC,IECPC,IEC,GASMAS,WCOMP,WEXP,NCEXG,
     #          WNET,WLOOP,PSPS,ML
      COMMON/ABCD/DN,ITETA,ITETA3,L
      COMMON/STORE/PRR(800),TEMP(800),HRR(800)
      COMMON/ARRAY/DELV(750),DV(750),P(800),DELN(800),DELP(800),
     #          THETA(800),V(800)
      COMMON/MATRX/CRANG(800),PRESS(800),VOLRAT(800),TMPR(800)
      COMMON/PROG/CM,BR,P3D
      COMMON/COMBUN/WCOMB,BRMAX
      COMMON/III/IFPCO
      COMMON/ANGLE/ICB,ICE,IMX,ID
      COMMON/COMOD/MODCOM
      IF(MODCOM.EQ.2) GO TO 736
      WRITE(11,991)
991   FORMAT(5X,'ANGLE',4X,'PRESSURE',6X,'VOLUME',6X,'TEMP'
     #          /5X,'(DEG)',6X,'ATM', 9X,'RATIO',6X,'KLEVINS')
      JJJ = IVC-719
      IF(IFPCO.EQ.0) JJJ = 1
      DO 990 I = JJJ,IBC,4
         WRITE(11,989) I,P(I),VDVBDC(I),TEMP(I)
989      FORMAT(/5X,I4,5X,F6.3,5X,F7.4,5X,F8.3)
990   CONTINUE
      WRITE(11,994)
994   FORMAT(//8X,'COMBUSTION STARTS'/)
      IF(BR.GT.BRMAX) GO TO 1
      DO 2 I = IBC,IEC
      WRITE(11,3)I,P(I),VDVBDC(I),TEMP(I)
  3   FORMAT(/5X,I4,5X,F8.3,5X,F8.4,5X,F8.3)
  2   CONTINUE
      GO TO 4
  1   DO 995 IM = 1,L
       WRITE(11,996)CRANG(IM),PRESS(IM),VOLRAT(IM),TMPR(IM)
996    FORMAT(/2X,F8.3,5X,F8.3,5X,F8.4,5X,F8.3)
995   CONTINUE
  4   WRITE(11,5)
  5   FORMAT(//8X,'COMBUSTION ENDS')
      IF(IFPCO.EQ.0) IIII = 360
      IF(IFPCO.EQ.1) IIII = EVO
```

```
      DO 997 I = IEC+2,IIII,4
      WRITE(11,998)I,P(I),VDVBDC(I),TEMP(I)
998   FORMAT(/5X,I4,5X,F8.3,5X,F8.4,5X,F8.3)
997   CONTINUE
      GO TO 50
C     ============================================================
736    CONTINUE
      WRITE(11,191)
191   FORMAT(5X,'ANGLE',6X,'PRESSURE',6X,'VOLUME',6X,'TEMP'
     #       /5X,'(DEG)',8X,'ATM', 9X,'RATIO',6X,'KLEVINS')
      JJJ = IVC-719
      IF(IFPCO.EQ.0) JJJ = 1
      DO 190 I = JJJ,IBC,4
        WRITE(11,193)I,P(I),VDVBDC(I),TEMP(I)
193     FORMAT(/5X,I4,5X,F8.3,5X,F8.4,5X,F8.3)
190   CONTINUE
      WRITE(11,294)
294   FORMAT(//8X,'COMBUSTION STARTS'/)
      DO 21 I = IBC,ICB,1
      WRITE(11,31)I,P(I),VDVBDC(I),TEMP(I)
31    FORMAT(/5X,I4,5X,F8.3,5X,F8.4,5X,F8.3)
21    CONTINUE
41    WRITE(11,51)
51    FORMAT(//8X,'COMBUSTION ENDS')
      DO 71 I = ICB,ICE,2
      WRITE(11,11)I,P(I),VDVBDC(I),TEMP(I)
11    FORMAT(/5X,I4,5X,F8.3,5X,F8.4,5X,F8.3)
71    CONTINUE
      IF(IFPCO.EQ.0) IIII = 360
      IF(IFPCO.EQ.1) IIII = EVO
      DO 297 I = IEC,IIII,4
      WRITE(11,298)I,P(I),VDVBDC(I),TEMP(I)
298   FORMAT(/5X,I4,5X,F8.3,5X,F8.4,5X,F8.3)
297   CONTINUE
50    RETURN
      END
C*****************************************************************
                    SUBROUTINE PRINT2
C*****************************************************************
      CHARACTER*10 XV,YZ
      COMMON/GEN/CB(40,4),A(10,16),C(5),D(5),EETAH,RAF,F(5),
     #           FPM,FVM,G(5),MEP,PID4,POWER,RPM
      COMMON/PRINTS/XV(16),YZ(32)
      WRITE(11,20)
20    FORMAT(///15X,'COMPARISON OF DIFFERENT DIESEL CYCLES'/
     #          15X,35(1H-)//70(1H*)
```

```
      #        //3X,'VARIABLES',11X,'ICS',10X,'FCS',14X,'PCS'
      #            11X,'ACS')
         DO 25 I=1,32
         IF(I.EQ.19) WRITE(11,20)
         WRITE(11,30)YZ(I),(CB(I,L),L = 1,4)
   25    CONTINUE
   30    FORMAT(/1X,A12,5X,F8.3,5X,F9.4,8X,F8.3,6X,F8.3)
         WRITE(11,35)
   35    FORMAT(//1X,66(1H*),//10X,8(1H*),' DENOTES NOT APPLICABLE ',//)
         RETURN
         END
C*********************************************************************
                                   SUBROUTINE PRINT3
C*********************************************************************
         COMMON/GAS1/THETAS,THETAU
         COMMON/GAS/PR(800),VOLD(800),TE(800),NV,T,PEVC,VOLEFF
         COMMON/ARRAY/DELV(750),DV(750),P(800),DELN(800),DELP(800),
      #                THETA(800),V(800)
         COMMON/SUCTION/THETA_SUC,PR_SUC,TE_SUC,VOLD_SUC
         IPR = 0
         DO 15 I = 1,NV
         IF(ABS(THETA(I) - THETAS) .LT. 1.E-3) WRITE(11,12)
         IF((THETA(I) - THETAU) .LT. 1.E-3) WRITE(11,14)
         IF(IPR.EQ.0) WRITE(11,10)
         IPR = IPR+1
   14    FORMAT(//20X,'BEGINNING OF EXHAUST STROKE'/
      #          20X,'GAS EXCHANGE PROCESS STARTS'/
      #          20X,'  THE FLOW IS  SUPERSONIC   ')
   12    FORMAT(//17X,'GAS EXCHANGE PROCESS CONTINUES'/
      #          17X,'   FLOW HAS BECOME SUBSONIC     '/)
   10    FORMAT(//6X,'ANGLE',5X,'PRESSURE',4X,'VOLUME',7X,'TEMPERATURE',
      #         /6X,'(DEG)',7X,'ATM',8X,'RATIO',8X,'KELVIN'/)
         WRITE(11,20) THETA(I),PR(I),VOLD(I),TE(I)
   20    FORMAT(5X,F7.3,5X,F7.4,5X,F7.4,9X,F7.2)
   15    CONTINUE
         WRITE(11,25) THETA_SUC, PR_SUC, VOLD_SUC, TE_SUC
  25     FORMAT(///5X, ' FRESH CHARGE SUCTION STARTS AT THETA = ', F7.3,'
      #DEGREES C.A', /5X, ' PRESSURE      = ', F8.3, ' BAR'
      # /5X, ' VOLUME RATIO = ', F8.3,
      # /5X, ' TEMPERATURE  = ', F8.3, ' KELVINS' )
         RETURN
         END
C*********************************************************************
```

Meaning of major variables used in the program

ACPA	coefficient in the calculation of variable specific heat of air
ACPF	coefficient in the calculation of variable specific heat for different fuels
ACPN2	coefficient in the calculation of variable specific heat for N_2
ACPO2	coefficient in the calculation of variable specific heat for O_2
AEV	maximum area of opening of exhaust valve
AFR	air-fuel ratio
AH	coefficient in the calculation of variable specific heat for temperatures ≥ 1600
AIV	maximum area of opening of the intake valve
AL	coefficient in the calculation of variable specific heat in the temperature range $400 < T < 1600$
AM	molecular weight
AM	a factor used in the subroutine GASEX
AMOLWT	molecular weight
AREA	cross-sectional area of bore
B	bore
BCPA	constant in the calculation of C_p for air
BCPF	coefficient in the calculation of variable specific heat for different fuels
BCPN2	coefficient in the calculation of variable specific heat for N_2
BCPO2	coefficient in the calculation of variable specific heat for O_2
BDCMAS	Mass of the gas in the cylinder when piston is at BDC
BETA	valve seat angle
BH	coefficient in the calculation of variable specific heat for temperatures ≥ 1600
BL	coefficient in the calculation of variable specific heat in the temperature range $400 < T < 1600$
BM	bore in metres
BMEP	brake mean effective pressure
BPOWER	brake power
BR	burning rate
BRMAX	maximum allowable burning rate
BRTHEFF	brake thermal efficiency
C10H22	diesel
CAINT	crank angle interval
CH	coefficient in the calculation of variable specific heat for temperatures > 1600
CL	coefficient in the calculation of variable specific heat in the temperature range $400 < T < 1600$
CL	low temperature coefficient for C_p and C_v
CM	scaling factor
COMDUR	combustion duration

CPA	C_p of air
CPN2	C_p of N_2
CPO2	C_p of O_2
CPR	C_p of product
CR	compression ratio
CRIT	critical pressure rate
CRL	connecting rod length
CV	C_v
CVG	C_v of products
CVR	C_v of reactants
DC	duration of combustion
DELP	Δp
DELTAN	Δn
DELTAT	ΔT
DELTAV	ΔV
DELTE	$\Delta\theta$
DELTP	Δp
DELTPH	ΔpH
DELTT	ΔT
DELTV	ΔV
DELV	ΔV
DMDDT	dm/dT
DPMAX	Δp_{max}
DTH	$d\theta$
DTHDDT	$d\theta/dt$
DTMAX	maximum time interval
DVDTH	$dV/d\theta$
DWELAE	dwell angle for exhaust
DWELAI	dwell angle for inlet
EETAH	thermal efficiency
EETATH	thermal efficiency
EFOCOM	isentropic efficiency of compressor
EFOTUR	isentropic efficiency of turbine
EQR	equivalence ratio
EVC	exhaust valve closing angle
EVO	exhaust valve opening angle
FMEP	frictional mean effective pressure
FMEP1	friction due to gas pressure behind rings
FMEP2	friction due to wall tension of rings
FMEP3	friction due to piston and ring friction
FMEP4	blowby loss
FMEP5	inlet and throttle losses
FMEP6	friction due to valve gear
FMEP7	pumping loss
FMEP8	bearing friction
FMEP9	combustion chamber and valve pumping loss

FMEPC	calculated frictional mean effective pressure
FPM	multiplication factor for pressure
FVM	multiplication factor for volume
GASMAS	mass of the exhaust gas
GH	number of inlet valve per cylinder
H	inlet valve diameter
HR	heat release rate
HRMAX	maximum heat release rate
HRPF	calorific value of different fuels
HTMOD	HT model code
HTRANS	heat transfer
I	do loop index
IBC	start of injection
ICE	end of combustion
ICOMBM	index for the combustion model
ICS	ideal cycle simulation
IEC	end of combustion
IFPCO	code for stroke
IMEP	indicated mean effective pressure
INCR	increment in crank angle for calculating pressure
INDF	index for the fuel
INMASS	mass of fresh charge inducted during intake stroke
IPRINT	index controlling the print out
ISUPCH	a logical variable to operate the engine by a gear driven supercharger
ITMT1	index for taking into account fuel vapourisation effect
IVC	inlet valve closing angle
IVO	inlet valve opening angle
K	do loop index
KA	ratio of specific heat for air
KP	ratio of specific heat for product
KR	ratio of specific heat for reactant
MC	mole numbers of carbon
MECHEF	mechanical efficiency
MEP	mean effective pressure
MH	mole numbers of hydrogen
MO	mole number of oxygen
MODCOM	combustion model code
MODEL	model number used in the subroutine progressive combustion in the calculation of n
MODFHT	model for heat transfer calculation
MODFRP	model for friction
MODFVA	model for calculation of valve area
MODHR	model for heat release
MOLWTP	molecular weight of the product
NA	kmole of air taken in during suction

NADNAX	N_a/N_x
NCEXG	number constituent in the exhaust gas
NCYCLE	number of iteration cycles for convergence (FCS subroutine)
NITRN	number of iteration in Newton-Raphson method (FCS subroutine)
NMDNMX	$N_m/(N_m + N_x)$
NMO	N_{mo} (refer section 7.3 in the text)
NP	N_p (refer section 7.3 in the text)
NPO	N_{po} (refer section 7.3 in the text)
NPR	number of moles of the product
NPR	number of piston rings
NPT	total number of product
NX	N_x (refer section 7.3 in the text)
OMEGA	ω
P1	pressure at IVC
P3D	pressure p_3' [refer eq.(8.1)]
PA	atmospheric pressure
PEMF	exhaust manifold pressure
PEVC	pressure when the exhaust valve closes
PIMF	inlet manifold pressure
PMAX	maximum pressure in the cycle
PMOLWT	molecular weight of the product
POWER	power
PR	pressure
PRESS	pressure
PS	mean piston speed in m/minute
PSL	piston skirt length
PSPS	number of power strokes per second
PVPRNT	a variable to activate pressure-volume print out
QV	Q_v (refer section 2.2.2 and 2.3 in the text)
R	universal gas constant
RLITAT	universal gas constant in litre-atmosphere
RMIX	R for the mixture
RMOLWT	molecular weight of the reactant
RPM	speed in revolution per minute
S	stroke
SAREA	surface area
SM	stroke in metres
T	temperature
TA	atmospheric temperature
TE	temperature at the end of ignition
THETA	θ
THETAR	θ in radian
TM	manifold temperature
TPMAX	maximum temperature in the cycle
TREF	reference temperature
V	volume

VBDC	volume when the piston is at bdc
VDISP	displacement volume
VDVBDC	V/V_{bdc}
VOLEFF	effective volume
VTDC	volume when the piston is at tdc
WCOMB	workdone during combustion
WCOMP	workdone during compression
WEXP	workdone during expansion
WLOOP	intake-exhaust loop work
WNET	net work
Y	oxygen-fuel ratio
YCC	chemically correct oxygen-fuel ratio
YMIN	minimum oxygen-fuel ratio for combustion

BIBLIOGRAPHY

Akram, S., Henin, N. and Bryzik, W., (1990), Review of Simple Heat Release Calculations, *SAE Paper* **900445**.

Annand, W.J.D., (1963), Heat Transfer in the Cylinders of Reciprocating Internal Combustion Engines, *I.Mech.E.*, **177**, 36, 973-990.

Bracco, F.V., (1985), Modelling of Engine Sprays, *SAE Paper* **859394**.

Campbell, A.S., *Thermodynamic Analysis of Combustion Engines,* John Wiley and Sons, New York.

Chen, C. and Veshagh, (1991), A Premixed Turbulent Burning Velocity Model Based on Dimensional Reasoning, *SAE Paper* **910077**.

Chiu, W.S., Shahed, S.M. and Lyn, W.T., (1976), a Transient Spray Mixing Model for Diesel Combustion, *SAE Paper* **760128**.

Cho, I.Y., Fujimoto, H., Tanabe, H. and Sato, G.T., (1990), Similarity of Law of Entrainment into Diesel Spray and Steady Spray, *SAE Paper* **900447**.

Dent, J.C. and Sulaiman S.J., (1977), Convective and Radiative Heat Transfer in a High Swirl Direct Injection Diesel Engine, *SAE Paper* **770407**.

Dent, J.C. and Pramod S. Mehta, (1981), Phenomenological Combustion Model for a Quiescent Chamber Diesel Engine, *SAE Paper* **811235**.

Ferguson, C.R., (1986), *Internal Combustion Engines, Applied Thermodynamics*, John Wiley.

Gosman, A.D. and Harvey, P.S., (1982), Computer Analysis of Fuel-Air Mixing and Combustion in a Axisymmetric D.I. Diesel, *SAE Paper* **820036**.

Goyal, M., Glem Scharpf and Borman, G.L., (1967), The Simulation of Single Cylinder Intake and Exhaust Systems, *SAE Paper* **670478**.

Heywood, J.B., (1988), *Internal Combustion Engine Fundamentals*, McGraw Hill.

Hiroyasu, H. and Kadota, T., (1974), Fuel Droplet Size Distribution in Diesel Combustion Chamber, *SAE Paper* **740715**.

Hiroyasu, H., (1985), Diesel Engine Combustion and its Modelling, Diagnostics and Modelling of Combustion in Reciprocating Engines, *COMODIA* **85**, 53-75.

Hiroyasu, H., Arai, M. and Tabata, M., (1989), Empirical Equations for the Sauter Mean Diameter of Diesel Spray, *SAE Paper* **890464**.

Hohenberg, G.H., (1979), Advanced Approaches for Heat Transfer Calculations, *SAE Paper* **790825**.

Lefeuvre, T., Myers, R.S. and Uyehara, O.A., (1969), Experimental Instantaneous Heat Fluxes in a Diesel Engine and their Correlation, *SAE Paper* **690464**.

Mehta, P.S. and Gupta, A.K., (1985), Modelling of Spray Swirl Interaction in Direct Injection Diesel Engine Combustion Chambers, *I.Mech.E.*, **199**, D3, 187–199.

Millington, B.W. and Hartles, E.R., (1968), Frictional Losses in Diesel Engines, *SAE Paper* **680590**.

Miyamoto, N., Chikahisa, T., Murayama, T. and Sawyer, R., (1985), Description and Analysis of Diesel Engine Rate of Combustion and Performance using Weibe's Functions, *SAE Paper* **850107**.

Rajagopal, K., (1991), *Three Dimensional Modelling of Incylinder Flows, Fuel-Air Mixing and Combustion In a Four Stroke Compression Ignition Engine*, Ph.D Thesis, Madras, India.

Ram Reddy, P., Mohan Krishna, D., Govinda Mallan, K.R. and Ganesan, V., (1993), Evaluation of Combustion Parameters In Direct Injection Diesel Engines – An Easy and Reliable Method, *SAE Paper* **930605**.

Ram Reddy, P., (1993), *Modelling of Combustion, Performance and Emissions in a Four-stroke D.I. Diesel Engine*, Ph.D. Thesis, IIT Madras.

Ramos, J.J., (1989), *Internal Combustion Engine Modelling*, Hemisphere Publishing Corporation.

Shipinski, J., Uyehara, O.A. and Myers, P.S., (1980), Experimental Correlation between Rate-of-injection and Rate-or-heat-release in a Diesel Engine, *ASME*, **68**-DGP-11.

Shrirakawa, S., Ohsawa, K. and Aoyama, T., (1987), Simulation of Spray Combustion in an Axisymmetric Small Direct Injection Diesel Engine, *I.Mech.E.* C01/87.

Sitkei, G. and Ramanaiah, G.V., (1972), A Rational Approach for Calculation of Heat Transfer in Diesel Engines, *SAE Paper* **720027**.

Tatsu Oguri and Shigewo Inasa, (1972), Radiant Heat Transfer in Diesel Engines, *SAE Paper* **720023**.

Taylor, C.F., (1968), The Internal Combustion Engine in Theory and Practice, **11**.

Taylor, C.F. and Toong, T.Y., (1957), Heat Transfer In Internal Combustion Engines, *ASME Paper* **57**-HT-17.

Watkins, A.P., (1989), Three-dimensional Modelling of Gas Flow and Sprays in Diesel Engines, *Computer Simulation of Fluid Flow, Heat and Mass Transfer and Combustion in Reciprocating Engines*, N.C. Markatos, (ed.), Hemisphere, 193-237.

Watson, N., Pilley, A.D. and Marsout, M., (1980), a Combustion Correlation for Diesel Engine Simulation, *SAE Paper* **800029**.

Webber, H.G. and Borman, G.L., (1967), Parametric Studies using a Mathematically Simulated Diesel Engine Cycle, *SAE Paper* **670480**.

Wilson, N., Pilley, A.D. and Marzank M., (1980), a Combustion Correlation for Diesel Engine Simulation, *SAE Paper* **800029**.

Wolfer, H.H., (1959), Ignition Lag in Diesel Engines, *VDI-Forshung sheft 392, 1938*, Translated by Royal Air craft Establishment, Farnborough Library No.358, UDC 621-436.047.

Wong, C.L. and Steere, D.E., (1982), The Effects of Diesel Fuel Properties and Engine Operating Conditions on Ignition Delay, *SAE Paper* **821231**.

Woshni, G., (1967), A Universally Applicable Equation for the Instantaneous Heat Transfer Coefficient in the Internal Combustion Engines, *SAE Paper* **670931**.

Index